AGEING IN URBAN NEIGHBOURHOODS

Place attachment and social exclusion

Allison E. Smith

This edition published in Great Britain in 2009 by

The Policy Press
University of Bristol
Fourth Floor
Beacon House
Queen's Road
Bristol BS8 1QU
UK

Tel +44 (0)117 331 4054
Fax +44 (0)117 331 4093
e-mail tpp-info@bristol.ac.uk
www.policypress.co.uk

North American office:
The Policy Press
c/o International Specialized Books Services (ISBS)
920 NE 58th Avenue, Suite 300
Portland, OR 97213-3786, USA
Tel +1 503 287 3093
Fax +1 503 280 8832
e-mail info@isbs.com

British Library Cataloguing in Publication Data
A catalogue record for this book is available from the British Library.

Library of Congress Cataloging-in-Publication Data
A catalog record for this book has been requested.

ISBN 978 1 84742 270 5 paperback
ISBN 978 1 84742 271 2 hardcover

Cover design by The Policy Press
Front cover: image kindly supplied by www.sxc.hu/photo/993619
Printed and bound in Great Britain by TJ International, Padstow

Contents

List of boxes, tables and figures

Box

Tables

Figures

Acknowledgements

There are a number of people whom I wish to thank. First and foremost are the older people who graciously gave up their time to talk with me and share some of their life stories. It was a privilege to have this opportunity. There are also a number of people, particularly in Vancouver, to whom I am greatly indebted for their support of the research – with special mention to Carolyn Innes and Dr Marlene Wickman.

I would like to thank Professor Judith Phillips at Swansea University, Luke O'Shea, formerly of the Department of Communities and Local Government, Professor Sheila Peace at The Open University and Professor Chris Phillipson at Keele University for their contributions to the book. In addition, I would like to thank Professor Anne Martin-Matthews at the University of British Columbia for support prior to and during my fieldwork in Vancouver, and my PhD supervisor Professor Thomas Scharf.

I would also like to thank my parents – Marius and Shirley Smith – for their unfailing support and encouragement.

Foreword

Judith Phillips

The study of ageing is continuing to increase rapidly across multiple disciplines. Consequently students, academics, professionals and policy makers need texts on the latest research, theory, policy and practice developments in the field. With new areas of interest in mid- and later life opening up, the series bridges the gaps in the literature as well as providing cutting-edge debate on new and traditional areas of ageing within a lifecourse perspective. Taking this approach, the series addresses 'ageing' (rather than gerontology or 'old age') providing coverage of mid- as well as later life; it promotes a critical perspective and focuses on the social rather than the medical aspects of ageing.

In this book Allison Smith provides new ways of understanding the relationship between older people and their environments, looking beyond the person–environment fit that has traditionally dominated the environment and ageing literature. By focusing on the experience of older people in deprived inner-city communities in Canada and the UK she takes an unexplored approach concentrating on the wider social environment. The book is informed through a rich tapestry of older people's biographies, case studies and illustrations, highlighting the importance of both lifecourse and 'place' in our analysis of ageing.

The book will appeal to academics interested in environmental gerontology, urban studies, town planning, housing and community development. It has considerable relevance to policy makers in the field of ageing, particularly those engaged in environmental and housing issues on both sides of the Atlantic.

ONE

Introduction

> Environment can have powerful enabling or disabling impacts on older age ... unsupportive environments (poor transport, poor housing, higher levels of crime, etc) discourage active lifestyle and social participation. Indeed, disability can be defined not as a physical state that exists without reference to other factors but as mismatch between what a person can do and what their environment requires of them. (House of Lords Science and Technology Committee, 2005, p 53)

Background

Since the 1970s, most Western nations have experienced a growth in inequality (Gordon, 2006; OECD, 2008b) and, in particular, a rise in the number of marginalised and deprived inner-city neighbourhoods (EC, 1997; Gordon and Townsend, 2000; Lee, 2000; Lupton and Power, 2002; Power, 2009). This has raised significant concerns related to the social and economic health of many Western countries (Barnes et al, 2003; Levitas, 2005).

Academic research and government policy have increasingly sought to focus on such areas (Power and Mumford, 1999; SEU, 2001a; Lupton and Power, 2002; see European Regional Development Fund, www.communities.gov.uk/citiesandregions/european/europeanregionaldevelopment/), as there has been, in particular, a growing need to better understand the experiences of those living in such places and find policy solutions that improve individuals' environmental well-being. In the UK, urban regeneration and renewal of deprived neighbourhoods has been a key policy focus of the New Labour government since 1997 (see SEU, 1998; SEU, 2001a). This focus has sparked wider public and academic debate about factors that underpin marginalisation and social exclusion of individuals and areas.

However, in the UK, academic research and social policy focus has largely been concerned with addressing the needs of children, young people and adults of working age living in these types of neighbourhoods (see the Policy Action Team reports: SEU, 1998–2000). Until very recently, the experiences and needs of older people living in poverty and social exclusion in these areas have been ignored (Scharf et al, 2002b; Phillipson and Scharf, 2004). Given the growth in both the ageing of the population and deprived inner-city areas, there is now an urgent need to better understand the situation of ageing in such places and to consider appropriate policy and practice solutions.

The need to better understand the experiences of older people is in part driven and supported by research that suggests that environment matters, such that those individuals living in deprived neighbourhoods are presented with more negative challenges (for example, high crime and antisocial behaviour, poor housing and infrastructure, and high population turnover) than people living in non-deprived areas (Atkinson and Kintrea, 2001; Brown et al, 2004). In addition, the research literature suggests that the increased losses associated with later life (for example, in terms of health; Kunzmann et al, 2000) and the quality and type of environment (McPherson, 1998; House of Lords Science and Technology Committee, 2005) become an important factor in determining well-being and independence, such that, as suggested by the House of Lords Science and Technology Committee (2005, p 53), ageing is a malleable process and 'Environments can have a powerful enabling or disabling impact on older age'.

Why should we revisit the relationship between the person and the environment?

The goal of environmental gerontological research, according to Lawton (1986, p 15), is to see a society better able to meet the needs of its ageing population:

> The vulnerability of this age group makes more compelling the search for ways of elevating behavior and experienced quality of life through environmental means. By this line of reasoning, if we could design housing with fewer barriers, neighbourhoods with more enriching resources, or institutions with higher stimulating qualities, we could improve the level of functioning of many older people more than proportionately.

This has social and economic consequences for society and governments. 'Ageing in place', and to some extent potentially 'place in ageing', implies an enabling and supportive environment, such that the 'staying put' philosophy of current social policy (Haldemann and Wister, 1993) needs to be guided by empirical and theoretical research.

Recently, environmental gerontology has received criticism for 'languishing' and a 'lack of innovativeness' in theoretical and empirical development (Kendig, 2003; Wahl and Weisman, 2003). While great gains in knowledge were made in the 1970s and early 1980s (see Lawton and Nahemow, 1973; Rowles, 1978; Lawton et al, 1982), much of the work since has sought to verify and replicate findings. This book comes at a critical time in the field of environmental gerontology and more broadly in the ability of nation states to prepare appropriately for an ageing society. There is a need to revisit the knowledge currently available in this area, identify gaps and set out a future direction of travel given trends data and policy agendas on environmental sustainability and ageing in place. The field of environmental gerontology has a responsibility and contribution to make to these agendas and policy development – how academics in this field and others choose to respond to policy makers can help to shape the process and experience of future ageing.

In a sense, environmental gerontology is languishing at a time when it should be flourishing. The demographic profile of older people has drawn international interest in preparing to meet the needs of an older society. According to the United Nations (UN, 2003), 'one out of every ten persons is now 60 years or above' and this is projected to increase in the proceeding years. In addition, more older people than ever before live in urban areas and this is expected to increase – over half the world's older population currently lives in urban areas (51%), and this figure is projected to increase to 62% by 2050 (UN, 2003). These trends should raise significant concerns given growing criticism and questioning of the age-friendliness of urban areas and the ability to meet the current needs of an ever-increasing urbanised ageing population (Zwingle, 2002).

Environmental ageing research is significant as spaces can affect many aspects of daily life, for example, physical and mental well-being, feelings of safety and comfort, the level of independence, and social support (Lawton, 1990). According to McPherson (1998, p 157, emphasis added), the environment can in turn be influential in the process of ageing: 'For older adults who experience changes in health, income, or marital status, the *type* and *quality* of environment may become an important factor in determining the level of personal well-being and independence'. In this context, Becker (2003, p 130) argues that examining 'the spatial contexts in which elders live and the meaning they attach to the places they call home is a critical component of studying the aging process'.

There is also a generally accepted notion that ageing in place is optimal from the perspective of both the individual and the state. However, the optimality of ageing in place has generally assumed that there is a particular quality to environments in which people age. We have yet to ask if there are particular environmental qualities that test optimality; specifically, given the multiple risks present in deprived neighbourhoods (for example, high rates of crime, poor infrastructure, disengagement of services and poor housing), can we consider ageing in place optimal? The aim of this book is to tackle the paucity of knowledge related to our understanding of the person–environment relationship and impacts on well-being in particular urban neighbourhoods – inner-city deprived areas. If environment matters in ageing, then we need to better understand the key factors that impact on this.

The book is unique in that it draws from new cross-national empirical research with older people in two countries across five deprived inner-city neighbourhoods;[1] not since the ground-breaking work of Peter Townsend in the 1950s have the experiences of older people living in environments characterised by multiple risks been examined in depth. The research findings aim to fill shortfalls in and build on knowledge around the lived experiences of older people in contemporary inner-city neighbourhoods. The book also draws on the author's own experience of working on social exclusion and older people policy in central government. The discussion and findings presented here will be of relevance to social scientists, in particular those with an interest in ageing, human geography and psychology; and those in the health professions, policy makers, city planners and architects.

Outline of the book

The objective of this book will be to build on and progress scientific knowledge in the field of environmental gerontology and address next steps in policy and practice in this area. However, before proceeding to outline this book it is important to clarify the use of the term 'environment' within this book. According to Peace et al (2006, p 8), environment is 'both the place and space that encompass the person and affect their understanding of themselves and the culture in which they live'. They go on to state that environments can be distinguished on the basis of macro- and micro-levels. Environment in this book would be classified as a macro-level and is loosely defined and characterised as the physical and social space of the neighbourhood where one lives (for example, local parks, shops and backyards/gardens). It is typically viewed as external to the private internal space of the home; 'beyond the familial, domestic or intimate world but influencing the creating of self-identity through spatiality' (Peace et al, 2006, p 8). However, the author takes the view that the macro- and micro-space are not mutually exclusive or distinctive from each other, rather, they interact to influence and determine the overall relationship an older person has with their neighbourhood.

This book is structured around three overarching parts and encompasses nine chapters. This covers ideas around the *revisiting*, the *rethinking* and the *refocusing* of the person–environment relationship.

Part One: Revisiting the person–environment fit

Part One revisits the literature and debates on the person–environment relationship.

Chapter Two reviews the theoretical and empirical literature on 'the person' and 'the environment'. This draws on literature from a range of disciplines over the last 40 years primarily in the US, the UK and Europe. The first part of the chapter re-examines the contribution of Lawton and Nahemow's (1973) *Ecological Model of Ageing* to environmental gerontological thinking; this focuses on concepts of *personal competence* and *environmental press*, and the *docility* and *proactivity hypotheses*. The second part of the chapter revisits the breadth of literature on 'ageing in place' and 'place in ageing', which draws primarily on the work of Rowles and his concept of 'insideness'. The chapter closes with an identification and discussion of shortfalls and gaps in knowledge within the current literature.

Chapter Three begins to unpick the experience of ageing in urban cities. It presents trends in demographic ageing (for example, growth in the numbers of older people and healthy life expectancy) and urbanisation. Consideration is given to factors that have been found to foster as well as hinder ageing well in urban centres. Concern is raised over the growth in particular types of urban neighbourhoods – especially the deprived inner-city neighbourhood – and the lack of knowledge in relation to the experience and impact on ageing.

Part One will help to address and answer the following questions:

- What does the current literature tell us about the person–environment relationship (for example, key conceptual and theoretical frameworks)?
- What are the gaps and shortfalls in knowledge?
- Given trends, what do we know about ageing in particular types of urban neighbourhoods?

Part Two: Rethinking the person–environment fit

Part Two offers new cross-national empirical research that supports the rethinking and reconceptualisation of the person–environmental fit paradigm.

Chapter Four profiles the deprived inner-city wards used in the research, based on a combination of government statistics and reports, historical references, media articles, and photographs and descriptive text from older residents living in some of the research areas.

Chapter Five presents the research evidence that supports the development of three new environmental categories – *comfort*, *management* and *distress* – which is illustrated through in-depth analysis of eight case studies.

Chapter Six discusses how the factors present in these types of urban neighbourhoods reveal new knowledge in our understanding of the person–environment relationship, for example, that the relationships between personal-competences and environmental presses, and individual reports of well-being, are not always unidirectional (for instance, environmental distress does not always denote reports of poor well-being). Rather, the relationship is complex and might be mediated by lifecourse and/or religion/spirituality. In addition, temporal factors – the position of time: past, present and future – also play an intervening role. A new paradigm or rethink of the complexity of the relationship is discussed and suggested.

Part Two will help to address and answer the following questions:

- What are the environmental experiences of older people ageing in neighbourhoods that present multiple daily risks? Are there cross-national differences?
- What underpins older people's desire or rejection of ageing in place?
- How does the new empirical evidence help to address gaps in knowledge and a rethink about ageing and place?

Part Three: Refocusing the person–environment fit

Part Three argues for a refocusing of the person–environment relationship. The implications of this research and the wider field of environmental gerontology are analysed in terms of what this means for further research, academic debate and development of social policy.

Chapter Seven seeks to refocus the direction of environmental gerontology by consideration of the current policy context and 'preparedness' of nations to address the aspirations of an increasingly ageing society. The chapter raises three key shortfalls in policy and practice and discusses the way forward.

Chapter Eight presents and considers possible influences acting on our interpretation of the person–environment relationship, such as romanticising place, and age, generational and period effects. In addition, the chapter assesses and speculates on future challenges; it examines the role of globalisation, technology and communications, and how the economic downturn might influence ageing and place.

In Chapter Nine, the key themes raised within each of the three parts of the book – *revisiting*, *rethinking* and *refocusing* the person–environment fit – are pulled together and summarised. It discusses the contribution of the book to advancing scientific knowledge and addressing the criticisms of a 'languishing' state within environmental gerontological literature. Critically – given trends in demographics and urbanisation – the chapter also gives direction and next steps to advancing policy and practice in this area, suggesting that society has reached a crucial junction in preparedness for supporting an agenda around ageing in place and more broadly creating positive, enabling and inclusive neighbourhoods for all.

The overarching aim of Part Three is to refocus the way in which we think about the person and environmental debate by addressing the following questions:

- What is the current policy context around the individual and the environment?
- What are the shortfalls and next steps to be taken in social policy?
- How might the person–environment relationship be influenced by future challenges and opportunities?

Note

[1] The research was an extension of the ESRC's Growing Older Programme (GO), Older People in Deprived Neighbourhoods – Social Exclusion and Quality of Life (with Thomas Scharf and Chris Phillipson).

Part One
Revisiting the person–environment fit

TWO

Environmental gerontology

> [T]he right to a decent environment is an inalienable right and requires no empirical justification. (Lawton, 1980, p 160)

Introduction

Society has reached a historical period in the demographic profile of the population, bringing into focus a need to prepare nations to support ageing and older people. Although Lawton (1980) stated that a decent environment is a right requiring no empirical justification (see quote above), social policy and social change needs to be driven by a better understanding of what constitutes a 'decent' environment in which older people are committed to ageing in place. Environmental gerontology can and must play a role in the supply of knowledge to inform the health and well-being of older people and ensure that policy and practice is driven by a strong evidence base.

This chapter reviews the stock of empirical data on the person–environmental fit over the last 40 years. Key conceptual theories and empirical data, such as M. Powell Lawton's (1980, 1982, 1990) *Ecological Model of Ageing* and Rowles' (1978, 1980, 1983a, 1993) concept of '*insideness*' are examined as to their contribution to our understanding of environmental gerontology. Connected to this, the chapter explores the concepts of 'ageing in place' and 'place in ageing' as they contribute to current debate and a wider policy agenda around 'staying put'. Importantly, this chapter discusses recent criticisms and shortfalls in scientific knowledge related to person–environment fit.

Over the last half-century, researchers have generated a wealth of data and developed a range of theoretical concepts and frameworks relating to the relationship between the 'ageing person' and the 'environment'. This relationship is seen as pluralistic, encompassing numerous disciplines, mixed methodological approaches and empirical findings (Wahl and Weisman, 2003; Scheidt and Windley, 2006), and hence has no uniform theoretical and methodological approach (Kendig, 2003); this provides both opportunities and challenges for understanding ageing and the environment. A variety of academic disciplines have in some form been interested in understanding the person–environment relationship. Given the enormity of this literature, the focus of this present literature review is largely on gerontological research that informs the dual concepts of 'ageing in place' and 'place in ageing' as this relates to understanding the relationship between the person and their environment. It addresses approximately 40 years of environmental science research and borrows from the disciplines of psychology, sociology, epidemiology, geography and anthropology.

Ageing in place is concerned with understanding the process of ageing in a familiar environment. This is in general considered optimal: 'older people, particularly as they grow more frail, are able to remain more independent by, and benefit from, aging in environments to which they are accustomed' (Rowles, 1993, p 65). This has largely attracted the attention of policy makers interested in assessing the economic costs of housing an ageing society (Haldemann and Wister, 1993; Cutchin, 2003; OECD, 2003) and meeting social care needs (Wanless, 2006).

According to Cutchin (2005: 121), place is defined as 'a concept that broadly refers to the ensemble of social, cultural, historic, political, economic and physical features that make up the meaningful context of human life'. *Place in ageing* is concerned with understanding the meaning of place in the process of ageing (Rowles, 1993) and has largely attracted the interest of the academic community. Connected to place in ageing is the idea of emotive connection to place or 'place attachment' (Wahl, 2001). When speaking of these two concepts together, for simplicity, the author will use the term 'place and ageing'; recognising the presence of physical and psychological factors in the person–environment relationship.

The first part of this review revisits the work of Lawton and Nahemow (1973) and Lawton's (1980, 1982, 1990) *Ecological Model of Ageing*. A key focus will be on the conceptual and theoretical underpinnings connected to our understanding and deconstruction of the person–environment fit; in particular, *environmental press* and *personal competence*, and the envisaged interaction of these two components. It then explores the literature around the themes of 'ageing in place' and 'place in ageing'. Specifically, it identifies what we currently know about these concepts, why they are important, what affects them and how they can be measured. This draws on North American, British and European research in this area. The final part of the chapter reviews current limitations in our knowledge of environmental ageing. It highlights and discusses three current limitations:

- gaps in contextual understanding;
- methodological shortfalls;
- lack of consideration of temporal dimensions.

Given the current demographic achievements and political interest in ageing and the environment (to be discussed more fully in Chapter Three), there is an urgent need now to address these shortfalls in scientific knowledge.

Revisiting the Ecological Model of Ageing

There has been an enormous amount of criticism of environmental gerontology in the latter part of the 20th and beginning of the 21st century. According to Scheidt and Windley (2006), the 1960s and 1970s produced a handful of early theories that drove policy and practice, but this had largely dissipated by the 1980s to the present. They suggest that research and practice since 'have been largely fueled by looser assumptions derived from these older grand-scale frameworks or from more specific models tailored to highly particularized contexts' (2006, p 106). In addition, they suggest that the 'absence of well-articulated theory useful for stimulating empirical research and practice continues to occupy discussion' (p 106) (see Wahl, 2001).

Early origins of the Ecological Model of Ageing are rooted in Lewin's ecological equation $B = f(P, E)$ – such that: 'Behavior is dependent on the qualities and dynamic interaction of both persons and environment' (Scheidt and Windley, 2006, p 106) – which drove the early origins and foundation on which early theories were built. There has been acknowledgement that iconic status of the model outstrips empirical validation of the assumptions, with findings being 'mixed' (read Scheidt and Norris-Baker, 2004; Scheidt and Windley, 2006).

In recent years there has been more of a reflective examination of environmental gerontology, a key criticism being that researchers have relied too heavily on this model because of an absence of others – 'adding to and changing taxonomic elements of each of its major environmental, individual, and outcome components in an attempt to revivify its empirical promise' (Scheidt and Windley, 2006, p 108).

The importance of the Ecological Model of Ageing, and hence the need to revisit it, cannot be underestimated. There are at least three reasons for this. The first relates to the predominance of the model. The concepts and frameworks have dominated the environmental gerontology discourse for over 30 years. Originally developed by Lawton and Nahemow (1973), the Ecological Theory of Ageing or Competence-Press Model continues to influence environmental science research and practice. Described by Kendig (2003), Schwarz (2003) and Wahl and Weisman (2003) as one of the most prominent and 'landmark' theories in the field, and by Golant (2003, p 640) as 'by far, the most referenced, interpreted, and applied theoretical framework', 'the competence-environmental press framework continues to remain a pivotal model of person-environmental research' (Gitlin, 2003, p 632). The second is the cross-discipline support for the model. The competence-press discourse and framework have been found to apply and be relevant across disciplines (for example, anthropology, geography, gerontology and psychology). And the third relates to the model's methodological flexibility. Although developed originally as a quantitative measure (see Lawton and Nahemow, 1973), the framework and concepts of competence-press appear to work well and help inform qualitative research (see Rowles, 1978; Rubinstein, 1986, 1988; Peace et al, 2003).

Lawton and Nahemow (1973) developed two useful concepts – personal competence and environmental press. *Personal competence* is generally recognised as something characteristic to the person, typically defined as external (for example, resources such as financial status and social networks) or internal (for example, personality). Lawton (1982) defines the processes of competence as related to biological health, sensory and perceptual capabilities, motor skill, cognitive capacity and ego strength. This may in part reflect his disciplinary roots in psychology. Others define personal competence in more social or subjective terms, such as stock of social support or capital, perceived financial management and functional health (Rowles, 1978; Rubinstein, 1990; Brown, 1995; Peace et al, 2003). Personal competence is viewed on a continuum from low to high, with low representing those with few resources (for example, poor health or lack of financial resources) and high referring to those with many resources (for example, good health and being financially secure) (see Figure 2.1).

Environmental press, originally credited to Murray (1938), examines the contextual demands of the environment and how the person responds based on their competence level (Lawton and Nahemow, 1973; Lawton, 1982). Environmental press is related to such things as the physical demands of the area, aesthetic appearance, amenities and fear of crime (La Gory et al, 1985; Brown, 1995). Lawton and Nahemow (1973) also include socio-environmental relationships in this definition, such as an individual's relationship with family, friends and neighbours, and membership of cultural or social groups (Lawton et al, 1982; Lawton, 1999). As with personal competence, environmental press is viewed on a continuum from weak to strong, with weak representing perceived low environmental demand or stimulus and strong indicating high environmental demand (see Figure 2.1).

Figure 2.1: Competence-press model

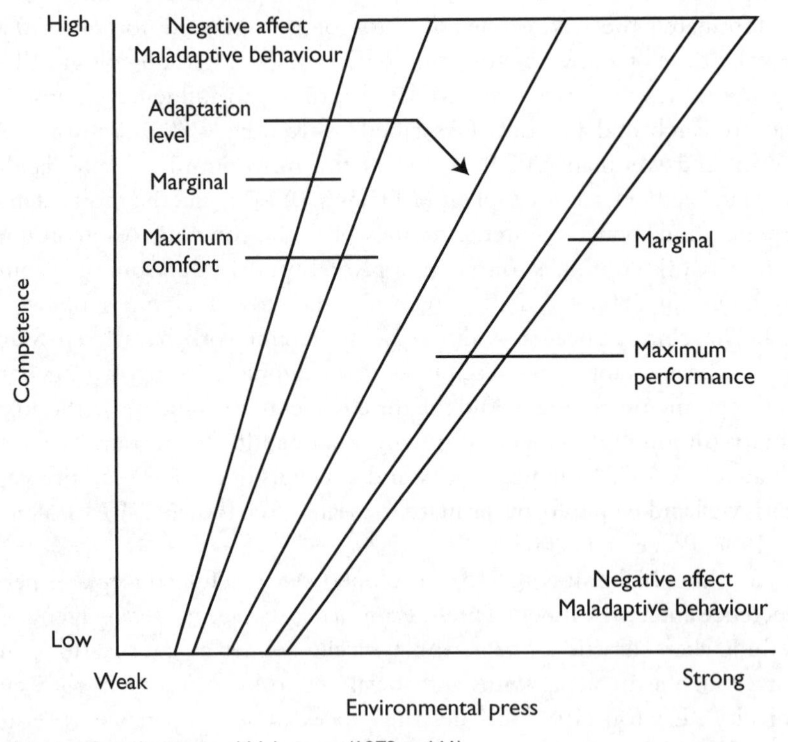

Source: Adapted from Lawton and Nahemow (1973, p 661)

The basic theoretical framework of competence-press was envisaged to function in the following way:

> [B]ehavior is a function of the competence of the individual and the environmental press of the situation ... a behavior (or affective response) is seen as the result of a combination of a press of a given magnitude acting on, or perceived by, or utilized by, an individual of a given level of competence. (Lawton et al, 1982, p 43)

For example, those with low competence encountering strong environmental press are more likely to have maladaptive behaviour compared with those having high competence encountering weak environmental press where behaviour is likely to be adaptive and positive. As suggested by Lawton (1986, p 11), the 'essential contribution of the model is to indicate that adaptive behavior and/or positive affect may result from a wide variety of *combinations* of individual competences and environmental press'. These combinations can be those experiencing low competence and strong press or high competence and weak press or a situation in which competence and press have reached a state of equilibrium or adaptation level. At this level, behaviour or transaction with the environment is viewed as automatic. Environmental press levels above the adaptation level – zone of maximum performance potential – are hypothesised to enable 'learning, novel behaviour, and mobilized energy, as well as positive affect' (Lawton, 1998, p 4), and press levels below adaptation – zone of maximum comfort – are associated with reduced energy output and, in general, positive behaviour. These combinations have been explored and found in a range of research literature (Rowles, 1978; Kahana, 1982; Nahemow, 2000; Peace et al, 2003).

The competence-press framework has led to the development of two key hypotheses: the environmental docility hypothesis and the environmental proactivity hypothesis. The *environmental docility hypothesis* states that:

> decreased personal competence leads to a greater likelihood that one's behavior or subjective state would be controlled by environmental factors, or alternatively, that a greater proportion of explanation for personal outcomes was due to environmental influence for less competent people. (Lawton, 1990, p 345)

This is similarly expressed by Rowles (1978, p 161): when 'physiological and health constraints upon agility increase, environmental barriers become more significant'.

The *environmental proactivity hypothesis* was developed after criticisms that the model was too environmentally deterministic and lacked consideration of individual agency. The hypothesis recognises that there is a reciprocal interaction: 'that older people, like all others, choose, alter, and create environments' (Lawton, 1999, p 94). The hypothesis states that 'environmental resources are likely to be better used by (and therefore more likely to be behavior-activating for) people of higher competence' (Lawton, 1985, p 507). This casts the person as the agent of environmental change, and recognises the bidirectional relationship between the person and the environment.

Ageing in place – physical

Research literature related to 'ageing in place' finds that the majority of older people would prefer to remain in their own homes and communities, even when faced with increased frailty (Haldemann and Wister, 1993; Rowles, 1993; OECD, 2003; Godfrey et al, 2004). Reasons underlying older people's desire to remain in their neighbourhood are investigated in the current literature review. Understanding these reasons might present insights into the reasons why some older people wish to age in place despite multiple physical and/or environmental risks or why some choose to reject remaining in place. Two factors that might present important reasons for ageing in place – physical necessity and spatial restriction – are discussed next.

Physical necessity

Ageing in place might have pragmatic reasons related to cost and convenience: 'remaining in a dwelling that is owned, mortgage free, in a location where one is fully aware of and integrated within a local service network and can receive practical assistance from friends and neighbors' (Rowles, 1993, p 68). However, discussion of the 'cost and convenience' of ageing in place seldom goes beyond a couple of descriptive lines. The focus of the research literature is primarily based on the physical necessity of people to age in a location with which they are familiar. Previous research has found that one of the principal reasons underlying a need to age in place relates to physical attachment (Rowles, 1978, 1983a, 1984; Lawton, 1985; Rubinstein, 1986, 1988; Mowl et al, 2000). Such attachment or physical-spatial knowledge is assumed to be gained through years of residence in a location and/or could be gained through frequent performance of an activity (Rowles, 1978, 1980). Research suggests that having this acute physical awareness of one's own environment is optimal as functional health declines, enabling the maximisation of physical function and the maintenance of independence. This is discussed in further detail below.

Rowles (1978, 1980) conducted a series of in-depth ethnographic studies of older people living in urban and rural neighbourhoods in the US. Coming from a human and social geographical perspective, Rowles (1978) interest was in exploring the geographical experiences – an 'individual's involvement within the spaces and places of his life' (1978, p 38) – of long-time community-residing older adults. Findings from this research revealed that older people form a physical attachment or what Rowles termed 'physical insideness' with their environment. It is suggested that we often take this for granted and tend not to think about it:

'over many years, each participant had developed an inherent "body awareness" of every detail of the physical configuration of this environment' (Rowles, 1983a, p 302). According to Rowles (1978, p 163), this has important implications for ageing in place as the 'lessons learned through repeatedly traversing familiar space facilitated continued participation in environments which might otherwise have been almost impossible to negotiate'. Put simply, having physical insideness with a familiar environment enables the masking of functional health declines and the maintenance of stable levels of physical functioning in the face of decline.

The development of a physical connection to the environment has also been explored by Lawton (1985). Using participant observation, Lawton found that community-residing people had over the years of living in a single location developed a 'state of residential knowing'. Lawton (1985, p 508) describes this as: 'Intimate knowledge of the idiosyncrasies of one's dwelling ... one gets to know how to find neighborhood resources, how to use transportation, and who one's friends and neighbors are'. Lawton suggests that the more people know about their environment, the more independent they can be whatever their level of personal competence.

In addition, having a physical awareness of the environment enables greater flexibility and accommodation to changes in the environment. This is evident in some of Rowles' (1978) case studies:

> To Stan the local environment was a series of resource nodes (bars) [pubs] embedded in space to be negotiated. Traversing this space involved a detailed awareness of the path to be taken under diverse circumstances. When there was snow he kept to the right of the path.... Around lunchtime he would be especially conscious of the traffic.... When it was hot he would take a shady route. (1978, p 166)

Physical spatial knowledge of the environment has been found to be related to ideas of control or autonomy (Francis, 1989; Oswald et al, 2003a; Phillips et al, 2005). From the psychology literature, control has been linked to a decrease in stress, to psychological well-being and to coping. According to Francis (1989), control is a key variable in the use and experienced quality of spaces and places. Control affects environmental use, perception, valued places and attachment. Elements of control might be necessary for daily functioning and meaning. Perceived control is an important prerequisite to form positive environmental experiences (Francis, 1989). Oswald et al (2003a) found control to be influenced by age, education and income. They found that advanced age, lower education and low income were associated with high external control beliefs or the belief that others have more power over one's situation. This suggests that ageing in place might pose negative challenges for these individuals. Based on this finding, one would expect that older persons living in deprived areas characterised by lower educational attainment and poverty might present greater challenges to ageing in place compared to those individuals living in non-deprived areas.

Spatial restriction

Another underlying reason to age in place might be a consequence of successful adaptation to increased spatial restriction brought about by declines in functional health. Previous research suggests that health restrictions and environmental barriers work to support increased spatial restriction with age (Rowles, 1978; Lawton, 1985; Rubinstein, 1986, 1988). Such research highlights a number of reasons to suggest that when spatial restriction occurs, the process of ageing is made easier if one remains in place.

The first of these relates to the ability of the older person to manipulate and control their physical environment through environmental restructuring (Lawton, 1985; Rubinstein, 1986, 1988; Peace, 1988). Lawton (1985) found that when functional health declined among community-residing older persons, they tried to maximise their physical living space by restricting mobility to their immediate surroundings (for example, the ground floor of their house) through environmental restructuring. This restructuring of their physical space enabled both more control over their immediate environment, and maintenance of their social world by continuing to live in their community.

A second benefit to ageing in place when spatial restriction occurs is presented by Rowles (1978). In his in-depth study and analysis of the geographical experiences of five older people living in an inner-city neighbourhood, Rowles identified the significant role played by 'fantasy' in relation to well-being and adaptation:

> As the person grows older there is a change of emphasis within the geographical experience involving a constriction in the realm of action which is accompanied by an expansion of the role of geographical *fantasy*.... There are consistent accompanying changes in the older person's orientation within space and in *feelings about the places of his life* reflecting a selective intensification of involvement. (Rowles, 1978, p 202, emphasis added)

'Fantasy' is defined by Rowles as the recollection of the past. It enables the individual to be liberated from any spatial restrictions, with 'autobiography, personality and the limits of imagination' being the only boundaries. In the face of changes and adaptation to health decline, fantasy supports personal identity. It is suggested that this is accomplished by locating the person in the past as a healthy, active independent self, thus creating a continuity of self (this is discussed in more detail later). The literature suggests that environmental restructuring and fantasy might not be achieved outside a familiar environment (Rowles, 1978). Therefore, ageing in place might be a prerequisite for successful adaptation to increased spatial restriction (and hence physical attachment).

Spatial restriction, although generally viewed within the literature as a feature or consequence of physical health decline, might also have a psychological component. Consideration of psychological factors such as distress within restriction might be particularly probable in environments characterised by high press(es). Environments such as deprived inner-city neighbourhoods might fit this profile. In particular, fear of crime might put restrictions on mobility independent of any changes in functional health. This is an important consideration but remains largely neglected within the literature (Peace et al, 2006).

Spatial restriction was found by La Gory et al (1985) to be a possible protective factor for environment decline. Their empirical research suggests that persons with low competence (for example, poor functional health) may be unaffected by living in an inner-city neighbourhood: 'The urban pathology and distress predicted by classical urban theorists is apparently not experienced by the elderly with reduced physical, social and psychological resources and abilities' (1985, p 416). Conversely, those who were highly competent, and hence physically mobile, experienced significant environmental distress. La Gory et al suggested that a 'more active lifestyle is necessary for the individual to experience the press or overload of the city. In this sense, restricted spatial experience may serve a protective function' (1985, p 416). Consideration of this might be important in the analysis and interpretation of older people's perceptions of environmental demands and subsequently their relationship with their neighbourhood.

Place in ageing – psychological

In this section, the focus shifts to examine research related to more emotive or sentimental bonds that tie people to their environment. Unlike ageing in place, which relates primarily to the physical familiarity or process underlying physical attachment to place, place in ageing relates to the psychological reason underlying people's desire to stay in their present locality. Such understanding might be particularly salient when trying to analyse and understand the reasons why people may desire to remain in place despite the multiple risks present in their neighbourhood. According to Rapoport (1982, p 143, emphasis added), environmental stress is 'subjectively defined so that symbolic and meaning aspects become important ... *familiarity* may make environments of widely varying quality "good" and, therefore one must consider *meaning*'.

The literature discusses place in ageing in the following way. According to Taylor (2001, p 9), place 'encompasses vernacular architecture, landscape, social relationships with older people, and memories', and it 'can exist as remembered experiences in the minds of those at a distance'. Numerous studies have sought to understand place in relation to the development and creation of meaning. Terms such as *attachment to place*, *place attachment* and *sense of place* have all been used to denote the creation of positive experience or memories. Rubinstein and Parmelee (1992, p 139) define attachment to place as a 'set of feelings about a geographical location that emotionally binds a person to that place as a function of its role as a setting for experience'. Riley (1992, pp 13, 18) suggests that attachment is 'an affective relationship between people and the landscape that goes beyond cognition, preference, or judgement ... [and is] a complex set of threads woven through one's life'. Brown and Perkins (1992, p 284) argue that 'Place attachment involves positively experienced bonds, sometimes occurring without awareness, that are developed over time from the behavioral, affective, and cognitive ties between individuals and/or groups and their sociophysical environment'.

Failed or disrupted attachments to place are generally defined as harmful (Brown and Perkins, 1992; Rowles and Ravdal, 2002). Disruptions are thought to threaten the self-identity, stability and security of the individual, and disruptions can take many forms (Fried, 2000). For example, indigenous change refers to transformations of the environment or neighbourhood 'while the individual remains in place' (Rowles and Ravdal, 2002). This can result from deterioration of the area/dwelling, change in cultural and/or ethnic groups or physical disruption of the area brought on by structural change (for example, routing of a major highway through the area). Rowles and Ravdal (2002, p 88) suggest that geographical change can present a traumatic and stressful situation, arguing that for some people:

> particularly those who have resided in a single location throughout their lives, being in place fosters a strong sense of possessiveness, even territoriality. Such intense bonding with places leads to a reluctance to abandon them because, in an almost literal sense, to abandon them is to abandon the self.

The above explanations of place attachment generally consider attachment to be positive and disruptions to attachment to be negative. However, this might be a little oversimplistic. Fried (2000) challenges the notion that place attachment is always positive and disruptions are always negative. He suggests that place attachment is a 'primordial sentiment', which carries deep psychological feelings. This sentiment can be significant for positive well-being or can be dysfunctional. A danger of place attachment is that people become 'addicted to encompassing forms of continuity in community attachments' (Fried, 2000, p 193) and are unable to take opportunities that might improve their situation. For example, when an individual rejects attempts at improving their environment and/or personal resources for the sake of ageing in place, there is a need to consider dysfunctional forms of place attachment.

Relevance of place and ageing issues

Within the literature, a number of reasons are given that support the idea that place is important in ageing. The most frequently referenced relate to notions of place and identity. Development and maintenance of identity is believed to be contextually situated in place. This is appropriately articulated as follows: 'If you draw a map of everywhere you have ever been they say you draw your own face' (Shakespeare, 2002, introduction/scene 1). This quote parallels much of the research findings within this area. Essentially, place is argued to provide an individual with a rich 'tapestry' of lifelong experiences and memories; as one ages and possible health problems challenge identity, place can work to reinforce one's life, as it was in the past, and help the individual manage their present or future self (Rubinstein and Parmelee, 1992). The physical environment can present a backdrop against which the individual chooses to accept or reject the self (Howell, 1983). This is why place in the ageing process might be particularly significant.

Identity and place

A significant contribution to academic understanding of the importance of place in ageing can be credited to Rowles' (1980, 1983a, 1983b, 1984, 1993) ethnographic research. Adopting an explorative investigative approach, Rowles spent several years studying the phenomenological experience of attachment to the environment and self-identity of Appalachian rural older people in the US. This work is presented in detail below because it provides useful insight into, and explanations of, place attachment and identity among older people (Rowles, 1980), and because much of the research since appears either to borrow from this work and/or establish similar findings (Rivlin, 1987; Taylor, 2001; Peace et al, 2003, 2006).

Rowles' (1978, 1980, 1983a, 1983b, 1984, 1993) research and analysis revealed that older people who have lived in one locality for a long time develop a physical and psychological attachment to their environment. This is particularly pronounced with advanced age and/or health challenges. Rowles framed ideas of attachment within the term 'insideness'. Physical insideness has previously been discussed in relation to ageing in place. Rowles developed two other types of insideness relating to the emotive or sentimental meaning given to place in ageing; these are social and autobiographical. Social insideness relates to the propensity to form social affinity with a place or 'integration within the social fabric of the community' (Rowles, 1983a, p 302). For example, this includes daily routines, rules and norms that operate and develop between others in the household or outside the home with neighbours: 'Individuals are enabled to develop a sense of "belonging" through participation in local culture, and through sharing in nurturing the neighborhood's sense of group identification with place' (Rowles, 1993, p 66). Autobiographical insideness concerns the personal history of the individual in relation to place. Accordingly, it is proposed that autobiography might present the greater insight into older people's attachment to place and identity, because such an insideness and its recall is highly personal (Rowles, 1983a, 1993). As Rowles (1993, p 66) suggests, 'Our images of self and sense of identity as we grow older, and as those around us age, are inextricably intertwined with the places of our lives' and 'as we grow older and remember the events of our lives, places are selectively recalled as we reinforce our image of who we are'. As a consequence, unlike physical and social insideness, autobiographical insideness can rarely be created in a new environment (Rowles, 1980). This 'grand fiction' of the past is believed to be reinforced through three mechanisms operating within the environment: preservation of artefacts (for example, photographs), ongoing participation in a familiar setting, and shared history or experience of the community among older residents (Rowles, 1980, 1983a). Autobiographical insideness is connected to the earlier notion of geographical fantasy, therefore as functional health declines autobiography might take on a new significance in sentimental attachment.

Concepts of social and autobiographical insideness present a useful framework for the consideration of place attachment among older people. However, insideness might conceivably be a feature or consequence of a specific geographical location. In Rowles' case, it might typify conditions present in a rural environment. Conditions present in other environments, such as urban settings where change is more prevalent, might challenge concepts of insideness. This could present a different way to assess the strength of, or disruptions to, place attachment.

Rowles' research suggests that for older people, specifically those who have lived in their neighbourhoods for a long period of time, persons and place can become important sources of self-identity and support. Taken together, Rowles (1993, p 66) suggests that while:

> not exclusively an aging-related phenomenon, our ability to develop and maintain a sense of attachment to place, to sustain a sense of physical, social, and autobiographical insideness, and to organize the space within our home in a manner consistent with our needs and personality, may as we grow older, become increasingly significant in preserving a sense of identity and continuity amidst a changing world.

Social and autobiographical insideness raise some important issues with respect to understanding the importance of place in the ageing process and present issues that require consideration in the current research. Specifically, place is characterised by collective and personal/individual affinity.

Within a British context, environment and identity maintenance has been investigated by Kellaher et al (2004) and Peace et al (2005, 2006). Using a mixed qualitative approach, 54 older people living across three different geographical locations – metropolitan/urban areas, towns and semi-rural villages – were interviewed. Findings revealed a dynamic relationship between older people and their social and material environment. According to Peace et al (2005, p 200), there appears to be a comfort level for environmental connectedness (or insideness) that enables a person to maintain a balance between the self and society:

> [P]eople find that over time the number and quality of their attachments to environment become compromised by decline in their own competence and/or the demand characteristics of environment. The point at which these attachments become insufficient for tolerable living equates to the point where adaptive behaviour cannot rebalance environmental press.

In this situation, older people are found to create new, or reinforce old points of place attachment, through modification in personal behaviour (for example, physical or cognitive/imaginative) or environmental changes. Individuals successfully engaging in new or reinforced points of attachment were seen to have maintained mastery over their environment and a life of quality: 'life of quality is one where mastery is maintained over the strategies necessary to make attachments/connections – to have the capacity to attach to social and material "fabric"' (2005, pp 200-1). Peace et al (2005) also make the point that the relationship is dynamic such that the process is constantly changing as health declines or improves or as needs within the environment change. This introduces a temporal dimension into the relationship that has often been neglected in the literature. This is discussed in more detail later with reference to Golant's (2003) work.

Environmental challenges to identity were also studied by Scheidt and Norris-Baker (1990). In an analysis of declining rural towns they found that when community identity was challenged by negative changes (for example, economic decline, population decline), older residents either sought to re-establish the community of the past or create a new identity: 'Some older individuals have forged a regional sense of community which includes one's own town as well as more viable nearby communities' (1990, p 18). They suggest that this was necessitated by the economic and psychological benefits of being associated with a more viable community. However, these findings might be in part a feature of the rural areas. For older people who have invested all or a substantial part of their lives in one location and where there is little interest in moving or lack of opportunity to move, the continued development of a sense of community identity and attachment in any form might be important for psychological well-being. This might also be usefully extended to urban areas in which older people have spent all or a substantial part of their lives; similarly having invested in these neighbourhoods, older people might willingly challenge negative perceptions of the area.

It is also important to make the point that place can undermine identity. Feelings of displacement have the ability to evoke painful memories of past places and people. Becker's (2003) study of the meaning of place among three groups of older immigrants living in an inner city identified significant feelings of psychological distress related to feelings of displacement from the environment. According to Lambek and Antze (1996, p xvi), 'while memory should support the dominant view of our identity ... it always threatens to undermine it, whether by obvious gaps, by uncertainties, or by glimpses of a past that no longer seems to be ours'. This might be particularly relevant in the consideration of older people living in deprived inner-city areas, where the experience of significant, unpleasant social and physical changes to their neighbourhood might be a feature of individuals' biographies.

Identity and ageing

Another consideration is the connection between identity and ageing. The understanding of identity and how it relates to or is affected by the ageing process has been a focus of significant research (Kaufman, 1986; Brandtstädter and Greve, 1994; Smith and Freund, 2002). Interest has centred on understanding how changes associated with ageing (for example, decline in health, bereavement) challenge or put strain on people's continuity of self. In *The ageless self*, Kaufman (1986, p 7) concedes that 'when old people talk about themselves, they express a sense of self that is ageless – an identity that maintains continuity despite the physical and social change'. This continuity of self is maintained by:

> [drawing] meaning from the past, interpreting and recreating it as a resource for being in the present. It also draws meaning from the structural and ideational aspects of the cultural context.... Old people formulate and reformulate personal and cultural symbols of their past to create a meaningful, coherent sense of self, and in the process they create a viable present. In this way, the ageless self emerges: its definition is ongoing, continuous, and creative. (Kaufman, 1986, p 14)

This was similarly expressed by Brandtstädter and Greve (1994, p 72), who found the self to be a dynamic structure, 'involved in the representation, evaluation, and active control of personal development over the life span, and which exhibits distinctive features of self-organization, self-reproduction, and self-stabilization'. Despite challenges accompanying later life, older people exhibit 'remarkable stability, resilience and resourcefulness of the ageing self' (Brandtstädter and Greve, 1994, p 72). This is also supported by cross-sectional and longitudinal analysis from the Berlin Aging Study. Smith and Freund (2002) found older adults (aged 70-103) to actively achieve maintenance or accept changing selves in the presence of physical health decline. Extending challenges of the self as not only those encompassing personal changes (for example, health, loss of friends) but also the environmental context might need to be considered. This is addressed in the work of Peace et al (2006), which finds that when environment fails to meet the needs of an individual, they engage in *option recognition*. This allows individuals to preserve identity and well-being by adapting the environment or considering more appropriate housing options. This might be particularly pertinent in an environmental context, which might present multiple challenges and risks.

Life review

Life review might be another important feature. Although it has been mentioned above in the context of identity, it deserves some brief mention here. Place can be argued to provide life review, particularly for those who have remained in a single location for most of their lives. As Rubinstein and Parmelee (1992, p 147, emphasis added) suggest: 'Place and things are important symbols of the self, *cues to memories of significant life experiences*, and a means of maintaining, reviewing, and extending one's sense of self'. Place is envisaged to provide the backdrop against which life events can be remembered and replayed; attachment to long-ago places keeps the past 'alive' and provides continuity of identity in the face of functional decline. The lifecourse is proposed to be intertwined with environmental meaning, such that by listening to and examining the individual's organisation of self and life, environmental meaning can be found (Rubinstein, 1990). Some of the examples given in the literature include the local park where they played as a child, the local church where they got married or the local school that their children attended.

Life review fits closely with Rowles' concept of autobiographical insideness, in that it is contextually specific and seldom replicated elsewhere. Life review has also been found to be important for psychological health (Butler, 1963; Blane et al, 2004) and enhancing quality of life (Borglin et al, 2005). Facilitating life review through ageing in place might present an important consideration for the well-being of older community-residing residents.

Quality of life

The relationship between 'place and ageing' and quality of life presents another important consideration. Research supports a connection between these concepts (Farquhar, 1995; Raphael et al, 1999; Hannan, 2001; Scharf et al, 2002a, 2002b; Stevens-Ratchford and Diaz, 2003; Gabriel and Bowling, 2004; Wiggins et al, 2004; Scharf et al, 2005). Place was an important factor in Farquhar's (1995) study of older people in Hackney (London) and Braintree (Essex). For those living in Hackney, an inner-city borough with high rates of deprivation, older people reported a poorer quality of life compared to those in Braintree, described as a semi-rural affluent area. Gabriel and Bowling (2004, p 675) found 'living in a home and neighbourhood that is perceived to give pleasure, feels safe, and has access to local facilities and services' to be important themes in older people's reports of quality of life.

Ageing, in particular declines in health, is also important in ratings of quality of life (Bowling, 1995). Findings from the Berlin Aging Study established that age per se was not a cause of lower levels of well-being, but that health constraints were (Kunzmann et al, 2000). Borglin et al (2005), in an in-depth study of quality of life among those aged 80 and over, found 'that quality of life in old age meant a preserved self and meaning in existence' (p 201); suggesting that quality of life is driven not only by health status, but also by a positive psychological sense of self. However, it should be noted that quality of life is a complex concept (Smith, 2000) and, while a link has been found with place and ageing, other themes have also emerged. Quality of life has been found to be temporally located (Blane et al, 2004) and affected by social comparisons (Gabriel and Bowling, 2004; Graham and Kenealy, 2004). Social comparisons might be particularly relevant to understanding older people's perceptions of quality of life, given that evaluations are likely to be made within the context of those around them (for example, neighbours, peers).

Influences on place attachment

The previous section was focused on understanding the importance of place with respect to the identity and lifecourse of the ageing individual. This section is concerned with addressing possible influences on the development of place attachment. Understanding these influences might generate important insights for this study, in that the characteristics of deprived urban areas might present challenges to sentimental attachment.

Place attachment research has found a number of factors that affect its development, including:

- length of residency (Rowles, 1978, 1980; Young et al, 2004);
- social support, contacts and integration (Shumaker and Taylor, 1983; St. John et al, 1986; Rivlin, 1987; Mesch and Manor, 1998; Cattell and Evans, 1999; Fried, 2000; Phillipson et al, 2001; Cattell, 2004; Godfrey et al, 2004; Helliwell and Putnam, 2004);
- perception of area (Mesch and Manor, 1998) or perceived rewards of living in an area compared with other areas (Shumaker and Taylor, 1983);
- access to services and amenities (Kasarda and Janowitz, 1974; Shumaker and Taylor, 1983; Rivlin, 1987);
- neighbourhood satisfaction (Kasarda and Janowitz, 1974);
- functional distance (for example, proximity to social encounters) (Rivlin, 1987; Sugihara and Evans, 2000);
- perceived control over the environment (Pellow, 1992);
- perceived choice in the selection of residence (Shumaker and Taylor, 1983);
- community participation (Francis, 1989);
- public spaces (Francis, 1989; Armstrong, 2000; Mumford and Power, 2003);
- lifecourse or life history (Western, 1993; McHugh and Mings, 1996);
- cultural influences (Taylor, 2001; West, 2002);
- location (Fried, 2000; Corcoran, 2002; Parkes et al, 2002; Airey, 2003; Helliwell and Putnam, 2004; Burholt and Naylor, 2005).

Length of residency has already been discussed with respect to ageing in place. Living in a single location for many years can support a number of underlying factors associated with place attachment such as established social networks, area knowledge, physical insideness and development of life history. Cattell and Evans (1999), in a study of residents living on two estates in East London, found friendliness, good humour, reciprocity and support of neighbours to strengthen residents' sense of attachment. Area perception or perceived rewards of living in the area were found to undermine or aid in attachment. These 'rewards' might be decreased or increased personal dependence and/or environmental presses. As long as the perceived rewards were viewed as higher or the same as other areas, place attachment was not undermined.

Access to services and amenities has also been identified as important in place attachment. According to Rivlin (1987, p 14), when needs are 'concentrated and a local area becomes the context for servicing the major domains of life, that area will assume a particular importance to residents, in contrast to instances where people go all over a city to fulfil their needs'. When people use the services within their area they contribute to sustaining the local economy and build social and community capital through these transactions. We know from much of the research data that social support is a significant factor in place attachment (see Shumaker and Taylor, 1983)). According to Rivlin (1987, p 14):

> [if] an area has been the context for meeting needs over time ... [and] where concentrated use of the neighbourhood has built sets of relationships, habits, and memories that have developed, over time, and where group affiliations have existed, over time, the combined power of each domain is likely to have created strong attachments to the place and its people.

How this might change through the use of technology (for example, shopping online) is discussed in Chapter Eight.

In recent years there has also been interest in assessing public place quality and use (see Altman and Zube, 1989; Low and Altman, 1992; Worpole and Knox, 2007) and attachment (Francis, 1989). It is suggested that the ability to form public place attachments might foster and enable greater connectedness to an area. Public space attachments have been found to increase or develop when residents are engaged within spaces of their neighbourhood. In particular this has been studied in relation to community gardens and parks. In a redevelopment of Battery Park in Lower Manhattan, New York, for example, the participatory process was found to have enhanced attachment to the community (Francis, 1989). Participatory benefits of public space, such as gardens and parks, have also been shown to increase community action to solve other issues important to the neighbourhood (Armstrong, 2000). The involvement of people within the public spaces of their community has the ability to create a level of personal investment and establishment of personal control, each found to be potential sources in place attachment. Research findings support a link between plants/gardens and psychological well-being (Milligan et al, 2004), suggesting a basis for the fostering of place relationships (Brook, 2003). In addition, public places are a backdrop against which social meetings with friends and family occur (Stedman et al, 2004) and where intergenerational and cross-cultural relationships can be fostered (Holland et al, 2007; Worpole and Knox, 2007). Therefore, the public spaces might be significant as an underlying factor in place attachment.

Lifecourse or life history has also been shown to affect place attachment. In a study of attachment among older American retirees who travel south for the winter, referred to as snowbirds, McHugh and Mings (1996) found that those couples who moved more frequently through their life histories were less rooted to any one specific place on retirement, compared with couples who had lived in one place most of their lives. For the latter couples, attachment was still very strong towards the neighbourhood that they had left. Similarly, Peace et al (2003, p 204) found participants who had migrated to Britain as adults who described their own place identity as '"in limbo" between cultures'.

Place attachment has also been closely linked with geographical places. This suggests that certain environments might create greater or lesser degrees of attachment. Childhood places have been suggested as creating the foundation of place attachments in adulthood (Chawla, 1992; Cooper Marcus, 1992). Public places and participatory activity in parks and community gardens have been found to increase community involvement and attachment (Francis, 1989; Armstrong, 2000). Research connected to particular types of areas – rural and urban, affluent and deprived – display equivocal results. While Rowles (1980) and Scheidt and Norris-Baker (1990) found a strong sense of place attachment among rural older people despite environmental challenges, urban research tends to be more unclear. Some studies identify a greater sense of place attachment (Fried, 2000; Parkes et al, 2002), while others report challenges to place attachment (Corcoran, 2002; Airey, 2003; Stafford et al, 2003; Brown et al, 2004).

Another factor to consider with regard to place attachment is the role played by culture. This might be particularly pertinent to the present study as it not only entails cross-national comparison, it also entails cross-cultural comparison. Of particular relevance within a cultural perspective is the spiritual relationship with place. This is supported within the literature and defined as 'place cosmology' (West, 2002). West (2002) suggests that place might be particularly relevant in those cultures relying on place as a source of subsistence and healing. This perspective has largely been neglected within the place attachment literature, possibly because of a generally narrow focus (discussed in detail later).

Geographical issues in place and ageing

Of particular significance within this research is how location affects place and ageing. Therefore, the rest of this discussion will focus on empirical findings arising from research conducted in differing geographical locations. Rural environments, in particular, have attracted substantial research on place attachment. These environments are seen or believed to present favourable conditions for attachment. For example, when combined with population stability and relatively long lengths of residency, the small, concentrated geographical setting is perceived as creating opportunities for frequent social contact. As previously discussed, Rowles' (1980) findings on 'insideness' evolved out of in-depth research on rural older people. Such results, Rowles suggests, could be a function of the conditions of rural environments. Even in rural environments that present older people with challenges – poverty, prejudice and ill-health – Taylor (2001) reported that older African Americans were able to retain a positive self-image, sense of place and well-being because of the ability to remain in their familiar locale in which cultural and historical ties among its members were strong.

If urban areas present challenges to place attachment, the question arises of what the literature has found regarding deprived inner-city areas. A number of studies have explored these challenges (Fried, 2000; Phillipson et al, 2001; Corcoran, 2002; Parkes et al, 2002; Scharf et al, 2002a; Airey, 2003). Parkes et al (2002, p 2413) found that those living in less affluent areas were more sensitive to unfriendliness and crime, concluding that for 'those in deprived areas, the neighbourhood is likely to be a more dominant aspect of life than in more affluent areas, where residents with more resources can look beyond their immediate surroundings for services and social life'.

Fried (2000) discusses his observations on 40 years of his work in environmental psychology and offers a number of important considerations relevant to the discussion and debate on place attachment and geographical expression. Fried suggests that people living in deprived areas might be more sensitive to aspects of the environment. Specifically, 'Place attachment might be greater for people who have few physical, economic or social opportunities other than place around which to focus a sense of social belonging' (2000, p 197). Those with greater resources have the freedom to engage in activities elsewhere and hence have a more attenuated form of attachment to neighbourhood. A further reason given by Fried for greater attachment in deprived areas relates to human coping and adaptation: 'More generally, discrimination, derogation, diminished opportunity, whether for ethnic minorities, women, the elderly, or for those of lower social class levels, accentuated the need for shared conditions like those of community' (2002, p 201). In a situation in which people might feel stigmatised, family and friendship/neighbour ties might take on a greater significance and source of support within the immediate community.

However, such ideas have been challenged. For example, in a study of older people living across deprived and middle-class/affluent areas, Phillipson et al (2001) identified differences in social network types between neighbourhoods. In Bethnal Green, a deprived inner-city area in London, family and friendships appeared more fragmented and tenuous, particularly among white participants. A possible explanation for this might relate to the health and mortality of participants/residents, whereas older people in more affluent areas are able to maintain more members of their social network (Phillipson et al, 2001) because of better health outcomes.

As part of the Culture of Cities Project, Corcoran (2002) studied the meaning of place attachment and personal identity across deprived areas of six European cities – Dublin, Lisbon, London, Toulouse, Turin and Umea. Findings revealed that attachment to place was a dynamic process created through a person's lifecourse: 'Attachment to place seems to derive from composite memories of people and experiences ... continuing sense of place is predicated on sedimented memories ... which are laid down over time' (2002, p 56). Although some residents were found to express 'placelessness' and a desire to move, Corcoran reported that others countered their sense of alienation or placelessness with either physical action or verbal defiance. Some people became civically involved in changing their community, a strategy Corcoran suggests illustrated people's resistance to broader social issues of individual and neighbourhood marginalisation and exclusion. This was similarly found by Becker (2003) in a study of older minority ethnic groups living in deprived inner-city areas of the US. Resistance to marginalisation was shown to represent a strategy for overcoming a sense of displacement.

In a study of 12 women living in two 'less affluent' neighbourhoods of Edinburgh, Airey (2003) found evidence of 'distancing strategies'. The women's discourse revealed that the localisation or locating of social problems tended to be outside their own concept of their neighbourhood or immediate surroundings. According to Airey (2003, p 135), this allowed people to dissociate themselves from features of 'their' neighbourhood that were stigmatising:

> It would appear that the purpose of constructing imagined limits to 'their' neighbourhood at such a micro-scale was to enable the women to be able to exclude from their sense of neighbourhood those features of the wider social environment that they perceived to be negative, stressful and thus potentially harmful to their sense of well-being.

Corcoran's (2002) study revealed another significant finding related to deprived areas. It established that people's ability to cope with deleterious environmental change is believed to result from memories, experiences and perceived identity that have developed over their lifecourse. Her research suggested that coping for some residents might, in part, be a function of not engaging with 'reality': 'self-image of themselves in relation to the collective memory of the place gives them the ability to differentiate themselves from their current environment and draw the strength to resist from the memory of "how things used to be"' (2002, p 57).

This idea is very closely linked with Rowles' (see 1978, 1980, 1983a, 1983b) notion of 'fantasy' or 'autobiographical insideness', as previously discussed. In Rowles and Ravdal (2002; taken from Rowles' 1978 original research):

> [L]ifelong older residents of Winchester Street, were able to sustain a strong sense of attachment and belonging to their neighborhood because they were able to retain a shared sense of the community as it had been ... the neighborhood of the past still existed; it continued to live in their consciousness and conversations and to have great meaning. (p 95)

However, in order for there to be a collective memory or shared history there must be a group or cohort of peers who can share these memories (Rowles, 1978, 1980). The absence of a peer group might further serve to isolate older people. Again this suggests that autobiographical insideness might prove to be the more significant factor in explaining place attachment and psychological well-being in the face of marked indigenous change and unwillingness to relocate. However, as previously noted, memories can also harbour negative images that might strengthen attachment or resolve to the current place despite poor environmental conditions. This was evident in Becker's (2003) study of older immigrant groups living in deprived inner-city neighbourhoods of California. Memories of home evoked negative images of daily subsistence struggles and civil unrest for this group.

Summary: what we know

Before discussing some of the limitations in the current research literature, it will be useful to summarise the key features associated with contemporary debates linked to place and ageing. The adoption of the 'personal competence(s)' and 'environmental press(es)' discourse and framework gave initial structure to 'our' understanding of the person–environment components. Justification for the adoption of these concepts relates to the predominance of these components across time and diverse disciplines, methodological flexibility and the use of these concepts within particular geographical localities.

The literature associated with ageing in place suggests that the process of ageing is made easier if one remains in place. There are two underlying reasons for this:

- First, 'physical insideness' or intimate physical knowledge is argued to facilitate management of increasing functional health decline. This allows independence, a stable level of environmental control or mastery, psychological well-being by continuity in perceived self and knowing what to expect.
- Second, coping with 'spatial restriction' is found to be made easier if one remains in place. Having intimate physical knowledge of the environment enables people to gain control of both their physical and/or psychological 'deficits', and by doing this influence their environmental use, perception, attachment and psychological well-being (Francis, 1989).

The literature associated with place in ageing suggests that place is an emotive factor that is important in the process of ageing. Research on place attachment provides a framework from which to understand older people's psychological relationship with place:

- First, place attachment is considered an emotive bond between the person and the environment (both physical and psychological). Place attachment can be positive or negative, and not being attached to place does not always denote maladaptive behaviour.
- Second, place and ageing were found to be important for a number of reasons. Reification of identity, lifecourse or life review, and quality of life might only

be achieved when the individual ages in place. For older people this might be particularly significant. For those who have remained in place for a significant length of time, place provides a backdrop from which to reify past selves and enable life review.

- Third, place attachment has been found to be influenced by a number of factors, including length of residency, social integration, environmental barriers and geographical locality. Such characteristics have been found to be particularly challenged in deprived inner-city areas, raising the prospect that living in these areas might challenge place attachment.

Current analysis needs to be cautious about romanticising people's connection with place, and possible generational effects. Future research will need to consider the effects of globalisation, technology and communication, and the possible effects of the recent economic downturn on the relationship between the person and the physical environment. This will be addressed more fully in Chapter Eight.

The above literature provides a useful foundation from which initially to understand the person–environmental relationship. However, there still remain a number of gaps in scientific knowledge related to our understanding of older people's connection to their environment, particularly in places presenting multiple personal and environmental challenges. These are explored next.

Limitations of the current literature: what we do not know

In 1998, Lawton stated that he is:

> tinged with disappointment at the progress of theory development in environment and aging over the past two decades. Policy and practice seemed to benefit early from the person-environment perspective, but succeeding years failed to provide validation for the continued success of theory in directing practice.... Advances in environmental knowledge have *not* been matched by advances in knowledge regarding the person and individual differences in the person-environment transaction. (1998, p 2)

As such, environmental gerontology has been criticised for a lack of innovativeness in theoretical, methodological and empirical development (Kendig, 2003; Wahl and Weisman, 2003). Wahl and Weisman (2003), in a stocktake of environmental gerontology at the beginning of the new millennium, suggested that it is a field high in conceptual aspiration but low in application and respect of its theoretical achievements. In addition, much of the research undertaken in the 1990s sought only to replicate current knowledge. Such criticisms have caused scholars to reflect on the shortfalls with respect to the research process and current scientific knowledge. The aim of this section is to review limitations of the current place and ageing literature, specifically, contextual, methodological and temporal shortfalls, in the hope of moving this debate and thinking forward.

Gaps in empirical knowledge

Despite over 40 years of environmental gerontology research, a number of gaps in empirical knowledge relating to the relationship of the ageing individual and place remain. Given the current policy context, there is a need to address this. The first gap concerns contextual limitations. First, given that the roots of environmental gerontology are based in the US, it is perhaps not surprising that empirical and theoretical knowledge in this area has predominantly come from studies of older Americans. In a critique of American environmental ageing research, Parmelee (1998, p 179) suggests that a:

> benefit of an 'internationalization' of environmental gerontology would be simply to learn how generalizable our findings are: Are we observing culturally universal behavior patterns that are intrinsic to spatial behaviour in late life or simply the effects of being old and North American?

Another contextual shortfall relates to the geographical locations of past empirical research. Much of the person–environment literature has been conducted in institutional locations (Lawton, 1975; Calkins, 2003) and in rural settings (Rowles, 1980, 1983a, 1984, 1990; Scheidt and Norris-Baker, 1990; McAuley, 1998; Taylor, 2001; Oswald et al, 2003b; Burholt and Naylor, 2005; Joseph and Cloutier-Fisher, 2005). Given that the majority of older people reside in the community, institutional settings only address a small minority (Findlay and McLaughlin, 2005). Rowles (1984, p 148) cautions that the components of attachment observed in rural older people are likely a feature of the neighbourhood:

> [C]ertain characteristics of rural environments, physical and demographic stability and a social context conducive to being 'known' and to the maintenance among peers of shared memories of past events that transpired in particular locations, do provide particularly strong nurturance to such feelings.

The situation in urban environments might present a different understanding of attachment (Rowles, 1983b). In this respect, urban neighbourhoods have largely been ignored (Peace et al, 2003; Scheidt and Windley, 2006). According to Peace et al (2004, p 79), 'neighbourhood has been relatively under-emphasised, yet it is clear that as people age the salience of neighbourhood increases'. Added to this is a lack of research in deprived inner-city areas (Rubinstein and Parmelee, 1992). As suggested previously, these areas might present unique challenges within the context of place and ageing. With growing numbers of older people living in urban areas and increasing spatial inequalities, understanding place in the process of ageing and vice versa is increasingly significant. This has, in part, been studied in an English context in the research project to which this study is linked (see Scharf et al, 2001, 2002a, 2002b; Scharf and Phillipson, 2003; Smith, 2004).

Importantly, knowledge is also lacking with respect to comparative research. Few studies in the area of environmental gerontology have sought to develop cross-national perspectives on place and ageing. Given the criticisms in recent years of environmental gerontology as lacking innovativeness (Wahl and Weisman, 2003), advances in scientific knowledge are urgently needed. Understanding the experiences of older people in differing social, political and economic contexts can allow exploration of existing knowledge and new knowledge to emerge. The literature currently knows little about place in ageing and ageing in place across and between differing countries, and therefore could benefit from a more global comparative approach.

Methodological limitations

A methodological limitation within the current environmental science research is the predominance of quantitative studies and a lack of methodological advancement. According to La Gory et al (1985, p 416):

> [I]t is necessary to go beyond the survey research methodology on which this and most other such studies are based ... they do not provide the rich detail needed to understand the environmental experience. Future efforts should make greater use of intensive interviews with selected subgroups of older respondents.

A mixed-methods approach has also been advocated by Parmelee and Lawton (1990).

Methodological approaches, particularly in environmental gerontology, have been criticised for 'languishing' (Parmelee and Lawton, 1990) and a lack of innovativeness (Wahl and Weisman, 2003). According to Parmelee and Lawton (1990) and Wahl and Weisman (2003), despite the significant achievements in environmental gerontology research over the last two decades, there remains no cure or remedy. Critics suggest that there has been too heavy a reliance on past methodological designs and that, if environmental gerontology is to grow and has the aim of better understanding the person–environment relationship, new methodological approaches need to be adopted.

Temporal dimension

A criticism of environmental gerontology theory is the failure to adequately incorporate time or temporal dimensions (Fried, 2000; Golant, 2003). Although there has been discussion of the significance of time within the person–

environment relationship, few empirical studies have theoretically or analytically incorporated this dimension (Golant, 2003). As place and people are temporally located and time occurs within a geographical context, researchers might be neglecting a significant factor in the understanding of place and ageing. According to Golant (2003, p 639):

> [I]t becomes crucial to focus on the temporal aspects of older people's environment and aging relationships. Failing to do so is to treat older persons' transactions with their environments, settings, or situations as merely contextual snapshots or temporally static episodes rather than frames of an ongoing environmental movie.

Golant's criticism of the neglect of temporal dimensions in the person–environment relationship is mainly focused on the avoidance of an individual's history or past and the individual in the future.

Individual history

The past

In assessing an individual's current and future relationship with place, past experiences need to be understood (Rivlin, 1987; Evans, 1999; Wachs, 1999; Fried, 2000; Cutchin, 2003; Golant, 2003). According to Rivlin (1987, p 14), time is critical in understanding community attachment:

> If an area has been the context for meeting needs over time ... and where concentrated use of the neighborhood has built sets of relationships, habits, and memories that have developed over time, and where group afflictions have existed over time, the combined power of each domain is likely to have created strong attachments to the place and its people.

Assessing time or temporal dimensions might be particularly significant in that older people have a lifecourse or life history that might have an impact on needs or expectation of needs based on experience, changes in health and interpersonal relationships, which might affect environmental interaction: 'The temporal dimension is obviously of utmost importance for persons who by definition have lived long enough to have accumulated a rich reservoir of experience and insight' (Rowles, 1978, p 36). According to Cooper Marcus (1992, pp 88-9), 'times, people, and places in our personal past are critical to our emotional well-being; they allow us to weather the swells and storms of change that are components to a greater or lesser extent of every life path'.

There are at least three factors that make consideration of the past important. First, the past might make an individual more or less sensitive to the current environmental milieu, such that the present environment might be an improvement on previous environmental experiences or might better aid or thwart adaptation or expression (Golant, 1998, 2003; Wachs, 1999). Wachs (1999), in trying to understand how past experiences influence the current evaluation of place, found that past experiences and past environmental supports either increase or decrease an individual's ability to cope with their current environmental situation. Past environments that present challenges to the individual might further need to be judged on the 'type and duration' of environmental stressors: 'Both the type and the duration of environmental stressor exposure and organism sensitivity to some physical conditions of the environment may vary with developmental status' (Evans, 1999, p 269).

The second factor concerns the continuity and discontinuity of the environment in the past (Wachs, 1999; Fried, 2000). This might relate to changes or stability within a community (for example, population turnover) and/or changes and stability due to individual mobility.

A third factor in the consideration of past experiences encompasses individual perceptions. How an older person perceives change is crucial. According to Golant (1998, p 642), those older 'individuals whose self-concepts are strongly rooted or anchored to past experiences and behaviors (the proverbial "living in the past") may experience the most difficulties' upon environmental change. Change could also force an unwanted re-examination of the self as the environmental (people and built structure) cues that at one time automatically reinforced the self and self-worth are gone. Individuals are left to try to make sense of their lives in the absence of a supportive environment (Golant, 2003). Although the literature predominantly focuses on negative environmental change, positive change can occur when the individual feels that they will gain greater control of their environment now or in the future. Older people living with increasing functional health problems and/or within deteriorating environments might actively seek environmental change or, as previously discussed, engage in 'option recognition' (Peace et al, 2006).

The future

Consideration of the future is another factor neglected within theoretical and empirical environmental research (Cutchin, 2001; Golant, 2003). Cutchin (2001) calls for a shift in focus on the past, which characterises humanistic research (for example, Rowles), to include the future. Cutchin argues that while the past is important, there is a need to understand the individual as part of a continuous process in place, comprised of the past, the present and the future. Consideration of the future appears particularly relevant when place becomes a problematic situation for a person. Cutchin suggests that when people experience a change in the environmental relationship (for example, because of health) and are unable to successfully reintegrate, the person–place relationship is weakened and the person contemplates action: 'Place attachment erodes because one cannot see a way or achieve a way to reintegrate into a meaningful relationship with place' (2001, p 40). Such a situation might impact on well-being and self-identity. Therefore, consideration of the future is significant in understanding the person–environment relationship.

Golant (2003, p 643) suggests that the assessment of the person–environment relationship should include a 'trajectory of change'. Such an analysis 'will depend not just on the current level of competence of older persons but also on how the capabilities of the older person have recently changed and are likely to change in the future'. This enables the extrapolation of the person–environment relationship, which might be significant to understanding the current person–environment situation.

Another consideration suggested by current research relates to return migration. If an individual is considering a future return to their home country this might in part explain a lack of, or ambivalence to, attachment to their present location. This was found by Western (1993) in his study of attachment of African Caribbeans living in Notting Hill in London. Despite almost 30 years of residence they still viewed themselves 'only as sojourners in Britain, who will before long return home to Barbados' (Western, 1993, p 147). Consideration of individuals' future plans is therefore critical to the understanding and analysis of place attachment.

Conclusion

The aim of this chapter has been to present a review and discussion of the environmental science literature to date. The first part of the chapter revisited the Ecological Model of Ageing and the contribution of this model to current knowledge and thinking. Key conceptual terms such as *personal competence* and *environmental press* still find empirical support. The next part of the chapter examined factors underpinning ageing in place and place in ageing, specifically physical (for example, physical necessity and spatial restriction) and psychological (for example, identity and place, identity and ageing, quality of life) aspects of place and ageing. The literature has illustrated the complexity of the person–environment relationship, and the fact that diverse disciplines have been involved in the construction of knowledge in this area.

While there is a breadth of environmental psychology and gerontological research on the relationship between the person and the environment, there still remain a number of gaps in scientific knowledge, particularly related to context and the dimension of time. Relatively little is known about ageing in specific environmental locations, including deprived urban areas. As discussed earlier, deprived neighbourhoods might present a series of additional challenges for older people. Moreover, there is a marked absence of cross-national and cultural research in the field of environmental gerontology. The next chapter takes a closer look at the situation of older people in urban cities, specifically asking why urban ageing is important and what factors foster and hinder ageing well in urban cities.

THREE

Urban ageing

Introduction

The previous chapter reviewed the last 40 years of empirical literature related to our understanding of the relationship between the older person and their environment. While this yielded a breadth of knowledge, there remain some substantial shortfalls within empirical knowledge that require urgent focus, particularly set against a context of other trends, in particular population ageing and urbanisation.

The focus of this chapter is on examining ageing in urban environments and what this means for the person–environmental fit. The first section of the chapter briefly examines trends in both population ageing and urbanisation. The next section discusses factors present in urban spaces that might support and hinder ageing, and what is currently known about older people ageing in urban centres. Critically, the chapter raises the question of the current 'optimality' of urban neighbourhoods to support the health and well-being of those ageing in urban centres.

Trends in urban ageing

> Population ageing and urbanization are two global trends that together comprise major forces shaping the 21st century. (WHO, 2007, p 6)

Trends in population ageing and urbanisation make the understanding of urban ageing highly relevant to the agenda on sustainable development. Urban development has been described as 'one of the most powerful of the forces which are shaping the geography of the contemporary world' (Clark, 2000, p 15); transforming the lifestyles of almost half of the world's population. A recent report by the United Nations Population Fund (UNFPA, 2007) predicted that by 2008, for the first time in history, more than half of the world's population – 3.3 billion people – would live in urban areas, and by 2030 this figure is expected to be almost five billion (see Figure 3.1).

In Europe, almost 75% of the population already live in urban areas (for example, 80% in the UK, 77% in France and Spain, 73% in Germany and 68% in Italy). Canada and the US have similar percentages of the population living in urban areas, 81% and 79% (2008 figures).[1] There has also been a rise in megacities – cities with a population of 10 million or more – and this is expected to rise

Figure 3.1: World population, total, urban and rural, 1950–2030

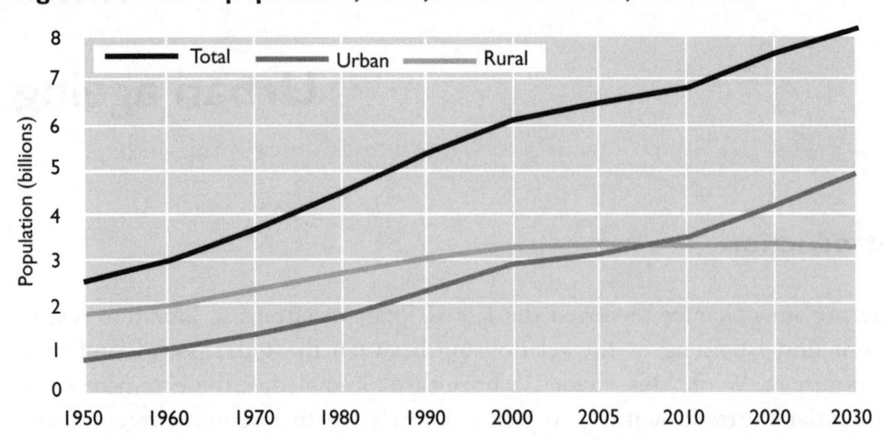

Source: Printed with permission: 'World population, total, urban and rural, 1950–2030', *OECD Environmental Outlook to 2030* (OECD, 2008, www.oecd.org/environment/outlookto2030)

further in the coming years. The United Nations predicts that by 2015, 23 cities will be defined as megacities, of which most will be in the developing world (UNFPA, 2007); and by 2030, three out of every five people will live in urban areas (WHO, 2007).

Population ageing represents a significant trend shaping urban areas. One out of every 10 persons is now 60 years old or above (UN, 2003) and this is projected to increase in the proceeding years; with the proportion of the global population aged 60 and above more than doubling from 11% in 2006 to 22% in 2050 (WHO, 2007). In countries of the Organisation for Economic Co-operation and Development (2007), the percentage of the population aged 65 and over has grown in comparison with those under the age of 65 (see OECD, 2007, population pyramids for 2000 and 2050). For G7 countries, from 2008 to 2060, the share of people aged 65 years and over is projected to rise from 17.1% to 30.0%, with those aged 80 years and over projected to triple from 21.8 million to 61.4 million in the EU27 countries (Eurostat, 2008).

More older people than ever before are found to live in urban areas and this is expected to increase in the coming years (UN, 2003; Rodwin and Gusmano, 2006). Figure 3.2 illustrates the growth in the numbers of those aged 60 and over living in urban areas across more developed and less developed countries. Less developed regions will see the greatest growth in those aged 60 and over in urban areas. The World Health Organization (WHO, 2007) suggests that in developing countries, the percentage of older people residing in cities matches that of younger people, at around 80%.

Life expectancy is an important contributing factor to the increasing numbers of older people; in most countries, life expectancy at birth is continuing to rise. According to population projections for the UK, life expectancy at birth for those born in 2006 is projected to be 88.1 years for males and 91.5 years for females.

Figure 3.2: Population aged 60 and over living in urban areas: world and developing regions, 1950–2050

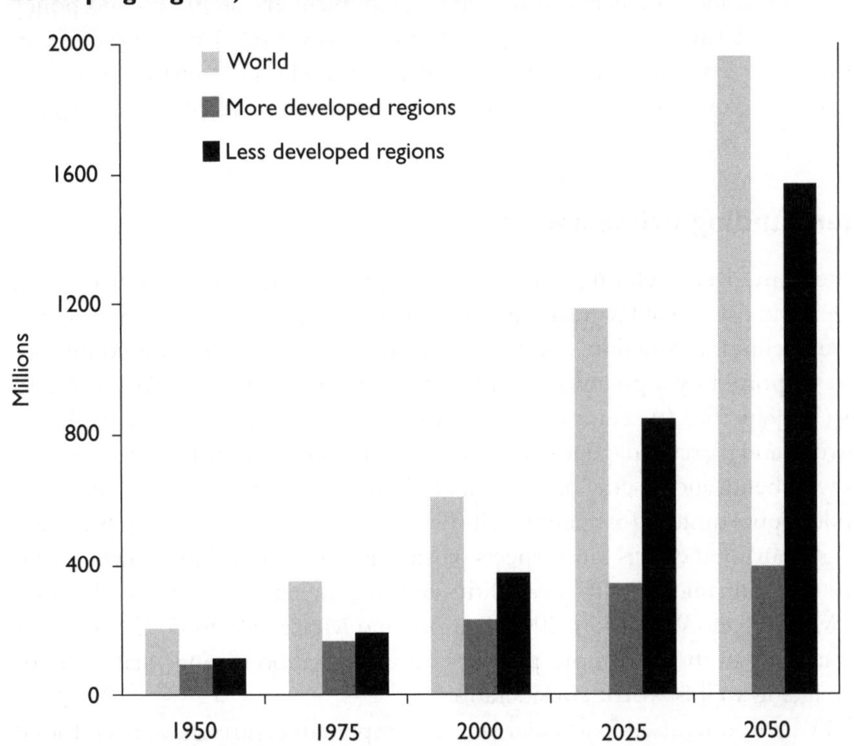

Source: Printed with permission: Population Division of the Department of Economics and Social Affairs of the United Nations: *World Population Ageing 1950–2050* (United Nations, 2002, Sales No E.2. XIII.3)

For those aged 65 in 2006, males are projected to live for another 20.6 years and females another 23.1 years. In addition, a greater number are reaching later life: for those born in the UK in 2006, 91% of males and 94% of females have a chance of reaching age 65 (Office for National Statistics [ONS] figures using 2006 base; Interim Life Tables 2005–07). Similar trends exist in other Western countries (Eurostat, 2008).

Understanding trends in healthy life expectancy (HLE) and disability-free life expectancy (DFLE) has implications for urban areas. Trends reveal that DFLE tends to be lower than HLE or years spent in good or not good health. In the UK (using 2004–06 figures), males can expect to live in good or fairly good health (HLE) for 68.2 years at birth and 12.8 years at age 65, for females this is 70.4 and 14.5 years. However, DFLE for males at birth is on average 62.4 years and at age 65, 10.1 years; similarly for females 63.9 years and 10.6 years (Smith et al, 2008, using ONS 2004–06 figures). Trends for those at birth show a greater gain in life spent free from disability than projections for those currently aged 65, particularly for females (Smith et al, 2008). Healthy life expectancy shows similar trends among most European countries (Eurostat, 2007).

Given trends in demographic ageing, including HLE and DFLE, and increased urbanisation, academics, health professionals, city planners, architects and policy makers should think more strategically about how each can contribute to improving the experience of ageing in urban cities. The next section examines some of the factors that have been found to both contribute to and hinder ageing well.

Understanding urban ageing?

The literature overwhelmingly supports the optimality of ageing in place, such that ageing in place enables greater physical mastery over the environment, despite possible declines in function, and fosters social and autobiographical continuity. This is supported by a policy agenda that favours ageing in place. According to Evans (1999, p 250), 'it seems reasonable to suspect that the human organism is sensitive to and partially dependent on certain dimensions of the physical environs for its well-being and healthy development'. And that the environment can create or hinder opportunities for ageing well (Phillips et al, 2005). A growing literature on neighbourhood effects links aspects of the environment to life chances, and is a social determinant in health inequalities and well-being (Atkinson and Kintrea, 2001; Marmot and Wilkinson, 2005; Stafford and McCarthy, 2005). Thus, better understanding of the conditions present in urban neighbourhoods that foster or hinder ageing well is worth consideration.

Urban environments, in particular large metropolitan centres, have been found to offer older people extremes:

> High levels of congestion, pollution, and crime in world cities, as well as social polarization and the high cost of housing, may undermine quality of life for older people. Yet these cities offer greater access to public transportation, pharmacies and stores, world-class medical centres, museums, parks, concert halls, colleges and universities, libraries, and theatres. (Rodwin et al, 2006, p 6)

The extremes present in urban centres can be seen to both foster and hinder ageing well. Factors that support and that hinder ageing well are discussed in more detail later.

Factors that foster ageing well

Given the population density of city centres, access to services and amenities tend to be supported and sustained, keeping people committed and engaged in their local community (Power and Mumford, 1999). Availability and access to services (for example, health and social care, post offices, libraries) have been found to be a key factor in ageing well and reports of quality of life (Godfrey et al, 2004), both supporting independence and people's feelings of social connectedness. As highlighted in Chapter One, neighbourhoods that are able to satisfy people's needs for basic living and pleasure are also more likely to encourage place attachment.

There is evidence of greater diversity and choice in urban living for older people when compared with rural living (Laws, 1993; Gitlin, 2007). Cities now present spaces and places that can support differing lifestyle choices (Savage et al, 2002), although this is typically for those who can 'elect', through financial means, to have such lifestyles (Phillipson, 2006). Some of the community and housing options on offer range from 'new urbanism' or utopian ideals of living to purpose-built age-segregated complexes. To illustrate, the town of Celebration built by the Walt Disney Company in Florida in the US (Frantz and Collins, 1999) and Poundbury in Dorset, England, adopt many of the principles of what is referred to as new urbanism. Despite the emphasis on 'new', the principles adopted have their roots in the turn of the last century. Emphasis is placed on how the built environment fosters community cohesion, creating more pedestrianised places and communal areas – with the idea that if you get people out of their cars and onto the streets and pavements they are more likely to have the opportunity to stop and talk with their neighbours.

There has also been a rise in housing specifically designed to meet the health and social care needs and/or active lifestyle choices of older people. Retirement villages aim to offer a lifestyle choice of ageing in place in a supportive, secure and independent environment. These villages have been found to play an important role in the promotion of health and well-being and help to address the shortage of suitable homes for later life (Croucher, 2006). However, there has been some criticism that studies of the effectiveness of these types of housing rely heavily on expressions of residents' satisfaction rather than more robust quality-of-life measures (Croucher et al, 2006). Retirement villages have also been criticised for being exclusionary, promoting unrealistic images of ageing and creating tensions between those who are 'fit' and those who are 'frail' (Bernard et al, 2007).

Globalisation is also argued to have had an enormous impact on urban places and ageing. Giddens (1990) defines globalisation as the intensification of worldwide social interactions that work to link distant places in a way that each impacts on the other. According to Phillipson (2007), globalisation has transformed urban spaces by creating greater diversity in the social, cultural and economic spheres; this has given rise to new types of movement in later life, which enable the construction of new and multiple spaces, communities and lifestyles. For some, globalisation has enabled greater opportunity: 'Older people in developed countries become aware of the possibilities of travel, migration, and the potential benefits of global tourism' (Phillipson, 2006, p 48). For those able to adapt and respond to the changes of globalisation, possibly through health and financial capacity, well-being in later life is likely to be maximised. However, for others, globalisation might present greater risks (Phillipson, 2006, 2007).

Recently, there has been growing interest in what makes places 'good' and 'optimal' places to age. The World Health Organization, working with 35 cities in

22 countries, has developed guidance on 'global age-friendly cities'. It describes an age-friendly city as encouraging:

> active ageing by optimizing opportunity for health, participation and security in order to enhance quality of life as people age.... In practical terms, an age-friendly city adapts its structures and services to be accessible to and inclusive of older people with varying needs and capacities. (WHO, 2007, p 1)

The World Health Organization has developed a checklist of essential features of an age-friendly city, which covers aspects of the built environment, service provision and participation (WHO, 2007). Some of the specific features of an age-friendly city are a pleasant and clean environment, adequate public toilets, safe pedestrian crossings, places to rest (benches) and access to green spaces.

The document (WHO, 2007) sets out eight areas that make an environment enabling:

- *housing* (for example, appropriate design, modifications, maintenance, enabling ageing in place, housing options, choice);
- *social participation* (for example, accessibility to events and activities, facilities and settings, fostering community integration, addressing isolation);
- *respect and social inclusion* (for example, respectful and inclusive services, addressing public images of ageing, promoting integration and family interaction, economic inclusion);
- *civic participation and employment* (for example, volunteering options, training, employment options);
- *communication and information* (for example, access to customer-friendly technology, a one-stop information centre);
- *community support and health services* (for example, service accessibility, professionals who are respectful and address needs appropriately, support to live at home);
- *outdoor spaces and buildings* (for example, a clean environment, green spaces, safe pedestrian crossings, adequate public toilets);
- *transportation* (for example, affordable, reliable, frequent, routes that go where older people need to go – hospitals, shopping centres, parks, accessible vehicles).

There has been some criticism of the methodological approach (for example, the ability of older people to drive key age-friendly themes), the appropriateness of the checklist for developing countries/cities and the empirical evidence behind it (Tinker and Biggs, 2008). Specifically, there is a lack of evidence on the impact of 'age-friendly' checklists on the experience and process of ageing. However, despite these criticisms, the global age-friendly guidance has been significant as far as a conscious-raising exercise about the need to consider the built environment in the process of ageing.

Factors that hinder ageing well

Empirical evidence has also revealed a number of risks associated with ageing well in urban places. For some, the environment has been found to present a greater or lesser amount of what has been labelled 'daily hassles'. According to Phillips et al (2005), daily hassles include neighbourhood problems such as overcrowding, noise, air pollution and congestion. Hassles that relate to managing and traversing the environment, such as 'negotiating hilly and/or uneven terrain and worries about being able to sit down whilst out shopping' (Godfrey et al, 2004), in addition to access to and provision of public toilets, have been found to make many city centres difficult to manage (Phillips et al, 2005; WHO, 2007) and work to reduce social inclusion. Equally, the level of perceived environmental press(es), such as the physical demands of an area – fear of crime, access to high-quality services and aesthetic appearance – have been found to affect older people (La Gory et al, 1985; Brown, 1995).

Globalisation, as previously discussed, has had a significant impact on urban areas and the experience of ageing. While the previous section highlighted the opportunities this offered some older people, a critical view of the impact of globalisation is that it is working to reconstruct ageing as a risk factor. According to Phillipson (2006), in the 1990s ageing moved from being a national burden on economies to being a worldwide problem, and responsibility for financial care moved from institutions to individuals and families. And while some people have been able to adapt to the changes brought about by globalisation and capitalise on opportunities, for others it is a destabilising force and there are worries that it is generating new social divisions: 'between those able to choose residential locations consistent with their biographies and life histories, and those who experience rejection or marginalisation from their locality' (Phillipson, 2007, p 321).

Evidence has also shown that there has been a rise in the geographical disparity and polarisation of neighbourhoods in many Western countries (EC, 1997; Gordon and Townsend, 2000; Lee, 2000; Lupton and Power, 2002; Power, 2009), with poorer neighbourhoods becoming more acute and concentrated (Lupton and Power, 2002). Massey (1996, p 395) has suggested that we are living in an *age of extremes*, where from the 1970s, 'the promise of mass social mobility evaporated and inequality returned with a vengeance, ushering in a new era in which the privileges of the rich and the disadvantages of the poor were compounded increasingly through geographic means'. Similarly, Wacquant (2008) in *Urban outcasts* takes a new and critical perspective of the construction of exclusion and poverty in current Western countries. He suggests that urban centres are heading towards increased *advanced marginality*, where the social and political structures in society are not enabling the reintegration of populations cast out in particular territories, creating a rise and spread of urban marginality. This presents a significant concern given the growth of urban areas and the demographic profile taking place internationally.

Deprived urban inner-city areas are typically described as having the following characteristics (Hatfield, 1997; SEU, 1998; Gordon and Townsend, 2000; Langlois and Kitchen, 2001; Johnson et al, 2005):

- high unemployment;
- lack of community spirit;
- low educational attainment;
- litter/poor general appearance;
- drug problems;
- unsupervised youngsters;
- poor public transport;
- vandalism/threatening behaviour;
- poor/lack of shops;
- high crime and feeling unsafe;
- low income and poverty;
- a high percentage of overcrowding;
- poor housing stock;
- a high percentage of benefit claims/government transfers/social programmes;
- high rates of morbidity and mortality;
- a high population turnover.

Understanding the characteristics of neighbourhoods is important because geography or where people live has been found to influence their life chances (for example, education, health, life expectancy; Marmot and Wilkinson, 2005) and risk of social exclusion (Lupton and Power, 2002). According to Lupton and Power (2002, p 140), '[p]oor neighbourhoods are, in a sense, a barometer for social exclusion'. The exclusion of individuals from society presents a particular concern as it:

> involves the lack or denial of resources, rights, goods and services, and the inability to participate in the normal relationships and activities available to the majority of people in a society, whether in economic, social, cultural or political arenas. It *affects both the quality of life of individuals* and the *equity* and *cohesion of society as a whole.* (Levitas et al, 2007, p 9, author's emphasis)

Thus, neighbourhoods with such characteristics are likely to present their residents with numerous risks to daily life. For older people, deprived areas are likely to present additional challenges and barriers to ageing well.

The study of older people living in deprived urban areas has not typically received the attention afforded other age cohorts (Phillipson and Scharf, 2004).

However, there are some studies that have sought to examine older people living in these types of neighbourhoods (Townsend, 1957; Corcoran, 2002; Scharf et al, 2002a, 2002b, 2005). Peter Townsend's (1957) seminal book *The family life of old people* was one of the first to capture the situation of older people living in poverty in Bethnal Green in the East End of London. Interviews with over 200 older people who lived there produced a rich dataset on the impact of poverty on family life, living arrangements and health.

However, little is known about the experience of older people living in contemporary inner-city areas and its impact on quality of life. One of the few studies to shed light on this was carried out by Scharf et al (2002a, 2002b, 2003a, 2005), who examined the social exclusion and quality of life of people aged 65 and over living in three urban cities in England. The study surveyed over 600 people living in nine of the most deprived electoral wards in England; in-depth interviews were also conducted with approximately 140 people. The data produced an account of the daily life of older people living in neighbourhoods characterised by multiple risks. Of the sample, 45% were found to be in poverty, which was defined as lacking two or more socially perceived necessities.[2] Poverty had a significant impact on people's self-reported quality of life, with 66% of those in poverty reporting a poor or very poor quality of life, compared with 34% not in poverty. Of the sample, 40% reported being a victim of at least one type of crime (for example, property or personal theft) in the previous two years. Being a victim of crime had a statistically significant impact on reports of both quality of life and neighbourhood satisfaction: 57% reported a poor quality of life and 56% reported dissatisfaction with the neighbourhood. For people who had had no experience of crime, these figures were 43% and 44% respectively.

Building on the work of Scharf et al (2004), Barnes et al (2006) analysed the degree and characteristics of social exclusion using the English Longitudinal Study of Ageing (ELSA). Social exclusion was measured across seven domains:

- social relationships (contact with family and friends);
- cultural activities (cinema and theatre);
- civic activities (voting and volunteering);
- access to basic services (such as health, social care and shops);
- neighbourhood exclusion (fear of crime);
- financial products (bank account, savings);
- material consumption (household amenities, holiday).

Findings revealed that those living in the most deprived area had a greater risk of experiencing multidimensional exclusion and having higher rates of exclusion across each of the measures. As noted earlier, Lupton and Power (2002, p 140) suggest that '[p]oor neighbourhoods are, in a sense, a barometer for social exclusion'.

Enabling urban environments

The previous subsections aimed to highlight factors that foster and hinder urban ageing. These factors might become even more significant when length of residence and time spent in a neighbourhood are considered. The evidence around area effects can be argued to disproportionately affect those who spend more of their day within their neighbourhood, such as those who are retired from paid work. Findings from Baltes and Baltes (1990) revealed that older people spend the majority of their time (between 70% and 90%) within their immediate home environment.

Although there is a lack of literature on people living in deprived areas and time spent in the neighbourhood, it would be reasonable to assume that those with less financial resources living in these types of places have less opportunity to escape on a daily or weekly basis. Given this, the quality of environment surrounding the individual might be particularly important to maintaining well-being. For some, deprived areas might present greater challenges to notions of ageing well – such as fear of crime and antisocial behaviour, high population turnover and poor access to services and amenities. It is reasonable to assume that ageing – successfully, well or optimally – requires an enabling environment where residents feel secure and supported. But with a rise in unsupportive environments, for example deprived inner-city areas, this challenges the optimality of the ageing in place agenda.

Over 25 years ago, Lawton (1982, p 33) claimed that the physical environment of older people had 'been typically ignored or at best implicitly assumed'. To a certain extent this situation has changed in recent years. There has been a breadth of research aiming to better understand older people's relationship with their home and objects within the home. However, there has been some criticism and call for a focus on other aspects, such as the neighbourhood. Within environmental gerontology, the neighbourhood has not been as well studied as the home environment (Scheidt and Windley, 2006); given gaps in knowledge it is important that we move quickly to understanding the impact of deprived inner-city neighbourhoods on ageing well not least to look at mitigating against any harmful factors but also to look at the opportunities presented in such neighbourhoods.

Conclusion

Over the last half-century there have been important changes in both the growth of urban areas and the demographic profile cross-nationally. The developed (and developing) worlds have increasingly become urbanised and with a greater proportion of older people living within these centres, as stated by the World Health Organization (WHO, 2007), population ageing and urbanisation are major forces shaping the 21st century.

Urbanised areas present both benefits and risks to ageing. Population density supports the provision of and access to services (for example, hospitals) and amenities (for example, theatre, museums), which are important for maintaining well-being and critical for building attachment to place and people. Equally, big cities are also associated with high levels of congestion, crime, and social and geographical polarisation.

Globalisation has been argued to have a significant impact on urban ageing. For some, it has generated enormous opportunities, creating a greater diversity of social, cultural and economic spheres and the possibility for older people to have new lifestyles and occupy new spaces through global tourism. However, for those unable to adapt and take up the opportunities of globalisation (for example, through lack of financial resources or poor health), this has presented greater risks for ageing.

Increases in the number of marginalised inner-city neighbourhoods have raised particular concerns given the growth of urban ageing. Characteristics of such neighbourhoods present particular risks for older people – specifically, poor access to services, poor infrastructure (for example, uneven pavements, poor lighting), crime, poor housing and antisocial behaviour. There are concerns that such environments go against notions of optimal ageing (House of Lords Science and Technology Committee, 2005) and challenge the agenda around ageing in place. Such neighbourhoods also go against factors found to be critical for creating 'age-friendly' communities (WHO, 2007).

Shortfalls in knowledge that were highlighted in Chapter One, coupled with a growth in geographical polarisation and demographic shifts, should raise concerns among academics, policy makers and planners as to the preparedness of society to meet the needs and aspirations of an ageing population. There is an urgent need to better understand the relationship between place and ageing in environments that present multiple daily risks; specifically, what factors underline the desire for or rejection of ageing in place in these types of neighbourhoods, and what is the impact on quality of life? These issues have important implications for understanding and supporting urban ageing, neighbourhood sustainability and addressing the social exclusion agenda. The next three chapters aim to readdress shortfalls in knowledge by presenting and examining new empirical evidence on the experiences of older people living in five deprived inner-city neighbourhoods across two countries.

Notes

[1] Data from Global Health Facts: urban population (% of total population living in urban areas) 2008 figures; www.globalhealthfacts.org/topic.jsp?i=85, last accessed May 2009.

[2] For more information on 'socially perceived necessities', see Gordon et al (2000).

Part Two
Rethinking the person–environment fit

FOUR

Skid row? Area profiles

Introduction

This chapter through to Chapter Six draw on new cross-national empirical research on older people living in deprived urban neighbourhoods in England[1] and Canada. The aim of this research is to build on the relative paucity of current research on 'ageing in place' and 'place in ageing' in these types of neighbourhoods, and as a consequence argue for the rethinking of the person–environmental fit paradigm. This chapter presents descriptive profiles of each of the cities and neighbourhoods in which the research was undertaken. It draws on both historical and contemporary sources, in addition to pictorial and descriptive accounts from older residents living in some of these localities.

Area profiles

There is some evidence which supports an *area effect*, specifically, those individuals living in deprived neighbourhoods are presented with more negative challenges than people living in non-deprived areas (Atkinson and Kintrea, 2001; Brown et al, 2004). In addition, the literature suggests that the increased losses associated with later life (for example, in terms of health) can influence well-being (Kunzmann et al, 2000). How these influence the relationship between place and ageing is of significant interest given the trends presented in the previous chapters.

An initial challenge of the present research was to identify comparable areas in England and Canada in which to conduct an empirical study of place and ageing. The study areas in each country were required to meet three criteria: be politically defined (for example, defined electoral boundaries); be located in an inner city; and have particular characteristics associated with deprived urban areas.[2]

Historically, the UK has had a long tradition of poverty and deprivation research (see Booth, 1886–1903; Townsend, 1957). This is in contrast to the situation in Canada, which has tended to be subsumed under the US discourse on income poverty (Yeates and Garner, 1976; Hajnal, 1995). This has resulted in the development of different measures of area-based 'deprivation'. Despite these differences, broadly comparable indicators could be used for identification of 'deprived' neighbourhoods, such as a high percentage of people living in low-income households, poor-quality housing stock and low educational attainment. This approach ultimately led to the selection of three wards in Manchester, England, and two wards in Vancouver, Canada, in which to conduct the study.

A brief description of each city and neighbourhood is given below. These profiles provide a context from which to better understand the research findings, and hence the experiences of living and ageing within this type of community.

Manchester, England

The discussion of Manchester and the wards of Cheetham, Longsight and Moss Side is organised around three approximate time periods: mid-19th to early 20th century, 1914 to late 20th century, and the present day (early 21st century). It is presented in this way to highlight each area's unique historical development and then to contrast this with an almost analogous development of decline in the post-war era.

Historical development (mid-19th to early 20th century)

In 1844, Friedrich Engels presented one of the earliest accounts of Manchester during the Industrial Revolution. His description of the living and employment conditions of the working class appeared bleak:

> I am forced to admit that instead of being exaggerated, it is far from black enough to convey a true impression of the filth, ruin, and uninhabitableness, the defiance of all considerations of cleanliness, ventilation, and health which characterise the construction of this single district.... And such a district exists in the heart of the second city of England, the first manufacturing city of the world. (Engels, 1892, p 53)

The development of Cheetham, Longsight and Moss Side occurred at different historical time periods and for different reasons. Cheetham, located approximately two miles north of Manchester city centre, is one of Manchester's oldest districts (Manchester, 2003b). The area was named after a wealthy family who owned much of the land in the area around the 16th century (Dobkin, 1984). In the early part of the 19th century, Cheetham was still largely a residential area, made up of primarily wealthy landowners wishing to escape the city. According to the historian Dobkin (1984, p 20):

> Cheetham Hill was described at this time as a genteel neighbourhood and it certainly merited this description. The largest houses along the main road had been built in the last decades of the eighteenth century by the first of the wealthy merchants and manufacturers and five of their residences occupied almost the whole of one side of the road. Halliwell Lane and Tetlow Lane had a similar group of lordly mansions, as did Smedley Lane. Some twenty of the early beneficiaries of the Industrial Revolution resided in Cheetham Hill and Cheetham,

> enjoying a lifestyle similar to that hitherto enjoyed only by the landed gentry.

During the Victorian era, Cheetham established itself as a desirable place to live (Manchester, 2003b) and the area continued to expand into the early 20th century. Development between the city centre and Cheetham (Hill Road) grew, establishing new residential areas for the middle and working classes – terraced housing – and some industry.

With regard to Longsight, according to Sussex (1983), there is little written history about it; in part because it was often subsumed under neighbouring areas (for example, Gorton, Kirkmanshulme and Rusholme). A key factor in Longsight's development was an improvement in transportation links with the city of Manchester in the mid-19th century. This linked the two areas, creating increased employment opportunities and growth in small industry. However, Longsight – approximately two miles south-east of the city centre – still remained for much of the 19th century underdeveloped compared with areas in closer proximity to Manchester city centre. According to Sussex (1983, p 29): 'In some ways it is a dormitory suburb; people who moved out of central Manchester in the 1860's and 1870's were looking for somewhere to live'. Longsight continued to expand in commerce and industry up until the First World War.

Moss Side was one of the last areas around central Manchester to be developed. This in part reflected its physical geography – largely marshy land, around one mile south of the city centre – that was unsuitable for building. Any substantial development in Moss Side did not take place until the second to late part of the 19th century. Census data indicate that in 1851, 943 people lived in Moss Side; by 1901, this figure had grown to 26,583 (Makepeace, 1995). With this growth in population, Moss Side developed substantial residential areas and retail businesses. It became an important shopping centre in the early 20th century. According to Makepeace (1995, p 63), 'it was possible to purchase almost anything'. Early accounts in the development of Moss Side, specifically in relation to housing stock, indicate a mix of housing types for those employed in manufacturing and more middle-class housing for those involved in small local businesses. Although much of the housing stock in Moss Side was of poor quality, Makepeace (1995, p 63) suggests that there was evidence of middle-class housing along Great Western Street: 'some of the terraced houses were aimed at a better type of resident, having small front gardens, which could be regarded as status symbols'. Moss Side's development continued up until the outbreak of the First World War (1914–18).

1914 to the late 20th century

Up until the end of the First World War, all three wards had differing developmental origins, as was illustrated above. Cheetham was developed for the affluent gentry who wished to escape the city, Longsight for the upper-middle classes, and Moss

Side appeared to house a mix of middle-class and factory workers. However, after the First World War, the areas appeared more uniform in their development. This can be attributed to two main factors. The first was Manchester's economic base and rise in slum areas, and the second, global events. Renowned for being the first industrialised city in the world, much of Manchester's early 20th-century economy was built on manufacturing (Manchester, 1999). Employment opportunities created by the development of industry caused a large growth in population migration into the inner-city areas, and consequently a rise in slum areas: by 1914 just under half of the properties, 80,000 of the 180,000, were classified as slum dwellings (Williams, 1996).

The outbreak of the First World War precipitated the start of a long period of economic decline for Manchester. It marked the start of the decline of Manchester's main industry – cotton and textiles. This was principally due to lack of investment in more advanced technology, increased international competition and disruptions to supply routes during the war (Manchester, 2003a). Economic recovery was made difficult in the interwar years by the Depression of the 1930s. The immediate period following the Second World War also posed a range of challenges. The first was the rebuilding of Manchester's infrastructure after the 1940 Blitz. The second was the decline of manufacturing and a shift to service industries. Third, the 1960s witnessed a project of slum clearances. This affected all three Manchester wards (Sussex, 1983; Boardman, 2003). Moss Side (and Hulme) were part of the largest slum clearance in England (Sussex, 1983; Manchester, 1999). The large-scale reconstruction of Manchester following the war created numerous employment opportunities. Inability to fulfil these employment needs brought a significant degree of in-migration, specifically from the West Indies and the Indian subcontinent (Manchester, 2003a). People from the West Indies tended to settle in Moss Side, and those from the Indian subcontinent in Cheetham and Longsight.

Continued economic decline and adjustment from a manufacturing base to a service base, through the mid-1970s and 1980s, continued to present challenges to Manchester. Unemployment rates were above the national average, particularly during the 1980s; Cheetham Hill and Moss Side had an unemployment rate of 44% at this time, with youth unemployment being particularly acute in Cheetham Hill, at 59% (Manchester, 2003a). The continued growth in unemployment, coupled with issues over race, inequality and policing fuelled increased social unrest; in 1981, Manchester, in particular the wards of Cheetham and Moss Side, saw violent street riots (Manchester, 2003a).

In the 1990s, Manchester witnessed a decrease in unemployment rates and a slight increase in overall population (Manchester, 2003c). This reversal might have been the result of a number of events in the late 1990s, specifically a government commitment to the revitalisation and regeneration of inner-city areas (SEU, 2001a), public–private partnerships (Manchester, 1999) and a wider European and international commitment to the rejuvenation of deteriorated urban environments (for example, by the European Regional Development Fund [ERDF], the United Nations Environment Programme [UNEP] and the World Health Organization's

Protection for the Human Environment [PHE]). In addition, the 1996 IRA bombing that devastated much of the city centre and preparation for the 2002 Commonwealth Games targeted public and private funds at redevelopment.

The present day

Manchester

In recent years, media and popular culture magazines have used terms such as 'renaissance' and 'reinventing' in their description and reporting of Manchester (see Wainwright, 1999; Parker, 2000). It has been argued that in the last 10 years the city has been transformed from a declining industrial city to a vibrant, modern and successful regional capital (Manchester, 2003d). This 'rejuvenation' of Manchester – both the central-city and inner-city areas – has been a consequence of local, national and European initiatives to regenerate the city's deprived urban areas.

Manchester is the third largest city in population size in England, with a population of just under 400,000, and approximately 2.6 million living within the Greater Manchester area (ONS, 2003). Manchester's population is ethnically diverse. Ethnic groups in the inner-city districts comprise almost 13% of the area's population; with one in eight of all Pakistanis and one in 12 of all Bangladeshis in Britain residing in Greater Manchester (ONS, 2002).

As a whole, Manchester has seen a turnaround in population and economic activity in the latter half of the 1990s. In 2000, Manchester experienced a growth in population for the first time in over a decade (ONS, 2002). Economically, after years of reliance on manufacturing, Manchester has made a shift to a more service-centred economy. More than 30% of employees are now employed in clerical, secretarial or managerial/administrative jobs as opposed to under 17% who are employed in manufacturing (ONS Regional Trends 34, 2000, cited in Manchester, 2003c). However, despite an upturn in some economic indicators, Manchester still has high rates of those of working age unemployed and claiming benefits (using 2006 data), and more than double the national average of those aged over 60 living in households that are income deprived (using 2004 data) (see Audit Commission Area Profiles data). Manchester's 20th-century struggles are still reflected in many parts of its inner-city neighbourhoods.

Longsight – showing dumped rubbish (2002)

Cheetham, Longsight and Moss Side

The electoral wards of Cheetham, Longsight and Moss Side still mirror Manchester's economic challenges in the post-war era. Although each of the wards is now part of renewal and regeneration initiatives, at the time of this research these wards still ranked as some of the most deprived in England. This is evident from 2001 Census data, which show that these areas still have a number of characteristics of deprived areas, such as high rates of unemployment, low rates of owner-occupation, high rates of rented accommodation, high rates of lone-parent families with dependent children, low educational attainment, poor health and low property prices (this is presented below). In addition, the media and popular culture images of the wards continue to highlight gang- and drug-related incidents of crime, perpetuating a negative image of these neighbourhoods (see Heaney and Wainwright, 2000; Thompson, 2002).

At the time of the study, the wards' populations ranged from approximately 11,000 in Moss Side to approximately 16,000 in Longsight. All of the wards are ethnically diverse, with approximately 50% of residents classified as White, and the remainder belonging to Asian/Asian British or Black/Black British groups. In Cheetham and Longsight, the predominant minority group is Pakistani and in Moss Side it is Black Caribbean. The unemployment rate in each ward is higher than the city and national average; in Cheetham and Longsight it is 7% and in Moss Side it is 8%. This is approximately double the national average of 3.4%. All three wards also report a higher percentage of people with poor health and limiting long-term illness compared with the national average. The number of people with no educational qualifications is highest in Cheetham, at almost 15% more than the national average; the respective figures are 11% in Longsight and 9% in Moss Side. Rates of owner-occupation are lower in all wards compared with city and national averages. In comparison with the national average (69%), owner-occupation ranges from 25% in Moss Side to 39% in Cheetham. The majority of housing in all three wards is rented from the local authority, housing association or private landlord. Rates of lone-parent households with dependent children are in all wards double or more the national average. (The source for the above statistics comes from ONS, 2003.)

Moss Side (2002) – showing a boarded-up house in between occupied ones

Moss Side (2002) – showing metal doors to protect traders from crime

Vancouver, Canada

Reflecting upon the stainless steel glass towers that dominate the downtown skyline, Vancouver author Douglas Coupland (2001) described Vancouver as the 'City of Glass'. Vancouver is located on the west coast of Canada. Much of its development has only occurred in the last 100 years. In 1901, the city had under 50,000 residents (Vancouver, 2002b), and today Vancouver is the third largest city in population size in Canada, with around half a million people living in the City of Vancouver and almost two million living within the Central Metropolitan Area (Vancouver, 2002b).

Traditionally, Vancouver's economy has been small-scale and less reliant on manufacturing than many other Canadian cities and in comparison with Manchester. Hutton (1998) describes Vancouver as a city that has bypassed the 'classic industrial' phase of development. This lack of manufacturing industry, compared with other Canadian cities, enabled Vancouver to sustain economic growth through the mid-1980s to the 1990s (St. Hilaire, 1998). This sustained growth in industry can be credited to a rapid increase in international migration to Vancouver, which started in the mid-1980s, or what Hutton (1998) refers to as 'economic' migrants from Asia (for example, entrepreneurs, investors, self-employed people). Immigration has primarily occurred from Hong Kong, and in more recent years from mainland China (GVRD, 2003a, 2003b).

While net in-migration to Vancouver remained stable through the 1970s (approximately 5,000 immigrants per year), the 1980s on average saw just under 12,000 immigrants per year and the 1990s almost 28,000 immigrants per year (GVRD, 2003a). In the 21st century, Vancouver's population profile is ethnically diverse, with almost half of the population defining themselves as belonging to a visible minority group. In the latest Canadian Census, the largest visible minority groups were Chinese (30% of the total visible minority population), followed by South Asian (6%) (Statistics Canada, 2003).

Vancouver's new economic migrants invested and established numerous businesses, and increased trade between Asia and Vancouver was established in the late 1980s. This growth in in-migration has helped Vancouver to be the sole Canadian city to sustain or experience an increase in employment growth in most of its major industries over the last 20 years, being associated with a growth in finance, insurance and real estate, construction (Hutton, 1998) and manufacturing (Hutton, 1998; Vindorai, 2001). However, because of Vancouver's established Asian-Pacific trade connection, the city experienced some economic decline when the Asian financial crisis occurred in 1998, principally in industries of primary resource exports (lumber, copper and so on), transportation and wholesale trade sectors, and a decline in Asian tourism. In the 2001 Census, the main industries in Vancouver were business and commerce, followed by the service sector, health and education (Statistics Canada, 2003).

Vancouver's rapidly expanding economy over the last 20 years has been accompanied by a variety of social problems (for example, an increase in poverty). According to Hutton (1998, p 29), the rapidly expanding service sector elite is increasingly polarised from the traditional blue-collar sector: 'The growing contingent of urban poor and the emergence of a distinct urban underclass appear in even starker contrast against the highly visible prosperity of much of the city'. A growth in poverty was a factor in Vancouver's drop from first to third in a list of the world's most desirable places to live (see Mercer Quality of Living Survey 2004 to 2007[3]). This polarisation is evident in the neighbourhoods of Downtown Eastside and Grandview-Woodland. Similar to the situation in Manchester, concern over the acute and growing problems in inner-city neighbourhoods has in recent years brought all levels of government – federal, provincial and municipal – together. The Vancouver Agreement committed these levels of government to a 'vision of creating healthy, safe and sustainable communities' in Vancouver, with an initial focus on problems associated with the Downtown Eastside (Vancouver, 2000; www.vancouveragreement.ca/TheAgreement.htm).

The Downtown Eastside

> It is perhaps inevitable that together with progress there will be decline. Urban 'plight' is one symptom of an expanding economy (City of Vancouver, 1965, p 1).

Housing and business premises (2002) – typical street scene

The Downtown Eastside (DES) is located less than a mile east of Vancouver's city centre. Of all 23 neighbourhoods in Vancouver, the DES is perhaps the most well recognised and notorious. Among the many social problems of the area – drug and alcohol abuse, prostitution and epidemic rates of HIV/AIDS – the DES is regarded as the poorest postcode in Canada (Synders and O'Rourke, 2001). Although once described as 'the fashionable heart of the city' (Vancouver, 1965), the DES has been subject to economic decline and major social challenges for almost 100 years.

Historically the original site of the City of Vancouver, the DES was a thriving urban area in the mid- to late 19th century. The centre of shipping trade and commerce, its proximity to the Burrard Inlet made the area a prime location for the construction of numerous lumber mills. Also emerging at this time was Chinatown. Many Chinese people migrated to Vancouver to work as labourers in local industries. The central streetcar terminus, coastal steamships and ferries brought a daily influx of people to the area. Hotels, banks, theatres, a library and department store were established along the Hastings Street corridor to accommodate the many commercial travellers and visitors to the area.

However, the prosperity and development of the DES changed in the late 19th and early 20th centuries due to the competing economic and political power of landowners in the present-day Granville area. The initial decline started with a shift in development westward (to the Granville area) from the DES. This appeared to have been caused by two factors. The first was the loss of the terminus point of the Trans-Canada railway from the DES to the Granville area, and the second was increasing structural and business development (for example, buildings, bridges) in the Granville area. The influx of people brought into the area by the railway continued to create demand for business and construction in the Granville area into the 20th century, gradually shifting what is known today as Downtown Vancouver from its original site in the DES.

Contrary to the growth and economic boom of the Granville area, the DES struggled to keep up with development and the loss of an increasing number of businesses westward. These local factors, coupled with international factors, including the 1912 recession, the outbreak of the First World War and the Great Depression, triggered the start of a long period of decline and neglect of the DES. The 1950s and 1960s saw continued area decline in contrast to the new site of Downtown Vancouver. The streetcar and the ferries stopped running into the area in the late 1950s because businesses relocated to busier thoroughfares. In the 1960s, private businesses, along with local and provincial governments, started putting money into the construction of new buildings in present-day Downtown Vancouver (for example, Pacific Centre and Eaton's department store). Growing development of more affluent residential communities, and a shortage of affordable residential neighbourhoods, saw an increase in lower-income people settling in the DES (for the source of the above historical information, see Synders and O'Rourke, 2001; Holt, 2002).

Between the Depression years and the 1960s, little was done to try to solve some of the economic and social problems of the area. Through these years the DES became associated with poverty, high rates of unemployment and transient populations. Only in the 1960s did the City of Vancouver become concerned with the situation in the DES. A 1965 report, prepared by the city's Planning Department (Vancouver, 1965), examined some of the problems in the area and presented possible policy changes. The social and economic problems listed in the report concerned issues of high unemployment, homelessness, chronic alcoholism, poor housing and high rates of people aged 65 and over who were sick and disabled. With regard to the needs of old-age pensioners, the report recognised the need to supply 'low-cost supportive housing':

> Improving housing for pensioners is necessary in this area.... These elderly men treasure their independence – it would be better to provide them with light housekeeping rooms in rooming houses or hotels.... Units should be small structures, but with enough rooms to be self-supporting. Adequate staff and recreation facilities should be provided, and perhaps even low-cost meals. (Vancouver, 1965, p 47)

It was not until the 1980s that facilities to house older people, specifically those envisaged in the 1965 report, were built in the DES (for example, Veterans Memorial Manor and Lions Manor).

The social challenges faced by the DES increased in the 1970s with the provincial government's decision to deinstitutionalise mental health facilities. The impact of this was significant for the DES; not only was there a lack of supportive community organisations to service the needs of people with mental health problems, but it further highlighted problems associated with the lack of affordable housing in Vancouver (Harvey and Greenwell, 1988; Jenson and de Castell, 2000). The DES was one of the only affordable neighbourhoods where many of these individuals could find housing.

In the 1980s, abuse of drugs, specifically intravenous drugs, was becoming an increasing social and health concern. The spread of HIV/AIDS and Hepatitis C became a provincial and federal issue. Crime also steadily increased through the 1980s and more small and large businesses moved out of the area (Synders and O'Rourke, 2001; Holt, 2002). According to Holt (2002), the DES began to be labelled as 'skid row'; a label that 'converted the area from a community to a dumping ground. Institutional uses, religious agencies and social services all began to locate here in disproportionate numbers bringing along with them transients which would perpetuate the area's bad reputation' (Holt, 2002, p 7).

Hastings Street (2002) – showing a number of boarded-up and abandoned businesses

Today, just over 5,000 people officially live in the DES. However, this figure does not take into account significant numbers of homeless people living in temporary shelters and detox centres. It is estimated that the figure might double with the inclusion of these groups (Vancouver, 2001). While the majority of the population are English speaking (47%), there is a large percentage of people who speak Chinese (23%). The DES has one of the highest percentages of people aged 65 and over, representing almost 25% of the local population, compared with an average of 13% for Vancouver. Over 80% of the population live in low-income households and the average household income is almost four times lower than the average for the City of Vancouver. Ninety-nine per cent of the accommodation is rented and is termed 'single room occupancy' (SRO), characterised as a small single room and usually with shared bathroom and cooking facilities (Vancouver, 2002a). The health of residents in the DES is generally considered to be poor. The spread of HIV/AIDS and Hepatitis C among intravenous drug users and sex trade workers has reached epidemic levels (17%–31% and 63%–92%, respectively; Health Canada, 2008). To help combat this situation, a safe injection pilot programme has been set up by the federal government (Health Canada, 2003).

The image of the DES is predominantly a negative one. Health Canada (2008) describes it in the following way:

> The DTE [Downtown Eastside] is one of North America's most impoverished areas and is known as 'skid row' to many of the locals. The majority of housing in the area is small, undesirable single person dwellings. Public self-injection, open drug dealing and prostitution are common. Many buildings are covered in graffiti and alleys tend to be used to discard needles and condoms.

In media reports, the area is often described as 'poverty stricken', 'seedy', 'notorious' and 'an embarrassment for the city' (see, for example, Bramham, 2003; Bula, 2003; Ransford, 2003; also, search www.FPinformart.ca for additional examples). Vancouver author Douglas Coupland (2000, p 87) refers to the DES as a:

> part of the city that is in chronic pain. The alleys feature snowdrifts of syringes, bleach bottles, alcohol swab wrappers, orange syringe tips and tiny plastic bags used to hold crack crystals. The amount of paraphernalia littering the place is astounding. You expect maybe a syringe or two and you see … *hundreds.*

However, as a one-time resident of the neighbourhood, Coupland admits to having some happy memories of the place: 'it's a place you should see, and not particularly fear. It's disturbing and intense, but the place is populated by people with souls just like anybody else. Wear sturdy footwear, lock the car, and open your mind and your eyes' (2000, p 87).

Sign going into local credit union and typical accommodation in the DES (2002)

Grandview-Woodland

Grandview-Woodland is located two miles east of Vancouver's city centre. The ward shares a border with the DES and some of that area's social problems, such as drug and alcohol abuse, prostitution and high crime rates. These two neighbourhoods, as previously noted, also have a similar sociodemographic profile (for example, low-income households, low-rental properties, population diversity and so on). However, their descriptive images are strikingly different. While the image of the DES is of 'skid row', Grandview-Woodland is often described as a 'bohemian enclave', and an area rich in 'history and cultural diversity' (Commercial Drive, 2003).

Grandview-Woodland is one of Vancouver's oldest neighbourhoods. Historically, the area was the first suburb to be developed outside the city, the DES being the second. Initially called Grand View, the development of the Grandview-Woodland area started to occur around the turn of the 20th century (Kluckner, 1982; Synders and O'Rourke, 2001). Before 1880, the area just east of the DES was an uncultivated forest: 'The first roads (later Victoria and Commercial Drives) were originally skid roads with paths running off them. Elk were hunted in the Grandview area and sold to settlers by natives when their stock ran out' (Vancouver, 1994). The area around Grandview-Woodland was initially used for logging; residential and business development did not occur until the extension of the interurban railway in the late 1880s (Synders and O'Rourke, 2001).

The railway, along with the construction of a number of roads, connected the city to Grandview-Woodland. This brought further business, industry, increased construction and settlers to the area. The area was promoted:

> as a middle-class alternative to the West End and Shaughnessy Heights. Lot sizes were very flexible, and the successful businessmen and industrialists who decided to move into the new area bought as many of them as they could, giving the area a hodgepodge of mansions, cottages, odd streets and blocks unlike any other area in Vancouver. (Kluckner, 1982, p 146)

The real estate and construction boom in the area continued until the 1912 recession, when factors similar to those that brought about change in the DES started to impact on development in Grandview-Woodland (Vancouver, 1994). This was then followed by the onset of the First World War and the 1930s' Depression. These events further debilitated development of the area and Grandview-Woodland gradually became a less attractive area for middle-class residents.

The composition of the population changed considerably over the years, starting in the late 1910s:

> The face of the community changed after World War I when Italian, Chinese and East European immigrants arrived in the area. After World War II, a second wave of Italian immigrants made the area home. This change in population composition brought about a change in the development of the area. They renovated old houses and noticeably changed the look of Commercial Drive with new shops and restaurants. (Vancouver, 2005)

In the 1950s and 1960s, the Chinese community increased in number and some of the earlier Italian and Eastern European settlers moved to other neighbourhoods.

Today, the population of Grandview-Woodland is almost 30,000. Although the majority are English speaking, the area is ethnically diverse, with 18% speaking Chinese, 5% Vietnamese, 3% Italian, 2% French and 2% Spanish. Most of the population is between the ages of 20 and 64, with just 10% being aged 65 or over. Forty-four per cent of the population live in low-income households, and the area has an average household income more than 15,000 Canadian dollars lower than the average for the City of Vancouver. Seventy per cent of the accommodation is rented, and belongs to a range of housing types (for example, apartments, houses) (Vancouver, 2002a).

The area is continuously and consistently celebrated for its diverse collection of nationalities, professions and ages, and its political activism. Grandview-Woodland is described as a 'charismatic area, with a diversity of people and housing, funky coffee bars, and unusual clothing stores and street activity' (Vancouver, 2005).

Discussion and summary of area profiles

The area profiles seek to provide a background against which the findings of the research can more clearly be understood. As has been shown in the area profiles, each of the study neighbourhoods has undergone a considerable process of change over the last century. This was particularly evident in the post-war period. Once-desirable areas have experienced a process of decline, as is illustrated in a number of theoretical models of neighbourhood life cycles (Hoover and Vernon, 1959; Downs, 1981; Smith and McCann, 1981; Bourne and Bunting, 1993). This process of decline was particularly evident in the wards of Cheetham, Longsight and Grandview-Woodland. All three areas were originally developed to cater to the needs of affluent landowners. By contrast, the neighbourhoods of Moss Side and the DES were originally developed to meet the housing needs of middle- or working-class people.

The process involved in the decline of neighbourhoods appeared dependent on wider city and/or global forces. Certainly, for Manchester the reliance on a manufacturing-based economy amidst decline in global demand for Western manufacturing precipitated and accelerated financial and geographical inequality. High unemployment in many of the research wards, in particular Cheetham and Moss Side, fuelled significant social unrest, possibly further reducing the 'desirability' of these areas as residential locations.

In Vancouver, the decline of the wards appeared to have been less tied to global economics and a set economic base (for example, manufacturing) and was more of a feature of local business interests and transportation issues. These events certainly precipitated the initial decline of these areas. In later years, in particular the post-war years, Vancouver's economy appeared diverse and generally stable compared with other cities in Canada. However, it can be argued that in the last

30 years, Vancouver's economy has expanded and become more global. Certainly this is evident in the expansion of trade between Vancouver and Asian markets from the 1970s.

The relative decline of the study neighbourhoods has implications for how older people might experience neighbourhood change. This applies in particular to factors associated with place and ageing. For example, negative changes that have occurred in these areas might challenge the relationship people have to space and place through disruptions to attachment and the ageing process.

Also evident in the previous descriptive profiles are differences in the types of deprived areas. Despite each of the research wards sharing similar characteristics associated with being deprived inner-city neighbourhoods, the degree and intensity by which each ward and its residents are influenced by these characteristics are differently shared. This is particularly evident in the descriptive profiles of the two Vancouver wards, where one neighbourhood – the DES – is often referred to as 'skid row', while the other – Grandview-Woodland – sharing similar social and economic issues, is referred to as being a 'bohemian enclave'. This might be particularly significant in understanding possible differences in the experience of place and ageing.

Expert area perceptions

According to Wang (1999, p 186), 'Images contribute to how we see ourselves, how we define and relate to the world, and what we perceive as significant or different'. This section presents a descriptive and pictorial account of deprived inner-city neighbourhoods from the perspective of three older residents – Mr Joseph Bennett and Ms Flora Clark from Vancouver and Ms Muriel Allen from Manchester.[4, 5] Each participant was asked to take photographs of places they both liked and disliked in their neighbourhood and then to write a description of each image they took. The text accompanying the photographs represents 'word for word' the participant's written description, including grammatical errors and exaggerated emphasis on particular words.[6] The photographs and text are followed by a brief discussion as to what can initially be drawn about older people's relationship with their neighbourhood.

Photographer 1

Mr Joseph Bennett, Grandview-Woodland, Vancouver, Canada

Mr Joseph Bennett is in his early seventies and has lived in the area for just over 30 years. For the past seven years he has lived in a one-bedroom apartment just off 'The Drive'. For much of his working life, Mr Bennett was a security guard. He never married and has no children.

A typical day for Mr Bennett starts early. He usually gets up just before 7 o'clock, and begins his day with a walk around the neighbourhood. Upon returning home he has breakfast and then decides what to do for the day. This might involve going to his local seniors centre, in which he is actively engaged. He enjoys many of the activities provided by this centre, in particular, lunch, day trips and educational classes. In the afternoon Mr Bennett takes another walk, usually down Commercial Drive to "see what is happening". Most of his days are spent within the neighbourhood.

Mr Bennett very much enjoys living in Grandview-Woodland and has no desire to move. He enjoys the friendliness of the area and the cultural diversity, proudly referring to it as "our own style of United Nations". He felt that living on 'The Drive' during the football World Cup (in the summer of 2002) was particularly exciting with all the different nationalities. He recalled that when Brazil won the competition, Commercial Drive filled with people cheering and partying: "I walked down The Drive to enjoy the atmosphere of the win, it was great".

Although Mr Bennett very much enjoys living in Grandview-Woodland, he feels that crime and drugs have become a particular problem. This problem he attributes to what he calls the "overspill" from the Hastings area (the DES). Although it seldom prevents him from going out, he is sure to avoid particular trouble spots in the area.

Photographs

"The community centre has activities for all age groups from pre-school day care to children of all ages, teenagers, adults and senior citizens. It serves the community well and is a very active place. Britannia Centre showing 'Family Activity Room' on the left and 'School and Public Library' on the right."
(Entrance to community centre and secondary school)

"This park has a children's playground and two sports fields designed for soccer and baseball games. An excellent family area and for organised sports during the day and it is safe because of the number of people using it but at night it catches some of the overflow of junkies and hookers from Hastings Street just two blocks away and sometimes drinking parties of rabble rousers."
(Woodland Park, one block west of Commercial Drive, between Adanac Street and Francis Street)

"Vancouver is the only city that maintains and cares for its cenotaphs through its parks department. In all other cities the Legions have to do it all themselves if they want one."
(Cenotaph at Grandview Park)

"Doctors and dentists, walk in clinic, physiotherapy, optical, all you need for health care."
(Vancouver Health Department, Commercial Drive)

"A large children's playground and an adults 'Bocce' court. This is a favourite Italian sport reflecting the large Italian population in this area often referred as 'Little Italy'.
'Note': Both Grandview and Victoria Parks are well used by families during the day and are usually safe during daylight. They are often used by drug addicts and drunks at night time. After the sun goes down they cannot be considered safe. Panhandlers are also a nuisance day and night."
(Victoria Park on Victoria Drive from Grant Street to Kitchener Street)

"One of the long-term care nursing homes in the Victoria Dr. area at Victoria Dr. and Napier Street. Notice it is well fenced with locked gates for security that is needed in this area."
(Nursing home)

"This building was originally a church (I went to Sunday school here when I was 4 years old, way back in 1934). It is now an entertainment centre promoting mostly local talent: musicians, actors, artists, etc. Clean entertainment and not a trouble spot."
(Vancouver East Cultural Centre at Venables Street and Victoria Drive)

"Directly across from Grandview Park, the busiest block in this area for entertainment especially in the evenings with coffee shops and restaurants, some with live music and other entertainments. Although this block is always busy and crowded at times, it is a safe area. The more good people on the street the safer for everybody."
(East Side of 'The Drive' from Charles Street to Williams Street)

"Joe's café caters mostly to younger people who are not all clean cut looking. They are not intentionally dangerous to other people but they do get noisy and boisterous at times and at night some drug addicts from the Park hang around and sometimes you can smell marijuana along this block. Better to avoid this area at night, William Street to Napier Street, panhandlers are a problem too."
(Joe's Café, Commercial Drive and Williams Street)

"Old original houses that have been repaired and repainted all different colours to add character and charm to one of the oldest neighbourhoods in the city. Some of these old houses have officially been declared 'Heritage Home' so they can never be torn down or altered."

"There are drug addicts and hippie types from here to Broadway. This area is not as dangerous as some areas in the city but it is risky after dark. In these grey areas of the city it is best to avoid them after dark if you can, otherwise 'proceed with caution'."
(Commercial Drive looking south from 3rd Ave)

"This entire area from Cambie Street to Nanaimo Street is catching the overflow of drug addicts, drug dealers, prostitutes, pimps and drunks from the Downtown Eastside and that unsavoury population continues to grow. Not a safe area! One block north of Hastings Street where this photo was taken is part of the infamous 'Kiddie Stroll' along Franklin Street, where child prostitutes are owned by pimps. This is a black mark of shame on the City of Vancouver and a disgrace to our politicians and judicial systems who refuse to do anything about it. The police cannot do anything when the courts refuse to prosecute and politicians only play lip service briefly then pass it off. There is a point in law that says 'Justice must be seen to be done' the way it 'appears' to honest citizens is the law protects criminals and to hell with the victims."

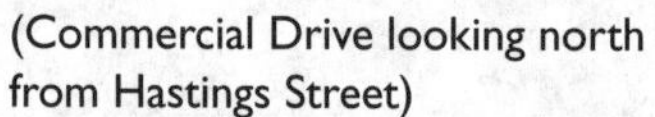

(Commercial Drive looking north from Hastings Street)

"These two old houses side by side were the original post office and postmaster's residence way back when Vancouver was in its infancy. Commercial Drive was then the longest and busiest commercial and retail street. That is why it was named 'Commercial Drive'. These two houses together have been declared a 'Heritage Site' to preserve part of our history."
(Old Post Office, Grant Street)

"The side streets off Commercial Drive are full of trees, giving a park-like appearance. A lot of houses have large hedges, shrubs and fences in front for their own privacy and appearance. These streets are quiet and peaceful-looking both day and night, giving the appearance of ideal family neighbourhoods. At night it can be quite different at times due to transient populations, different people moving in and moving out, and drifters from other areas. Each block has one street light at each end of the block and only one in the middle of the block. The large trees cause dark shadows on the sidewalks and the hedges, shrubs and fences provide hiding places for predators and thieves. Property crimes are less than in other parts of the city but still occur. There has been a few isolated incidents of women being accosted on these streets but they were saved by local residents. Like all communities women and children are not safe walking alone anywhere, especially at night. There is only safety in numbers. Vancouver is a major seaport, commercial and industrial city with ever-changing populations. People from other communities come here regularly for business, entertainment, and pleasure, and it has a high crime rate. There is no neighbourhood that can be considered 100% safe all the time."
(Side street, off Commercial Drive)

Photographer 2

Ms Flora Clark, Grandview-Woodland, Vancouver

Aged 68, Flora Clark emigrated from Scotland to Canada in the mid-1960s. Just over 10 years ago she moved from Eastern Canada to Vancouver to be closer to her children. She has one son and two daughters, all living in the Vancouver area. She is divorced from her husband, but appears to still have occasional contact with him. For much of her working life she was employed as an art teacher, and now in her retirement she enjoys painting and sculpturing.

Ms Clark has lived in the area only a year but seems already well integrated into the neighbourhood. Much of her daily schedule is organised around social engagements or her artwork. She appears to be very socially active, frequently meeting friends for coffee, enjoying activities at the local community seniors centre, such as day trips, computer lessons and creative writing courses, and does volunteer work a couple of times a week. When asked what she likes about living in her neighbourhood she said that she likes the affordable accommodation and the many activities going on in the area. She said that "if you are bored all you have to do is walk to the end of the street and you see friends or you see a poster on a lamp post advertising something to do, there is always music or an art show going on in the area". She feels very settled in the neighbourhood and has no desire to move.

One thing Ms Clark does not like about her area is the crime. She blames the proximity to the DES for many of the problems related to crime in her area. Despite being a recent victim of personal crime and worrying about it happening again, she feels that this has not prevented her from going out but has made her more aware.

Photographs

"Street Cleaners, Grandview Park, City Workers cleaning the Commercial Drive area."

"John outside Lucy's Café, an incredible story just by giving him "change" when he asked nicely said I'd do it if I could take his picture. He was dressed in what I would normally call 'street clothes' – i.e. nothing fancy, bandana around his head, beautiful eyes and he really looks you in the eye. He loves the Drive because it feels like Europe. I wish I had longer time to talk with him."
(Street person, Lucy's Café, below Grant Street)

"This man had just got into town from Winnipeg, he was hoping to get a window washing job around Metrotown. He was so cheerful I had to take his photo."
(Cheerful hitchhiker, Libra Room, Commercial Drive [2][6])

"A reminder of home. This shows some of the European mix of the area. It's a shame all the windows are smashed. Also a sign for Peg General Store Antiques."
(Red British telephone booth, Commercial Drive and Parker Street [2])

"A bright and beautiful Mural, it's so BIG. Amazing colours!"
(Mural, Circling Dawn, Organic Foods, Commercial Drive and Napier Street [3])

"Selling a range of ethnic clothing. A good place to buy gifts that are different."
(BECKS Women's Wear, Commercial Drive and Charles Street [2])

"Took a picture of a young man with dog and sign on cardboard decrying Premier Campbell's vicious cuts to the old and young – you name it everyone hates him now pretty much. This one made me sad. The sign reads 'End the war on the Poor'."
(Street scene, outside Liquor Store, Commercial Drive [2])

"Two men at Norman's Fruit and Salad Market, one of many in the area. Great fresh veg along Commercial Drive!"
(Norman's Fruit and Salad Market [2])

"They have the best and cheapest lattes in town!! I meet friends here."
(Joe's Café, Commercial Drive and Williams Street [2])

Photographer 3

Ms Muriel Allen, Moss Side, Manchester

As well as taking photographs and writing a description about each image, Ms Muriel Allen also participated in the face-to-face interview phase of the research and is one of the eight case studies presented and analysed in Chapter Five. Therefore, for information on her personal biography, see the section on environmental management in Chapter Five.

Photographs

"These are three[7] shots of the remaining woodland from which the park was created. In the spring and summer these views are fantastic! The park was created in about 1860 and at that time was very upper crust and was used mostly by nursemaids walking their charges. I spend a lot of time walking my dogs in this park and it's one of my favourite places!"
(Woodland, Alexandra Park [3])

"These are some shots of the pond in Alex. Park. There are different breeds of geese and ducks i.e. Canada geese, Mandarin ducks, water fowl and heron: large numbers of fish live in the pond and strangely a colony of large terrapins. I like this pond because of the wildlife and the view although I deplore the fishing which causes injury to the birds and is responsible for litter."
(Pond, Alexandra Park [3])

"This is a pile of rubbish which someone has dumped among the trees near the tennis courts. I've added a couple of shots of the unused pavilion and tennis courts. This whole area is a sad reflection on the maintenance and up-keep of parts of this park. I dislike the lack of care in this area which could be so attractive!"

"This is an area near the park entrance every day when I'm leaving the park I feed the magpies and pigeons. I took this picture of them feeding as I find a source of constant amusement."
(Alexandra Park)

"I've also added a couple of shots of the original gatehouse, now empty and neglected, but once a beautiful building. I would love to see this building restored and inhabited."
(Gatehouse)

Willow trees – three seasonal views, Alexandra Park: Spring
"Here are a couple of shots of the willow trees that grow at the waters edge, these are a beautiful sight in all seasons as they change so much."

Willow trees – three seasonal views, Alexandra Park: Summer

Willow trees – three seasonal views, Alexandra Park: Winter

"This is St Bede's College, which started out as an Aquarium in Victorian times, according to my granddaughters the inside has tiled walls depicting fish and other aquatic creatures. The outside of the building is decorated with small carving and statues of a religious nature. I like this building because it's unlike any other I know and harks back too a time when this area was upmarket!"

"This is a view of the sort of eyesores we have to put up with all the time in this area! The building and skips, the cars parked on and across the pavement. There is also litter (i.e. bones, broken bottles and cans on the pavement). This is a common problem in this area but nothing is ever done about it!"
(Problems in neighbourhood [4])

"This is a disused petrol station. It was only built 4 years ago and was closed in January '02 since then it has been left to rot although a light is on in the shop day and night with the original stock still on the selves! Obviously this is an eyesore and a waste which no one in this area likes!"

Discussion of the photographs

The use of photographs and descriptive text enabled further contextualisation of the study areas by including perspectives of older people living in these neighbourhoods. In addition, this method created added insight into 'place and ageing' factors, such as use of place and connection to place. This is discussed next.

Use of place

Use of place is evident by the location and variety of photographs taken. Mr Bennett's photographs reveal a broader use and knowledge of place than the photographs of the other two participants. In his collection of photographic images, he reveals both a variety of images and diverse locations spanning almost the entire neighbourhood. Mr Bennett's images centre around four themes: amenities and services, local parks (giving images of three parks and a local sports field), trouble spots or problem areas, and heritage sites. The locations of these sites are also varied in radius, from the north end of the neighbourhood (Hastings Street) to 3rd Avenue south, and McLean Drive west to Victoria Drive east. This represents almost all of the boundaries of the electoral ward. This can be contrasted with the photographs taken by Ms Allen and Ms Clark, which appear to have a much narrower focus; this is reflected in both the variety of images taken and location. Ms Allen's focus in her collection of images is on her immediate surroundings, specifically the local park (about a quarter-mile from her house) and problems found just outside her front door (petrol station, back ally). Similarly, Ms Clark's images are all focused around one region in her neighbourhood – Commercial Drive. Her images reflect the predominance of services and amenities located there but are different from those of Ms Allen and Mr Bennett in that the majority of photographs focus on people or have people within the image.

Photographs and text also reveal differences in the use of place. This is evident from the images of Joe's Café taken by Mr Bennett and Ms Clark. For Mr Bennett, it is a place where "younger people who are not all clean cut" go, where some drug addicts hang out and it is a place to avoid at night. Conversely, for Ms Clark, Joe's Café is a place where she meets friends and enjoys "the best and cheapest lattes" and is not viewed as a place to avoid.

Mr Bennett's photographs and descriptive text also reveal a strong sense of area knowledge and spatial hierarchy about certain parts of his neighbourhood. For example, some areas, such as the east side of 'The Drive' are viewed as safe because it is busy and there are a lot of good people around; whereas Joe's Café and Commercial Drive (from 3rd Street to Broadway) are considered "grey areas" and risky after dark, but "not as dangerous as some areas of the city". According to Mr Bennett, an area to be avoided in the neighbourhood is "the entire area from Cambie Street to Nanaimo Street", which he considered not safe at any time of the day.

Connection to place

Connection to place was evident in the type of images taken and the descriptive discourse. Elements of sentimental connection to place were found across all three participants' photographs and descriptive text. There was evidence of social connection being important. For example, Mr Bennett spoke fondly about the people in his area as "down to earth and friendly like a small town atmosphere inside a big city". He also spoke about walking down the street and enjoying the sight of "happy people" sitting in cafés along Commercial Drive. In fact, he became almost poetic about this: "so many people all talking happy talk at the same time, it sounds like a tree full of songbirds welcoming the morning sun". Mr Bennett also appears to be proud of the social diversity of the area and enjoys the idea of everyone "living together in our own style of United Nations".

Ms Clark's social connection to the area is evident from the type of photographs she took. Unlike Mr Bennett and Ms Allen, Ms Clark's focus is predominantly on people, with the neighbourhood as a backdrop. The ease with which she is able to talk with people in her area indicates a level of social comfort and integration. Her written description of Joe's Café also suggests a level of social support and connection to the area, by her stating that "I meet friends here".

Photographic images and descriptive text offered by Ms Allen do not directly present evidence of social connection to the area. However, we know from analysis of her case study that the park is a place where she meets many of her acquaintances for a chat, and in so doing might be out for "two hours rather than one". This is discussed in detail in the next chapter.

There is also evidence to suggest that an individual's past has implications for connection to place. This was found across all three participants. For Mr Bennett this was illustrated through photographs taken of the Cultural Centre, the cenotaph and Heritage Buildings. The Cultural Centre was significant because it was where Mr Bennett went to Sunday School at the age of four in 1934. A veteran of the Korean War and a member of the board of directors of Veterans Affairs Canada, the cenotaph at Grandview Park appears to be an important personal image for Mr Bennett. It provides both a connection to the past, when he was proud to serve his country, and continues to reinforce the self in the present through daily contact. He appears particularly proud of the fact that "Vancouver is the only city that maintains and cares for its cenotaphs", and having this located in his neighbourhood might have added to feelings of place attachment. Reference to the old houses and post office, which he describes as adding "character and charm to one of the oldest neighbourhoods in the city", appears to offer a certain pride about having a declared 'heritage site' in his neighbourhood.

For Ms Allen, images that reminded her of the neighbourhood and people of the past appeared to be important. For example, St. Bede's College "harks back to a time when this area was upmarket", the park used to be "very upper crust" and "was used by Nursemaids walking their charges", and the gatehouse was once a beautiful building. These images of the area as it used to be appear to provide some emotive connection and resistance to neighbourhood decline.

For Ms Clark, there is evidence to suggest that features of the neighbourhood might preserve a connection to her personal history and might aid in the development of attachment to area. For example, Ms Clarke's photograph of the British telephone box next to the antiques store, served as a reminder of her roots in the UK, but also might re-emphasise a certain sense of belonging in that she felt it reflected "some of the European mix of the area". Emotive sentiment to the area in this case might be gained not through years of residence like Mr Bennett and Ms Allen, but through proxy features such as physical features of the area that aid in the continuation of self and create well-being.

Negative images can also be viewed as an indication of connection to place, particularly when this is accompanied by emotive dialogue. Negative images and emotive text were evident from Mr Bennett and Ms Allen. For Mr Bennett, negative images and text related to concerns over crime, personal safety being a particular concern, and for Ms Allen, this related to the aesthetic features of the neighbourhood. "Black mark of shame", "disgrace" and "unsavoury population" are just a few of the statements used by Mr Bennett in relation to his description of crime in parts of his neighbourhood in the area. "Deplore", "eyesore", "dislike" and "lack of care" were used by Ms Allen to describe the appearance of her area.

This emotive dialogue, however, in combination with evidence of rationalisation and resistance, is argued to be evidence of place attachment.

In Mr Bennett's descriptive dialogue there is evidence of rationalisation in relation to crime. In particular, crime in the area is blamed on a "transient population, different people moving in and moving out, and drifters from other areas". When problems have occurred in the area (for example, incidents of women being accosted), they were "saved by local residents". Mr Bennett also considers crime a more general problem, in that "no neighbourhood can be considered 100% safe". It is suggested that this rationalisation helps to manage feelings of place attachment and well-being, by neutralising these negative challenges by perceiving them as caused by outside the area and by not being specific to the neighbourhood.

In Ms Allen's photographs and descriptive text there is evidence of resistance to negative environmental presses. Despite decline of areas of the park, she is able to view the area as it once was or could still be. For example, in the photographs presented of the unused pavilion and tennis courts, she is still able to see that the area with a little care could be "so attractive", and in reference to photographs of the empty and neglected gatehouse, she is able to see a "once beautiful building", which she would love to see "restored and inhabited". As previously mentioned, she is also able to visualise "Nursemaids walking their charges". In addition, her photographs reveal the importance of public spaces like parks in the development and maintenance of attachment. Of the 26 photographs taken, 22 of these related directly to the park.

Ms Allen's photographs also provide a temporal connection with the park, in that "the willow trees are a beautiful sight in all seasons, as they change so much". Ms Allen's inclusion of a few extra photographs from her own collection of this "change in seasons"', indicates the salience of this place for her throughout the year. In addition, the need to document these images long before this current photographic exercise indicates the significance of this place.

An important consideration in the analysis of these photographs and descriptive text is the length of residency of each participant. This might be a feature in both an individual's use of place and familiarity (for example, variety of photographs taken and location) and sentimental attachment (for example, emotive and descriptive text).

Analysis across the three participants reveals a difference, particularly in reference to use of emotive language and negative images, between Mr Bennett and Ms Allen, compared with Ms Clark. Mr Bennett and Ms Allen tended to be more descriptive in their explanation of photographs and also used a much stronger emotive dialogue in describing both positive and negative features of their neighbourhood, compared with Ms Clarke. This is particularly evident in the summary notes provided by Mr Bennett. A possible explanation might be a factor related to years of residency and hence the creation of a deep connection to area. Both Mr Bennett and Ms Allen have lived in their neighbourhoods for over 30 years, whereas Ms Clarke has only been a resident of the area for one year.

Therefore, their perspectives and points of reference based on years of residency might be different; in addition to their emotive bond to the area, and hence use of expressive language. While Mr Bennett and Ms Allen have likely witnessed 30 years of changes in their neighbourhood, Ms Clarke as a new resident has yet to experience any change or develop a point of reference, or strong emotive bond, from which expressive dialogue might be used.

In conclusion

These photographs and descriptive text proved a useful exercise to include and understand older people's perspectives in the profiling and contextualisation of their neighbourhood. And they revealed the diversity with which people use, experience and portray the places in their neighbourhood.

It can also be argued that this method may be more sensitive to the understanding of place and ageing issues compared with the interview data. Specifically, visual images have the ability to reach a greater audience, by evoking a greater connection than words. In addition, they provide direct knowledge on the specific objects within an area that are significant (for example, not just any park but a specific park) and enable 'outsiders' to see the neighbourhood through a resident's eyes.

A limitation of these data is that only three participants from two of the five areas took part in the photography exercise. Therefore it is difficult to assess any cross-national differences and/or similarities, and to extrapolate or generalise beyond these neighbourhoods. However, the purpose of this exercise was not to generate a large body of data based on a high number of participants. Rather, its importance lay in the inclusion of older people as active participants in data generation, methodological diversity and innovativeness, and its potential use as a valuable tool in current and future research.

As was evidenced by the perspectives and dialogue provided by the three participants and the analysis given, photography provides a useful way in which to study and understand older people's environmental perspectives. This supports Wang's (1999, p 186) statement that images 'contribute to how we see ourselves, how we define and relate to the world, and what we perceive as significant or different'.

Summary and conclusion

This chapter helps to set the scene and contextualise the research to be presented and discussed in the following chapters. The objective was to illustrate through historical and contemporary sources a descriptive profile of each study locality. This was supplemented with photographs and descriptive text from older people living in some of these neighbourhoods. Their perspectives help to shed light on the experience of ageing in deprived urban neighbourhoods. The next chapter aims to build on this by presenting analysis of 52 in-depth interviews with older people living in some of the most deprived inner-city neighbourhoods in England and Canada.

Notes

[1] The study builds on work that formed part of a larger research enterprise funded by the Economic and Social Research Council's Growing Older Programme. The 'Older People in Deprived Neighbourhoods – Social Exclusion and Quality of Life' study addressed the circumstances of older people living in urban neighbourhoods in some of England's poorest communities (Scharf et al, 2004).

[2] The English research areas were selected from the Department for the Environment, Transport and the Regions' 1998 Index of Deprivation, and the Canadian research areas were selected from Census data combined with the Statistics Canada LICOs (Low Income Cut-Offs). Selection of English and Canadian cities for comparison were made according to the following variables: population size, ethnic mix, industrial base, geography, language and area type (that is, most deprived in their respective country). Based on these variables, Manchester and Vancouver were found to be the most appropriate to compare. The selection of neighbourhoods was based on a similar process as the selection of cities; in England this was based on the 1998 Index of Deprivation and in Canada on Census data. Three electoral wards in Manchester and two in Vancouver were selected. In Manchester these were Cheetham, Longsight and Moss Side, and in Vancouver they were Downtown Eastside and Grandview-Woodland.

[3] The Mercer Quality of Living survey rates quality of living in 215 countries; this is conducted annually: www.mercer.com/qualityofliving

[4] All names have been anonymised.

[5] The author tried to recruit more participants to take photographs but many declined, fearing that taking photographs might draw unwanted attention and lead to victimisation.

[6] Some participants took multiple photographs of the same scene. For simplicity, the author has chosen to present only one image; selection was based on the clarity of photograph. Where more than one photograph was taken a number is given following the descriptive text.

[7] See note 6 above.

FIVE

Ageing in deprived neighbourhoods

Introduction

This chapter presents the results and analysis of face-to-face interviews conducted with older people living in deprived urban neighbourhoods of Manchester, England, and Vancouver, Canada. The aim of the chapter is to better understand some of the factors that underpin older people's desire to age in place despite multiple risks presented in their environment and conversely why others reject ageing in place.

The analysis begins with a summary of the key characteristics of the research participants in the two cities. This profiles the sample in relation to such factors as gender, age, marital status, ethnicity, health status, housing tenure, educational achievement and rating of quality of life. The discussion then focuses on the overall environmental expression of older people, which is found to fall into three categories – *environmental comfort*, *environmental management* and *environmental distress*.

To illustrate the environmental categories, the chapter presents an in-depth examination and discussion of eight case studies, four from Manchester and four from Vancouver. Each case study presents a detailed narrative of the participant's relationship with place, highlighting daily activities, social support, health status, financial concerns, feelings towards neighbourhood and well-being. Following each case study is an analysis and discussion of the issues and themes raised.

Sample characteristics

The sociodemographic characteristics of the 52 participants were broadly comparable between Manchester and Vancouver (see Appendix A). At ward level the three Manchester wards – Cheetham, Longsight and Moss Side – and the Vancouver ward of Grandview-Woodland shared the most similarities with respect to sociodemographic factors. However, the sample in Vancouver's DES differed with respect to gender, marital status, number of reported health problems, income and rating of quality of life. Many of these characteristics are reflective of people living in the area.

Overall, the sample had almost equal numbers of men and women. In all of the wards, except the DES, women outnumbered men. Conversely, in the DES, 14 of the 19 interviews conducted were with men, reflecting a predominance of men in the area (see area profile for the DES in Chapter Four). The mean age of the two samples were broadly similar; the Manchester sample had a mean age of 70, while the Vancouver sample had a mean age of 73. Both samples also reflected the ethnic diversity of the study areas. Six of the 26 participants in Vancouver belonged to minority ethnic groups – First Nation, Chinese/Other; in Manchester, 10 people in a sample of 26 were from the Black Caribbean group. All other participants in Manchester and Vancouver described themselves as White/Caucasian. The samples, except in the DES, were also comparable in terms of marital status, with just under half of the sample being widowed, and almost a quarter married. The DES had a greater proportion – eight out of 19 – reporting that they were single (never married). In terms of health, 43 participants reported a long-standing illness, of whom 34 reported that this limited them on a daily basis. The only difference found in reported health was in the number of self-reported health problems. Again, people living in the DES reported a greater number of health problems than people living in the other four neighbourhoods; 12 out of 19 residents reported having three or more health problems. The majority of the sample – 41 out of 52 – had lived in their neighbourhood for 11 years or more. Most participants – 38 out of 52 – were living in rented accommodation. The only difference found was in Moss Side (Manchester), where the majority owned their accommodation. The educational qualifications of the Manchester and Vancouver samples were broadly similar; just over 37 participants reported no qualifications and just six reported a City and Guilds or Trade certificate. Forty-seven participants were in receipt of a state pension. However, there was a difference in some areas with respect to additional sources of income beyond state benefit. In Cheetham, Grandview-Woodland and Longsight, almost equal numbers reported additional sources of income (for example, private or occupational pensions), whereas in the DES and Moss Side only a small number of people reported having income in addition to state benefits.

In ratings of quality of life, the majority reported very good or good quality of life – 31 out of 51 (one could not answer). However, when excluding respondents from the DES, 26 out of 31 participants rated their quality of life as very good or good. In the DES, most people reported their quality of life to be neither good nor poor – 10 out of 19 participants. In all, 10 of the 17 people who suggested that their quality of life was neither good nor poor lived in the DES. A possible reason for the dominance of this answer will be discussed in one of the case studies presented later. Almost equal numbers in each area reported having a poor or very poor quality of life (five people in total).

Sociodemographic variables also highlighted the heterogeneity of individuals living in these areas. There was a range of reported health states, years of residence in the area, quality of life judgements, marital status, ethnic backgrounds, type of housing tenure and income levels. Consideration of the heterogeneity of the population will have a variety of implications and influences on the study's findings.

Understanding environmental expression

The interviews with older people in each of the neighbourhoods sought to capture the relationship between the older person and their environment by asking them to describe their daily life, social support and networks, aspects of their neighbourhood they liked and disliked, their desire (or not) to move and how they would rate and describe their quality of life.

In total, 52 interviews were completed, 26 in each country. Themes emerged through inductive analysis (Holloway, 1997) of transcripts, the aim of which is 'the derivation of themes and constructs from the data without imposing a prior framework' (Buck et al, 2004, p 516). The author was conscious of the need to allow the older people's expression of their experience of living in their neighbourhood to evolve, with the only predetermined focus of analysis being the person–environment interaction. Short biographies were created for the 52 research participants. These biographies were structured around the person's relationship with their neighbourhood and factors that might affect this relationship, such as age, ethnicity, gender, years of residence in the neighbourhood, housing and name of neighbourhood/country (see Appendix B).

The 52 interviews were examined to reveal a range of environmental experiences. Transcripts revealed a division between those older people who were acutely aware of their environment because of negative features that impacted on their life, and those who were less aware or concerned with the environment because this did not negatively impact on their daily life. For those who were acutely aware of their environment, there was a further division between those who managed daily life and retained well-being, and those who expressed significant distress in daily life and challenges to well-being. This revealed three categories of environmental expression, termed *environmental comfort*, *environmental management* and *environmental distress*. Within each of these categories, a number of distinguishing characteristics evolved from the data. Although the categories evolved inductively from the in-depth analysis of the transcripts, the description and discourse used to explain each category borrows from the literature. As previously discussed in Chapter Two, Lawton and Nahemow (1973) and later Lawton's (1980, 1982) work on competence-press provides a particularly useful conceptualisation of older people in challenging environments.

The potential usefulness of these concepts should not be underestimated, particularly given the characteristics of the research areas in the present study. Conducting research in deprived neighbourhoods enables examination of extreme conditions – high press (for example, high rates of crime, lack of amenities and services, poverty) and low competence (for example, poor health, potentially limited social support). This is supported by the area effects literature (MacIntyre et al, 1993; Krause, 1996; Atkinson and Kintrea, 2001; Cohen et al, 2003). For example, Atkinson and Kintrea (2001) found that living in deprived areas creates additional problems for residents (for example, with regard to employment and health). Similarly, Krause (1996, p 349) found health to be negatively influenced by deteriorating neighbourhoods, arguing that 'these deleterious effects persist even after the influence of economic factors, as well as problems in key social relationships, have been controlled'. The apparent dichotomy to be found in these areas (high press and low competence) was judged to provide a useful basis from which to develop scientific understanding and analysis of place and ageing issues.

The categories to which participants belonged are descriptively defined as follows:

- *Environmental comfort.* The environmental comfort category is illustrative of cases in which there are low environmental presses matched against a number of personal competences. In this situation, the environment does not present significant, if any, negative challenges or presses to the individual. The environment in this category, compared with the environmental management and distress categories, takes on less of a significant focus within the construction of daily life. The person's personal competences, for example, social support, financial resources and health, are adequate for the perceived environmental conditions. There is evidence of place attachment within the immediate neighbourhood and there is no desire to relocate from the neighbourhood. Individuals in this category also express positive affect states and positive ratings of quality of life.
- *Environmental management.* The environmental management category is illustrative of situations in which there are strong environmental presses and adequate personal competences to cope with and adapt to everyday life. In this situation the environmental experience of the person is recognised to be difficult. However, the individual appears to have the resources or personal competences necessary to manage effectively. There is no or very little expression of psychological distress or inability to cope on a daily basis. While there is evidence of place attachment, this might not necessarily be to the immediate environment. Place attachment might exist in other areas previously occupied by the individual. The expression of the desire to move can vary, ranging from older people who wish to move to those with no desire to move. Those individuals expressing a desire to move are those who have formed place attachments beyond their immediate neighbourhood. In some cases there is evidence of protection and maintenance of self-worth and quality of life by the rejection of a neighbourhood.
- *Environmental distress.* The environmental distress category is illustrative of cases in which strong environmental presses are found to overwhelm the personal competences of the individual. In this category, participants are found to be acutely aware of their environment, such that it appears to negatively affect many aspects of daily life. There is often a disruption to routine or a restriction of activity based on environmental barriers (for example, fear of crime). There is evidence from the individual's discourse that place attachment does not exist or that there have been disruptions to place attachment, which once existed

but now works to undermine identity and well-being. There is expression of a strong desire to move but constraints are present that prevent the individual from relocating; in most cases this is restricted by lack of financial resources. Expressions of psychological distress are also evident, usually expressed through poor quality of life ratings and negative discourse on self-worth. Each category is summarised in Box 5.1.

Box 5.1: Summary of characteristics of environmental categories

Environmental comfort

- environment appears less significant;
- weak environmental press versus more than adequate personal competences;
- evidence of place attachment to immediate neighbourhood;
- no desire to move;
- ratings of quality of life – (in general) good to very good.

Environmental management

- acutely aware of environment;
- strong environmental press versus adequate personal competences;
- evidence of place attachment to immediate neighbourhood or place attachment outside neighbourhood;
- expressions of a desire to move or no desire to move;
- evidence of 'management'/strategies of daily living;
- ratings of quality of life – neither good nor poor, or good.

Environmental distress

- strong environmental press versus poor personal competences;
- no evidence of place attachment and/or evidence of disruptions;
- expression of a strong desire to move;
- evidence of minimal strategies of daily coping;
- ratings of quality of life – (in general) poor to very poor.

The categories within this analysis are not meant to be mutually exclusive and static, rather they are perceived as being dynamic and overlapping. As with all typologies, this represents a continuum where a few cases might fall on the borderline and may be less easily classified. The author recognises that individuals may move through a number of these categories throughout the lifecourse. This might be a function of personal changes associated with health and/or environmental changes. Within the current analysis, concern is centred around examination of *the present* (for example, in time and place) of the person–environment situation. However, in some cases, analysis extrapolates beyond the immediate category to suggest possible temporal changes in future environmental categorisation.

For this reason, a study investigating 'place and ageing' dimensions within some of the most deprived urban neighbourhoods in England and Canada represents an important contribution to informing and advancing gerontological knowledge.

Drawing on the literature review, there are two types of research questions to be addressed within this study. The first concerns shortfalls in empirical knowledge related to place and ageing, and the second addresses technical aspects of the research process and analysis.

In terms of empirical knowledge, there is a need for research that seeks to gain in-depth understanding of place and ageing within deprived urban areas across two countries:

- First, what factors are important in place and ageing in these neighbourhoods? Do potentially 'extreme' environments test the environmental literature and notions of ageing in place and place in ageing. In particular, this question seeks to understand the factors behind older people's desire to age in place in spite of the potential multiple risks presented in these neighbourhoods.
- Second, how does place and ageing influence older people's discourse and ratings of quality of life and self-perception/identity? This question explores the relationship between the environment and individual reports of well-being.

These research questions present the study's agenda for the type of knowledge to be investigated, while also setting the foundation for the type of methodological approach to be employed.

Case studies – Manchester and Vancouver

This section analyses data collected from 52 face-to-face interviews with people aged 60 and older living in the chosen study areas. Eight of these interviews are analysed in-depth using the case study method. The remaining interviews provide support for these case studies and are presented as short biographies in Appendix B. All 52 interviews were categorised into one of three environmental situations; this was in accordance with characteristics present within each transcript (for example, perceived environmental presses, personal competences, desire to move, evidence of place attachment – see Box 5.1 for a summary of environmental categories). Two of the case studies were selected to reflect an environmental comfort category (n=20). Four case studies illustrate differing forms of environmental management (n=23). The remaining two case studies illustrate situations characterised by environmental distress (n=9) (see Table 5.1). It should be mentioned that the environmental categories are not fixed; rather, they are considered to be dynamic or transitional and temporally bound. In particular, the categories represent a specific point in time and are not intended to suggest that the person's relationship with their environment will always be experienced in this way. All participants' names have been changed, as have references made to people (for example, neighbours, friends) and places (for example, streets, places of work) in order to protect individuals' identities.

Table 5.1: Summary of case studies*

Name	Key characteristics	Quality of life
Environmental comfort		
Mary Perkins	Aged 69, Black Caribbean, married, good health, 40 years in area, 4 children, Moss Side	Good
Jennifer MacDougall	Aged 90, White, widowed (15 years), health challenges, 40 years in area, 6 children, Grandview-Woodland	Good
Environmental management		
Muriel Allen	Aged 69, White, divorced, good health, 30 years in area, 5 children, Moss Side	Good
Berry Matthews	Aged 61, White, single, some health problems, 7 years in area, no children, DES	Neither good nor poor
Howard Adams Goodleaf	Aged 70, First Nation, separated, some health problems, approximately 40 years in area, 7 children, DES	Neither good nor poor
Helen Fox	Aged 78, White, widowed (4 years), poor health, 30 years in area, 1 child, Cheetham	Poor
Environmental distress		
Harold Waters	Aged 69, White, single, good health, over 30 years in area, no children, Cheetham	Poor
Elizabeth Laing	Aged 64, White, divorced, good health, 5 years in area, 2 children, DES/Grandview-Woodland	Good

Note: * All names have been anonymised.

Category 1: environmental comfort

Out of the total sample interviewed, 20 were found to belong to the category of environmental comfort. Some participants expressed feelings of love or like for their neighbourhood and others appeared less emotively governed or more 'neutral' with respect to feelings about their neighbourhood. Two case studies – Mary Perkins and Jennifer MacDougall – are presented and analysed below. They both show psychological connections to their environment. However, the way in which they traverse and manage their environment and daily activities differs.

Mary Perkins – Manchester

Mrs Mary Perkins is aged 69 and lives with her husband in a terraced house. Of Black Caribbean ethnicity, she has lived with her husband in Moss Side for over 40 years. She has four children, two of whom live locally and two of whom live elsewhere in England. She has few health complaints and enjoys good mobility.

Mrs Perkins enjoys many aspects of living in her neighbourhood, saying simply that, "I love this area":

> "I'm within walking distance of all the hospitals, the eye hospital, the foot hospital, the chest clinic, every one of the hospitals, the general hospital, like the Royal Infirmary. I am surrounded by everything that I need. Town is near and everything.... The market is near. We have one market up there and we have another one over there ... when I go to the market I catch the bus at the park and I go to the market, yes, without any problem, no problem, I go and I come back without any trouble."

For these reasons, Mrs Perkins felt that Moss Side is a particularly good neighbourhood for older people.

Most of Mrs Perkins' daily activities were usually undertaken within the neighbourhood or in the city centre. Typically in the morning she would wash up, have breakfast, and then sit and watch television or read her bible. Then she might go into town: "I browse around the shops just to see what's in the shops. Then when I get the money, I know exactly what I want". In the afternoon, she would have a rest and/or go for a walk; "I go to the park, I go to the museum, I go to the gallery. They're over there, across there ... just a few minutes". In the evening, she would usually watch television or goes to church or to visit friends. On alternate months she would attend a local residents' association meeting in which members discuss issues of concern, like crime and personal safety, and improvements to the area (for example, cleaning up alleyways).

Mrs Perkins appeared to have a very supportive social network. Family and friends visited her daily:

> "He [son] comes every day when he's not at work and then I have a brother who is retired, he comes every day without fail. My sister lives in Manchester, she comes sometimes. We have a very good friend, Mr Smith, he comes every day ... so I have plenty of visitors ... they'll sit down and talk and have a cup of tea, sometimes they don't want any tea, just to talk."

Mrs Perkins also enjoyed a very good relationship with her neighbours, most of whom had lived in the community for as long as she had:

> "My neighbours are very good. This one that lives next door to me, I have his keys, he has my keys, yes. And there is an old lady that lives [next door but one], I have to treat her like a mother. I cook and I give her and I shop and give to her and things like those and I have a talk … I could call on any one of them day and night and they'd be there to assist me."

Although very happy and generally content with living in her neighbourhood, Mrs Perkins recognised that there had been some unwanted, negative changes in the area:

> "When I first moved here the people were a lot more sociable. You could leave your door open and you could go anywhere. They used to leave bread and milk on the doorsteps. I used to go to work and come back and find it there. Nobody would break it, nobody would steal it and neighbours used to look after each other … your trouble would be my trouble, my trouble would be yours, we used to share but it's different now."

Mrs Perkins felt that the new residents, "young families", did not care for one another like the older residents: "they have no respect for us [older residents/people]". A recent incident with a neighbourhood youth appeared to reinforce Mrs Perkins' feelings: "one of them even threatened me that I would get shot … Tommy would circle around me on his bike and say 'you're going to get shot, you're going to get shot', so I called the police".

Despite this incident, Mrs Perkins was not overly concerned about her personal safety when out walking in the area. She felt that her long-time residency in the area had given her a certain level of protection from crime: "They all know me around here and I don't think they would attack me. They wouldn't do anything to me. It's like people that come from outside … those are the people that are vulnerable". Mrs Perkins felt that because a lot of the crime was related to gangs: "they know who they're looking for … we are safe … we would have to be in the wrong place at the wrong time to get hurt".

Mrs Perkins felt that her quality of life was good:

> "It's good because I have a roof over my head and I haven't got to pay a rent for that, it's my own. I have most amenities that would make me comfortable. I have central heating and I have gas fires. I have a cooker. Most things that would make you comfortable in the home I have. My husband has a car so I would say my quality of life is reasonable compared to some people."

Discussion

The case study of Mrs Perkins represents a situation in which there is a perceived level of comfort between an individual and their environment. Mrs Perkins appeared physically and psychologically uninhibited and unchallenged in the traversing and negotiation of her environment. In addition, there was strong evidence and emotive dialogue of attachment to neighbourhood – "I love this area".

The area's perceived environmental presses appeared to have a limited effect on Mrs Perkins' personal competences. The strength of her personal competences – good health, a strong social support network and being financially comfortable – was matched against what she perceived as the limited or low environmental demands made on her. She felt that she was able to enjoy a neighbourhood that had numerous amenities and resources, lacked a real threat of personal crime and enabled her to physically and psychologically manage on a daily basis.

Over 40 years of residence in the area, coupled with the unrestricted way in which Mrs Perkins experienced place and ageing, likely contributed to place attachment. Certainly this can be argued with respect to physical connectedness, which was evident in her knowledge of and familiarity with the area. Mrs Perkins had extensive knowledge of the amenities and resources that were available in or near her neighbourhood – eye, foot, chest and general hospitals, a number of markets, accessibility to the city centre, the park, museum and gallery. In her opinion, the area had "everything". She had no fears about leaving her house or issues of personal safety, and her physical-spatial knowledge appeared to lack limits – "there is no area I purposely avoid".

Social connection to the area was evident in Mrs Perkins' familiarity with local people. She "had plenty of visitors" on a daily basis; she also enjoyed a number of relationships with neighbours, many of whom were the "original" residents, having lived in the area the same length of time as she had. She appeared to have a particularly close relationship with one of her neighbours – treating her like a mother. Being a long-standing resident appeared to be significant for Mrs Perkins in creating feelings of social belonging, as she felt that the same level of neighbourliness could not be achieved with the newer residents in the area. She also appeared to suggest that her length of residency in the area and "being known" afforded her a level of protection from crime: "they all know me around here, it's people that come from outside, they are vulnerable".

Historical connection to the area was evident from Mrs Perkins' recollection of 'how things used to be'. She recalled how neighbours used to care for one another: "your trouble was my trouble"; and no one would steal from you: "you could leave your door open". Despite the presence of some negative changes, Mrs Perkins did not appear to be too disillusioned. This might be explained by a number of factors. The first was the availability of a peer group (for example, other original residents). This possibly enabled the neighbourhood of the past to be recreated and kept alive. Another factor evident from the interview was her ability to sustain a level of 'past' neighbourliness among her immediate older neighbours. Therefore, although she recognised negative changes with respect to new residents in the area, they appeared peripheral to her daily management within the area.

Consideration of temporal factors suggests that there was, in general, a manageable continuity between the past and the present. For Mrs Perkins, place and ageing was not significantly tested or affected by environmental demands or personal competence. This might have in part been aided by an ability to create continuity of the neighbourhood of the past through an established peer group (for example, old neighbours). Despite the recognition of some negative changes in the area, at least on her street, the neighbourhood of the past still appeared 'alive'. However, her future ability to do this might be challenged when the original neighbours die.

In summary, the case of Mrs Perkins illustrates a situation in which the experience of place and ageing is not limited by environmental or personal demands made on the individual. Mrs Perkins enjoyed living in her neighbourhood and was attached to the area. This case study was similar to a number of other interviews conducted in the Manchester and Vancouver neighbourhoods. These are presented in Table A1 in Appendix A and the biographies in Appendix B and apply to Joan Schofield, Leslie Johnson and Sydney Potter in Manchester, and Jean Gauche, Alistair O'Connor, Joe Dawson and Dorothy Dobson in Vancouver.

Jennifer MacDougall – Vancouver

Mrs Jennifer MacDougall maintained a very busy weekly schedule:

> "Most Mondays I play bridge. Tuesdays I do the same. I get up, make my bed and so on and go for a swim. I have been playing Scrabble in the afternoon but my Scrabble partner died, so that means Tuesday afternoons I have nothing to do right now, but, I got to find something. Wednesdays I have a girl come in, Wednesday at 8:00, and she does the cleaning of the bathroom and that for me, and then when she goes I go to 114 Riverview and play bridge. Thursdays I go for a swim, but tomorrow I am out for a picnic instead with a group of seniors. Friday I volunteer at a place up town, I play bridge with a couple of old men that can't find anyone in their building to play with, so I volunteer, it's kind of nice. Saturday, I do my washing and sometimes go out with family sometimes … in the summer I take the speed bus to North Vancouver and listen to the concerts there."

In the evenings, sometimes:

> "I go to the theatre or once in a long while I will have someone for dinner, not very often. I read the paper, I have a couple of shows I

> look at on the TV, and I also belong to a writing club so I do writing … I always have a book, I go through books; without books I would go crazy."

Although recognising at times that her schedule was sometimes physically difficult for her to manage, she felt that it was something she needed to do to keep going:

> "I am really on a tight schedule because if I get off it I will never get back on it, as long as I keep going. Like today, I thought I would never get up to the bus, but I have to keep going, I really push myself though … I don't want to start feeling sorry for myself. Once a senior starts to feel sorry for themselves they're done … I know I have two or three people I used to go around with and I can't stand them … they're blimming boring!"

A lack of immediate family around her was another reason Mrs MacDougall gave for keeping so busy:

> "Once in a while I feel lonely because the kids are quite a way from me and I don't have a family around me like I used to have. That is why I keep so busy is that I don't want to feel lonely and sorry for myself you see."

Mrs MacDougall still managed to drive, but was wary about using her car too often or driving long distances:

> "It is two blocks up to the bus that way and then it's a hard walk for me. I still have my car, but I don't drive it very far. I drive it to the swimming pool and I drive it to the library, and I drive it to get my groceries and that. I drive it about four days a week, but not very far. I haven't driven very far for the last four years, because my car is old and I am old, and I don't think it is right for me to take the road up."

She felt some pressure to give up her car, but was concerned by the fact that doing so would also restrict her ability to do some of her activities.

Mrs MacDougall has been an active participant and promoter of her neighbourhood. In the late 1980s, she helped form a theatre group for older people at her local community centre, and in the last couple of years has written a number of articles and a short story about her life in Grandview-Woodland. When asked what it was that she liked about her neighbourhood, she referred to one of the articles she had written:

> For me it had everything I needed to live a happy life. I needed transportation and also a community with lots of activity.... From my quiet apartment, I see the mountains – Grouse, Cypress Bowl and the Seymour ski lifts.... The Drive, as it is called, is a short stroll away. Commercial Drive has an incredible diversity of people, as well as restaurants and coffee houses, theatres and shopping. Everything I need is here: my doctor, banks, parks and entertainment. Then there is Britannia Community Centre. I go there to use the library, swimming pool, senior centre and secondary school for night classes. (dated March 2002)

She further elaborated on her article by saying that she enjoys the neighbourhood for its energy and vibrancy: "I also like the vitality, compared to the stuffed shirt atmosphere of the suburbs, suburbs are to bring up kids. Downtown cities are for seniors that are lonely". Mrs MacDougall also expressed a number of fond memories of the area, which she has illustrated in a short story entitled 'A walk down Memory Lane' (see Appendix C).

Although generally content and happy with where she lives, Mrs MacDougall expressed a number of dislikes about her neighbourhood. She felt that the ethnic mix of the building she lived in divided people into groups, to which she felt she was not included: "When they get together the ladies all, they are very happy giggling away, but they don't include me in anything. I have one friend up above ... and I go to the theatre with her once in a while" but other than that Mrs MacDougall felt that she could not rely on her neighbours for companionship.

Crime was another feature of her neighbourhood that she disliked. However, Mrs MacDougall saw this issue as not being specific to her area, but "like anywhere else in Vancouver". Although she felt that it was a "fairly safe" area and has never had any problems, she felt that it was still important to take some personal precautions. When she goes out she never takes a purse: "I have my keys, a handkerchief, a comb and some money in my pocket, that's all you need". Although she felt that it was important to be aware, she felt that this did not in any way prevent her from going out as and when she wished.

Family support appeared to be limited. Most of Mrs MacDougall's six children and their families lived in the US or elsewhere in British Columbia. One child lived locally, but was in her seventies and in poor health, so could only visit occasionally. Social support offered by friends was also limited:

> "You see all my really close friends, the ones that you make when you are younger when your kids are going to school, they are all gone, they are all dead, and the ones I make now are more acquaintances. I see them when I play bridge and whatever I do ... they don't come to my house and I don't go to your house, so you don't get really close."

Mrs MacDougall felt that her quality of life was good because she was 'very comfortable in her state of mind'. She was very happy with where she lived and her ability to get out. However, she felt that with a bit of extra money her quality of life would improve, because it would allow her to visit her family more frequently: "to be able to go and see my family and friends and invite them out for dinner and not worry about the cost, that would be lovely".

Discussion

Mrs MacDougall is illustrative of a situation in which someone is positively connected and integrated into their community. In this case study, ageing in place appeared optimal based on physical health and the management of a busy weekly schedule. Place in ageing was also recognised as significant in relation to Mrs MacDougall's present and future well-being and quality of life. In addition, this case study highlights the importance of the consideration of temporal dimensions and illustrates the dynamic relationship between place and ageing.

Physical connectedness or attachment appeared to be a key feature in this interview. Of particular significance was the level and distance of physical action achieved despite limited functional mobility. Certainly, Mrs MacDougall's in-depth physical knowledge allowed traversing of the neighbourhood and enabled maintenance of her busy schedule despite some limited mobility. The familiarity she had gained from years of residence in her neighbourhood likely enabled a greater level of physical function and achieved greater environmental comfort than might have been achieved in a newer setting. In reference to her short story, she was able to accomplish six tasks in "the allotted time of three hours", showing a significant level of 'residential knowing' and enabling greater physical function.

There appeared to exist an acceptable level of physical connectedness that Mrs MacDougall felt she needed to operate within. A prevalent feature in the interview and case study was the need to maintain a complete 'scheduled week' of activities. Her ability to maintain her week enabled her to physically 'keep going' and had a psychological element in that it prevented her from becoming lonely, in addition to creating a continuity of self. Changes to her scheduled week appeared to cause some distress. For example, after the sudden death of her Scrabble partner, Tuesday afternoons became an unwelcome, unscheduled part of her week.

Feelings of social integration or connectedness appeared to be lacking. Although there was likely to be a level of social integration gained through her activities and through the people she met when she was out, there was evidence to suggest that this did not satisfy her need for social support and contact. Within her building, she spoke about not being 'included' and having limited family contact. She also spoke about no longer having any close friends, just many acquaintances. Her expression of feelings of loneliness is likely a reflection of inadequate levels of social connectedness or sense of belonging.

There is evidence to suggest that personal history might offer greater insight into attachment to place than social or physical connectedness. This is certainly evident in Mrs MacDougall's case (see Appendix C). First, she recalled how 'miserable' she was when she moved away from the area, because it appeared to somehow remove or disconnect her from her 'good memories': "I came back because a lot of my good memories are connected to this area". In this case, happiness could only be achieved within the area, where she could connect with her good memories and retain continuity in her personal history. Second, Mrs MacDougall appeared to recognise the temporal value of memories. She was able to remember the area as it was in the past, "the lovely stately mansion and beautiful garden with the rowan tree". Despite the changes to the area, Mrs MacDougall was still able to recreate her neighbourhood: "I still have my memories of it firmly implanted in my memory bank". She was comforted by her memories in relation to the past and the present, and recognised their value to comfort in the future: "just maybe, I will have some warm memories of this day years from now when I might be feeling a little bit lonely". From this short story it is evident that her memories were specific and contextually bound in time to this neighbourhood, and that relocation produced significant psychological distress.

Consideration of temporal factors was particularly pertinent to this case study. Although Mrs MacDougall was classified as environmentally comfortable in the scheduled face-to-face interview, this view was challenged upon a later social meeting the researcher had with Mrs MacDougall a month after the original interview. This meeting is included for discussion here because the researcher feels that this presents an important opportunity to highlight the dynamic relationship between the environment and person, the positionality of individuals with respect to time and hence the importance of temporal issues in analysis.

In this meeting, the researcher encountered a much 'less energised self' of Mrs MacDougall and a significant change in her demeanour. Since the original meeting, Mrs MacDougall had experienced some health problems that resulted in her spending a number of days in hospital. This appeared to create doubts in her mind as to her physical ability to maintain her weekly schedule: "perhaps it is time to slow down". Her inability to find something (that is, an activity) or someone (for example, a Scrabble partner) to fill her Tuesday afternoons appeared a particular concern and source of distress for Mrs MacDougall; this appeared to present a further sign that she should slow down. In this meeting her ability to maintain a balance between her need to 'keep going' versus increasingly poor health and pressure to give up her car appeared to be fragile. This second meeting very much showed someone in a state of transition, where environmental presses appeared increasingly to challenge personal competence, resulting in 'less comfort' and more active management of her environment. This case study illustrates the importance of considering temporal dimensions, in addition to methodological and analytic claims, which position the individual in a specific time and place. This will be discussed further in Chapter Six.

In summary, Mrs MacDougall's case lends support to the place and ageing literature, and highlights the importance of temporal issues. Ageing in place appeared optimal, enabling greater physical activity amidst functional limitations.

The importance of place in ageing was evident in her discourse on the neighbourhood of the past and her need to stay in place. In this case, physical and historical connectedness was an important element in place attachment. Mrs MacDougall reported good quality of life and was able to maintain a level of continuous self through her weekly activities. This case study was similar to a number of other interviews conducted within this research study, most notably those with Theresa Blackbird (Vancouver) and Marva Collins (Manchester). These are presented in Table A1 in Appendix A and the biographies in Appendix B.

Category 2: environmental management

In 23 of the 52 interviews participants were found to 'manage' their environment (see Appendix A). Despite strong environmental challenges these individuals were able to adapt to these demands and maintain a positive level of physical and psychological functioning. Environmental management has potentially a number of combinations (see Box 5.1) and is conceptualised as overlapping with the environmental categories of environmental comfort and distress. Therefore, four case studies are presented and analysed here. Each illustrates a slightly different perspective on environmental management. In particular, Muriel Allen (already discussed in Chapter Four) took a very proactive stance to the management of her neighbourhood; Berry Matthews "learned by careful watching" to manage in his area; Helen Fox, despite profound health limitations, managed to live independently by the restructuring of her immediate living place; and Howard Adams Goodleaf managed his environment by being rooted spiritually in the "traditional Native North American way of thinking".

Muriel Allen – Manchester

Ms Allen's typical day usually starts around 9.00 or 9.30 in the morning. After she has breakfast – cereal with skimmed milk and a cup of coffee – she takes her dogs for a walk in the local park. These walks can last for an hour or longer: "Sometimes I meet somebody while I'm out and instead of being out an hour I'm out two". In situations in which she is out longer than expected, lunch is usually something quick ("I just sort of grab the nearest thing"), usually a sandwich, but generally "I always cook my meals … something like potatoes and cauliflower or cabbage … and some kind of vegetarian sausage". In the afternoon, Ms Allen's schedule varies. She might do some sewing, letter writing, gardening, shopping or visiting family or friends. Towards early evening, she is again off on another one-hour walk in the park with her dogs. Upon her return home, she makes something to eat and then sits down to watch television for the rest of the evening until it is time to go to bed.

Ms Allen has lived in rented council accommodation for over 20 years. She recalled: "I remember them building these. I remember passing on the bus and thinking those horrible houses with those tiny little slitty windows. I never thought I'd end up in one". Despite initial apprehension about living in her present accommodation and pressure from her daughter to move out to be closer to family, Ms Allen felt settled and defended her decision to stay. She felt that her "immediate area is not all that bad" and that moving did not necessarily equate with being better off, as the experiences of her daughter and friend had illustrated:

> "My daughter lives in Appleton and they own the house and it's sort of Edwardian-type three-storey house you know, and she's been burgled several times. I've only had the one burglary so really you know I might as well stay here … a friend of mine moved … she moved from next door actually … she'd only been there a year and her next door neighbour was murdered … so she would have been just as well staying here … it's better the devil you know, isn't it?"

As a long-time resident, Ms Allen has been witness to a number of what she views as negative physical environmental changes:

> "In this road here used to be chocked full of shops on either side.… People used to travel from different parts of Manchester like Wythenshawe and that area just to come down here and shop.… There was loads of shops. There was a dentist, a doctors, chemist … there was wonderful shops. There was a big furniture shop, a Woolworths, there was nightclubs you know the West Indian clubs, nightclubs. You could walk up there late at night and you'd hear the music and all the doors would be open and the lights, a bit like Soho you know, and that's all gone. There is nothing now."

There have also been a number of negative changes to the local park, which distressed Ms Allen (see photographs in Chapter Eight). She felt that negative changes had also occurred with people in the area and that neighbours are not what they used to be:

> "The actual streets and the people in them have changed. I mean when we lived on the other side of Moss Side in the older houses, neighbours used to sort of watch out for each other.… Like I used to go to work and when I got back from work somebody across the road would say 'oh there was somebody knocking on your door, he had a little red van' … or 'I've got a message for you', or if I went out and didn't let the cat out they'd say 'your cat's in our house, you know it was out in the rain'. Or if I had to go anywhere I could leave the key with somebody and say 'well if you know I'm not back will you let my daughter in when she comes home from school', things like that.… Now I'm here and people are not unfriendly, I get on with

> everybody, but I wouldn't dream of asking any of them to do me a favour, ever."

The way Ms Allen felt about her neighbours was not surprising given her experiences:

> "She's a drunk [referring to a next-door neighbour]. In the evening she's lying about in the back garden effing and blinding and fighting with everybody.... That house [referring to next door] has never had a normal person, when I first moved in there was a West Indian woman ... she had a toilet fear so she used to use the bucket as a toilet and toss it over the fence. The urine and the stench out there was unbelievable and it took me years to realise where it was coming from ... anyway I mean other than that she was harmless, she was all right."

Ms Allen recalled another neighbour who had been responsible for a series of break-ins on the estate, including to her house:

> "There was a fella, he's gone now ... he lived four doors up, three or four doors up, and he used to send these kids out.... He used to send them out and they used to steal stuff and take them to him and he'd buy it off them for peanuts."

It was this group of children that had broken into her house when she was out walking one of her dogs:

> "They burgled me and they wrecked everything ... they'd tried to set the house on fire. They'd put a pile of paper on the floor ... poured a bottle of turps over it. I'd got a painting on the easel that I'd been doing for a present for my son, and they'd thrown eggs at it. And I mean they were prepared to set the house on fire with a little dog in it.... They must have been in when I got back because they'd put the clip on the door ... I went to a couple of houses to ask them to phone the police and none of them would open the door. It's only about 6 o'clock at night you know, not in the middle of the night. Then the old man next door but one phoned the police."

Not surprisingly, Ms Allen felt that in an emergency she could not rely on her neighbours for help. Fortunately, because her children lived close by, she had peace of mind knowing that if she needed help they would be over quickly.

Ms Allen felt that gangs of children were still a threat on the estate. But unlike other older residents, she said that she refused to be intimidated by them:

> "Kids are still a threat round here ... I've had kids cheek me and that but I just give them as good as they get ... I just walk past but I mean I'm not infirm or anything. You know I'm quite fit and if they attacked me I'd give them a good fight 'cause I'm well able to take care of myself ... when I go out I've got to sort of push my way through them because there's no way I'm getting off the pavement onto the road just because of them ... [it is] not so much intimidating as annoying."

Socially engaged, Ms Allen had frequent contact with family, friends and acquaintances. She had two children who lived locally: a daughter she visited three times a week and a son she visited once a week. Her other children she saw less often, usually only on special occasions, and her friends she visited whenever she felt she needed a chat. Her visits to her children always occurred at their houses as they refused to visit her in Moss Side:

> "They won't come to Moss Side ... well they're scared ... they all used to come at one time. They all used to come every Sunday. But as things got bad, the drugs and the guns and that, they just keep away so that the only one who comes really is my son-in-law who drops me off but he never comes in."

Her one close friend had recently moved from the neighbourhood. However, she still managed to visit her every couple of weeks and had frequent telephone contact. Contact with acquaintances appeared to be a daily occurrence.

Despite the problems in her neighbourhood, Ms Allen did not feel defeated by these. Rather, she preferred to be proactive and tried to make improvements to her local area: "I just see all these things going on around me and I think oh it's terrible and they're so stupid and why are they doing it? So I have to let off steam". This is why she decided to join the local park committee. She wanted to fight the city council on what she viewed as destructive changes to the park:

> "It's a small group that have been, well we thought it was to help with improvements in the park and that, but all it is really is they want to make changes and they want us to agree to them and they want to apply to the Lottery for money and what they're doing now is just uprooting bushes. It's, I don't know but in my opinion this council is obsessed with grass.... Oh I have words every time I go. I had words with the park manager. I told him he was an idiot, it really upsets me. I go in and see all these bushes uprooted and trees chopped down and you know I've been going into that park so long and I've seen them make all these mistakes before and they just keep on doing it and it annoys me.... All they want is money off the Lottery.... They'll only waste it. I hope they don't get it."

Ms Allen also took in stray dogs until the council was able to pick them up and gave money to a number of charitable organisations.

Ms Allen felt that she enjoyed a good quality of life because she was able to take pleasure from her dogs and from the people she met:

> "My dogs, I get a lot of pleasure out of the dogs. I play football with them ... and talking to people. I've not got a lot of close friends, but I've got a lot of casual acquaintances. I talk to a lot of people so I enjoy that. I enjoy, you know, meeting people and they're not all, not all my age. I don't want to go to old folks' clubs and listen to a lot of old fogies moaning about their rheumatics, it's not my scene at all. So, you know, I mix with people of all different age groups. I mean I've got teenagers as friends and I've got people who are in their eighties and nineties and I just like to chat."

Discussion

Mrs Muriel Allen represents a situation in which numerous deleterious environmental challenges do not appear to have a negative impact on well-being. She appeared to be able to manage environmental demands through place attachment and through proactive management of her neighbourhood.

Ms Allen's experience of place and ageing appeared to be unaffected by strong environmental barriers. As illustrated, the environmental demands presented were numerous, from the general appearance and lack of vibrancy of the area, to changes in neighbourliness and increases in crime. However, despite these environmental presses acting upon Ms Allen, the use of place appeared not to be affected by these demands. Environmental management could be argued from her daily schedule. She was able to develop a level of physical familiarity or physical insideness, which enabled accomplishment of her needs (for example, walking her dogs in the park), which was in large part unaffected by environmental barriers (for example, crime). Her ability to 'manage' these presses might be a function of a number of personal competences, such as good functional health, few financial concerns and social support – that offered by family, a few friends, "numerous" acquaintances and her dogs.

The strength of Ms Allen's personal competences was remarkable in that they not only served to help her adapt to and cope with difficult environmental presses, they also enabled activism or environmental proactivity. Ms Allen was not content just to watch things decline in her neighbourhood, but rather preferred to become involved by sitting on the local park board and voicing her opinion. Ms Allen was very passionately and emotively engaged in trying to change things for the better in her neighbourhood, and despite the resistance she encountered she appeared not to feel defeated, but almost empowered by the challenge.

There was evidence of an emotive connection to her neighbourhood. This was found in relation to both a social and a historical connection she had with the area. A strong sense of social connectedness was found in her relationships with people and in her civic participation. In respect of social relationships, although she felt that she did not have a lot of close friends, she felt that she had "a lot of casual acquaintances" and talked with a lot of people. She boasted of having friends of all ages, giving self-affirmation that she was able to talk, identify and integrate with people of all ages. Her visits to the local park were significant in that she met many of these casual acquaintances/friends while also taking pleasure in walking in the park with her dogs. The sense of pleasure she derived from the park was also illustrated in many of the photographs taken by her (see Chapter Four).

Ms Allen's civic activities might be best illustrative of her attachment to place. Her attachment to the area can be argued through her need to try and improve her local area, in particular the park, and in her passionate attitude towards what she perceived as a hindrance to improvement. The level of her attachment or 'passion' was evident in some of the very vivid discourse she used about having to deal with the council and park manager: "I have words every time I go", "I have to let off steam" and referring to the council as "stupid" and the park manager as an "idiot". She also expressed feelings of psychological distress – "it really upsets me" – at seeing bushes uprooted and trees chopped down. Similar feelings were also evident in some of the photographs she had taken and the text she had written about the park.

Historical connection was also evident in Ms Allen's discourse relating to the neighbourhood and the neighbours of the past, and was evident in some of her photographs (see Chapter Four). The neighbourhood of the past was remembered fondly. It was an area of great activity and vibrancy, described as "a bit like Soho" with lots of shops and music, and the image of neighbours was one of caring: they "used to watch out for you". Some of Ms Allen's photographs also reinforced a sense of autobiographical insideness with the area, particularly in reference to the park and St. Bede's College. Reminiscence enabled the recreation of the neighbourhood as it was in the past when "Nursemaids walked their charges" and the "area was upmarket".

The park provided a significant focus for discussion within the interview, and featured in the majority of the photographs taken. The park appeared to be the main focus around which other daily activities were organised, such as lunch and visits with her daughter. For example, preparing a cooked lunch would depend on who she met in the park. If she was longer than an hour, she would just "grab a sandwich". The park was a place where Ms Allen spent time walking her dogs – an hour in the morning and an hour in the early evening. It also provided an opportunity to meet and have a chat with people, feed the magpies, enjoy nature, reminisce and escape into fantasy about how things might have been. This was evident in her photographs and accompanying text. Ms Allen's attachment to the park led to participatory behaviour to try and improve the park. This is suggestive of wider issues related to public places, specifically, place attachments to public places might encourage greater civic participation and the psychological well-being of area residents.

The consideration of temporal dimensions is significant in this case study. The past worked to help reinforce connections to the present and the future. Although recollection of the past in relation to the neighbourhood of the present suggests a certain level of loss, this loss appeared not to have disrupted present attachment to the area and there was no evidence of this affecting future attachment. This might in part be a function of rationalisation ("I might be not better off"), based on comparative references to her friend's and daughter's experiences of living in their neighbourhoods. Their experiences (a murder and break-ins) undoubtedly had an impact on Ms Allen's wish to age in place, as she reasoned that "it's better the devil you know". This statement is significant for a number of reasons. First, it recognises present and future commitment to age in place. Second, there is recognition that her area presents environmental challenges, but that familiarity has enabled management and adaptation in that she has come to know her area and what to expect. In this respect, Ms Allen has reached a level of physical insideness at which she has *learned* 'residential knowledge' that provides a level of both autonomy and security. This physical connection to the area allows not only acute awareness of the body, but also psychological well-being in that she feels able to traverse and negotiate the risks associated with place (that is, crime), thus allowing movement around the neighbourhood with an awareness of limiting possible personal safety risks.

In summary, despite the deleterious way in which she viewed changes to her present neighbourhood, coupled with the problems she had had with neighbours, Ms Allen did not appear to feel disconnected or disillusioned. Rather she appeared to manage her daily activities and was very committed to improving the area. Her case study illustrates a situation in which place in ageing is realised despite potentially numerous environmental challenges. A sense of attachment to place, construction of a positive-self identity and well-being/quality of life were achieved. This case study is similar to the situation of Mabel Smith (Vancouver) and Betty Wilson (Manchester). These are presented in Table A1 in Appendix A and the biographies in Appendix B.

Berry Matthews – Vancouver

Aged 61, Mr Berry Matthews moved to the DES seven years before the interview after the bankruptcy of his business forced him to relocate to more affordable housing. Never married, he lives in a one-room apartment in a purpose-built housing complex for older people. Greatly disliking the area, Mr Matthews described his ability to manage on a daily basis as a consequence of years of "watching what goes on" and "learning to live with it".

Mr Matthews felt that since moving to the area he has become more 'streetwise' through carefully 'watching' and 'learning' what goes on in the area:

> "They pick on the person that is the poorest and you know any predator, animal, man, any predator of any kind always looks for the

> weak spot, the weakest human.... You put someone down here with a weak spot, they get attacked, me, I got a fair size they don't bother me."

To avoid trouble, Mr Matthews does not make eye contact:

> "Eye contact is a no no. Ignore them and look like you are doing something, that's the key! If you look them in the eyes, they are either going to ask you for a cigarette, tell you all the problems they have in the world or ask you 'what the hell are you looking at?', you know, and then you are in trouble. You don't look at them, you just, if they talk to you just keep going. I've had lots of it. You just act like they don't exist and then they don't bother you."

At night, if he goes out, he has learned to avoid particular areas of the neighbourhood:

> "I am worried about it [going out at night], but I learn how. I know what happens. I've seen it happen, it's happened to me. There are certain areas you avoid, you know where the hot spots are. Like if you go down to the waterfront road down there, you are basically pretty good going towards Gastown, but I would not walk up Hastings and walk downtown on Hastings Street, not at night. This side of Main [Street] that's OK. The other side of Main, no, no!"

Concerns over crime and safety were likely linked to his experience of serious crimes in the area:

> "Last year, they shot the man four times in the stomach right in front of me. Two guys come across, you know, the Park right here ... two guys come from this side and pull out a gun and shot the guy four times right in the stomach.... The year before that I watched a guy trying to cut a guy's head off in the same park ... Oppenheimer Park.... He had a knife in his hand he was cutting.... This area most of these people here has seen the same type of thing. They won't tell you, they probably have been through it themselves, a lot of them ... very common to happen, very seldom reported."

Shopping in the DES was to be avoided according to Mr Matthews:

> "Ninety per cent of the stuff down here is rotten.... All of the crap that the other stores have, go to this store.... The stuff that comes down here, they would not sell any place else.... When you see the trucks coming and when they are unloading the trucks right there,

> you can see the stuff just dripping out of the boxes, and that is what they sell.... There is a store on the corner that I shop at once in a while for, like an ice cream bar or whatever, milk, eggs ... I will go there during the day, but it is a complete hassle, with all the druggies right in front of the doorway."

With the help of family, Mr Matthews travelled outside the area to do his shopping.

Mr Matthews appeared to have a supportive family network. He had regular contact with his brothers, a sister and numerous nieces and nephews. In addition, twice a month he met up with friends from his old neighbourhood for coffee. However, he was apprehensive about making friends in his present neighbourhood, because he felt that you could not trust the people who lived there:

> "They are acquaintances, yes I would put it that way, because every time so far that you have made friends they have always done something. They are always, they are crooked, people down here are down here for a reason and you know you really have to be careful. They can be the nicest person in the world and then you find out, like there is four people in the building that are murderers."

Mr Matthews did not feel at home in the DES and felt that he could not relate to the people:

> "I am not from here originally, right. I am from Vancouver, right, you know where City Hall is? That's where I grew up, and I grew up with people with the money, they had farms and that too, but I came down here because I went bankrupt, and I have not been able to get enough money to get out yet [laughs].... If you go out on the street and you hang around on the street or even in here actually, these people aren't just, you know, got a stomach problem or somewhere, there is an awful lot of people that just are not with it, right ... I am one of the luckier ones, I seem to have a head on my shoulders that I stay out of trouble."

Important for Mr Matthews was validation from others that he did not belong in the area: "I have been told to get out because, well even the doctors here they say like 'Why are you here?' [laughs] It's funny!".

To cope with living in the area, Mr Matthews spoke of two activities that he was passionate about – cycling and gardening. A couple of times a week he could be found riding his bike down to Stanley Park, which he enjoyed because it took him away from the area for most of the day. His other passion was gardening:

> "I am the gardener for the building. I have a courtyard garden. I do all the gardening, so I spend a lot of time doing that. I got two, one courtyard and then another floor of garden, so I spend most of my time gardening."

For Mr Matthews, gardening was therapeutic: "That is why I do it. Everybody thinks I am doing it for them, but it's for me [laughs]." Mr Matthews at one point even tried to help create a garden in Oppenheimer Park. However, he soon became disillusioned:

> "I helped with the garden there but I could not handle it. I helped a little bit, and then I just no no I ain't going, because you put it in and they pull it out. It did not matter what you put there, it disappeared.... Some of the stuff I planted is still there, but there was so much damage every day when you come back, that I ain't going to do that."

Despite Mr Matthews' experiences of living in the area and his desire to move, he was able to distinguish where he lived from the wider neighbourhood:

> "I can't complain about the place I live.... You see, it's fairly clean, and the roof view of the whole harbour and everything else is fantastic. You know, people pay a lot of money for that too, so I am not complaining too much, right. But if I could move out on an island or up the coast, something like that, but financially that is not in the books right now, but hopefully."

Mr Matthews even tried to rationalise that the neighbourhood was not that different from other areas of Vancouver:

> "You know, it's just as bad anywhere else. It's not as bad as here but I mean, anywhere in the whole lower mainland ... when you go to Surrey it is just as bad, in different parts ... it's bad everywhere you go."

When asked about quality of life, Mr Matthews was able to articulate what this meant for him. For him being able:

> "to do something, being able to eat or healthy enough to be able to do it, have enough money to be able to do it, not being restricted by either health or money or other people.... See if I want to go to the park, I can go to the park without being hassled or without having health problems or, you know if you are feelin' good and you go to the park you feel good, it's good! But there is not much quality if you go to the park and you are sick. You can't enjoy it even if it's the

> nicest thing in the world. You are not going to enjoy it if you feel like crap, you know, so you have to put everything together, good health, money, being active."

In rating his quality of life, Mr Matthews felt that it was neither good nor poor.

Discussion

The case study of Mr Berry Matthews represents a situation of environmental adaptation and management. Forced to relocate to the DES because of financial problems, Mr Matthews was able to manage daily life and prevent negative psychological well-being and/or maladaptive behaviour. His ability to associate and identify with places and people outside of this area enabled him to cope with and adapt to living in the neighbourhood.

Mr Matthews' experience of place and ageing was challenged by numerous environmental presses, such as being a repeated victim and witness of crime, not being able to trust people in the area and continuous issues over personal safety. Mr Matthews also had a number of limitations in personal competences, such as some mobility and financial restrictions. However, in spite of these presses and personal competence, he appeared able to manage to live in the area. His management of place might in part be related to his ability to establish a level of physical knowledge or physical connection. Physical knowledge appeared to have developed out of a need to satisfy concerns over personal safety, rather than functional health declines. This physical spatial knowledge was gained by the 'careful watching' of what goes on in the neighbourhood and his experiences with crime. Knowing the places to avoid or 'hot spots' and strategies of avoidance, such as "not making eye contact and walking with purpose", allowed some psychological sense of well-being and freedom of mobility. Mr Matthews' physical connection was also evident in his sense of acute physical awareness, particularly in relation to vulnerability to crime. In his 'watching and analysis' of the area he perceived that "they pick on the weakest person" and that with his "fair size [6 foot 4] they [criminals] don't bother [him]". This awareness of his body coupled with his avoidance strategies allowed him the freedom to negotiate and manage the demands of his environment. Although he still worried about going out, he felt that it did not significantly deter him.

Another important consideration of Mr Matthews' physical connection to his area related to the garden he created at the housing complex for older people where he lived. He was passionate about his garden, enjoying his morning coffee admiring it, and spent many hours of his day working on it: "Everybody thinks I do it for them, but it's for me". His physical connectedness with his garden might enable a greater level of environmental mastery, control and belongingness within this immediate place that would perhaps not be afforded if he left the residence.

Despite all of this, there was some evidence to suggest a past willingness to commit to the DES. It could be argued that Mr Matthews tried to create a sense of belonging or sense of place attachment within the DES but had been unable to do so because of environmental conditions that hindered his efforts. This was evident in his discourse around making friends and in his efforts to try and improve the local park. In discussion of his efforts to make friends, he mentioned the difficulty he has had in making friends, feeling that every time he has started up a friendship he has come to regret it because "they do something, they are crooked" and he felt that they could not be trusted. His voluntary efforts in developing a garden in the local park eventually stopped when he felt disillusioned and disheartened by continuous damage, "you put it in ... they pull it out ... there was so much damage every day".

Mr Matthews' inability to achieve attachments in this neighbourhood might have contributed to his need to find or reinforce connections outside the area, specifically the neighbourhood that he grew up and lived in before having to move to the DES. Perceiving himself as outside the neighbourhood or 'out of place' had a number of possible benefits related to identity and well-being. First, it enabled a level of achieved attachment and creation of belonging that might have been significant for psychological functioning. Second, it helped create a continuity of identity to his previous life (that is, prior to his bankruptcy). Third, it helped him in part to escape the stigma of living or being associated with the DES. A salient theme in the interview was the 'distancing' of himself from the neighbourhood and its people: "I am from Vancouver ... grew up with people with money ... I come down here because I went bankrupt" and "there is an awful lot of people that just are not with it ... I am one of the luckier ones". A further sense of validation of not belonging and distancing was reinforced by community workers: "I have been told to get out ... they say like 'Why are you here?'". This validation appeared to further reify the idea that he did not belong. Through the distancing of himself as 'unlike' the area and the people, and through connections made to his previous neighbourhood, Mr Matthews was able to make meaning and create a sense of belonging that retained continuity of self. His ability to connect to the neighbourhood he grew up in enabled him to maintain a positive self-worth and well-being amidst present environmental conditions that had in part limited physical geographical expression and hindered place attachment.

However, the degree to which Mr Matthews was emotively or sentimentally connected to his previous neighbourhood could be questioned. When asked where he would like to move to, he responded not by expressing a wish to return to the neighbourhood where he lived prior to moving to the DES and where he grew up, but rather a wish to move to "an island or up the coast". If Mr Matthews was sentimentally attached to this area, it might be expected that he would wish to move back to this area. Rather, it seemed that his old neighbourhood might have served more as a feature to disassociate himself from his present neighbourhood than as a source of emotive attachment.

Mr Matthews, like so many in the DES, rated his quality of life as 'neither good nor poor'. The dominance of this answer among participants living in this area warrants further analysis, and the case study of Mr Matthews illustrates some of the possible explanations. Although strong environmental presses and low to medium personal competences (for example, health, income) suggest a poor quality of life, this is not always the situation. This might be related to a balance between a number of consequences related to the individual, in this case Mr Matthews, and the environment. The first might relate to the difficulty in committing to the idea that your quality of life is poor, because this might present challenges to the self and ability at satisfactory life review. The second might be related to the idea that the situation could be worse. For example, despite disliking the area, Mr Matthews recognised that he lived in a nice, clean building with a "fantastic" rooftop view of the harbour that "people pay a lot of money for". The availability of good-quality, low-cost housing was a particular issue in the DES, and Vancouver in general. In addition, high rates of homelessness in the area might have created a social comparison and/or downward comparison between those who were 'lucky' to have housing and those who were not. The third might have related to the likelihood of moving in the future. For example, although Mr Matthews wished to move, it was "not in the books for right now". Knowledge of this might have created a need to establish an acceptable level of quality of life in order to maintain some positive level of psychological functioning. Fourth, although many discussed substantial environmental demands, many felt that this area was not that different to other areas of Vancouver. According to Mr Matthews, "it's just as bad anywhere else".

In summary, Mr Matthews' case study illustrates a situation in which strong environmental challenges have been matched by adaptation in which physical and psychological well-being has been established. Through distancing or the rejection of the neighbourhood and its people, Mr Matthews maintained a positive sense of self-identity and belonging. A strong sense of physical connectedness enabled the negotiation of the environment and a sense of emotional well-being. This case was similar to another interview conducted – with Keppol Polanski (Vancouver). This is presented in Table A1 in Appendix A and in the biographies in Appendix B.

Howard Adams Goodleaf – Vancouver

Howard Adams Goodleaf was raised in 'the North country' amidst what he referred to as the "traditional ways of the Native North American people". In his early twenties, Mr Goodleaf went overseas to fight in the Korean War. Upon returning to "his people" he found that things had drastically changed in the years he had been away:

> "I came back home. I went back to my people, but everything was changed there. Nobody spoke our native language any more, everybody spoke English, everyone had paper money.... Everything was more

> negative attitude among the family, everybody was arguing.... We used to live on buffalos and those were things that were of value to us as traditional people that we lived off the land, the value was turned right around into a monetary system."

Disillusioned with how his home had changed, Mr Goodleaf left and for the next 40 years lived periodically in the DES while working in commercial fishing and logging.

Mr Goodleaf chose to settle in the DES for a number of reasons: the availability of good-quality housing for older people, a strong First Nations community support centre and access to a number of amenities such as social services and grocery stores were important. In addition, the DES was close to his family, which enabled him to have frequent contact with his daughter and grandson. These allowed Mr Goodleaf to perform many of his daily activities within the area, which usually involved shopping "for fresh staple foods like meat and fish", visiting family and friends, leisure and volunteer activities. Mr Goodleaf enjoyed walking through the local parks: "Crab Park, it's a beautiful place, it's kinda right next to the ocean, it runs right into the water from a kinda gravel beach and it's beautiful there". Mr Goodleaf enjoyed going down there to pray or "to have a walk of peace". Although weary of Oppenheimer Park, Mr Goodleaf occasionally visited when there was "something special going on", like a "baseball game, lawn bowling, barbeque or when some other function is happening", but he did not tend to visit otherwise because "a lot of harsh things happen there". Mr Goodleaf preferred to do his activities during the day: "Once night time starts we usually try not to be out on the street too much.... It's just the daytime that's safer because everybody is about".

Central to Mr Goodleaf's life in the DES was providing support and counselling to 'street people'. Around three days out of the week he provided counselling at the native centre, and once a week helped run a 'ceremonial healing circle'. The support offered was rooted in what Mr Goodleaf referred to as the "traditional North American ways of thinking". He felt that "his people have become druggies and drunks because they have lost their way and are not guided by the traditional ways of thinking, which is peace oriented, practises forgiveness, and is oriented and rooted in the land and its creatures". Mr Goodleaf's belief was that:

> "We need to come together as human beings, respect and honour one another and pray together and say thank you for the air, the water, the fire and the earth, these four items is what we are made from as human beings, we have the spirit, we have the emotion, we have the physical and we have the mental, that's what we are, we're four components of creation and for these four components we come together in the ceremony, what we call a healing circle."

He felt that people are sick because of a negative attitude:

> "What is making our people sick is the attitude. A negative attitude is the worst sickness a human can have. You draw sickness and injury to your own self by having negative attitudes. Positive attitude is health, good health, well-being, good things happen. Our elders tell us, everything happens when this great spirit guides us."

Mr Goodleaf's involvement with the native centre and counselling was likely a consequence of a number of social and health challenges he had had to overcome. From his return from the Korean War until the early 1980s, he suffered from post-traumatic stress disorder and alcoholism. He felt that these illnesses were a product of his struggle between the culture and thinking he was raised in, and the European lifestyle he now lived. Although recovered from these illnesses, he still found that the life he wanted to lead was made difficult in the DES: "It's a struggle from the time you get up in the morning to when you lay down at night. It's a continuous struggle, you know, to maintain an adequate healthy way of life".

When asked what was important to have a good quality of life, Mr Goodleaf responded by saying:

> "For me to be able to help those who don't understand their tradition and their culture so that they can find a more balanced life of being, instead of being a druggy and drunk and stuff. To be a sober well-balanced human and community so that we put harmony back into our community instead of chaos, that's the way I understand it [quality of life]."

When asked to rate his quality of life, Mr Goodleaf appeared to find this a bit more of a challenge:

> "I think neither good nor poor would be the way it would be balanced, because being here is another thing too. This way I can help my daughter and my little grandson. That is why I am here. If it wasn't for that, North West Territories some place back there, retiring and kicking back. But I'd rather be helping my family. It's my job, that's what I want to do, it makes me happy when I help my children."

Discussion

Mr Goodleaf's experience of place and ageing presents a different perspective to the other interviews conducted within this study. The interview was unique in that Mr Goodleaf's life was governed and rooted in "the traditional Native North American ways of thinking". Spirituality played a significant role in the relationship and experience of the person with the environment.

Despite disliking the area in which he lived and wishing to move, Mr Goodleaf's daily activities were almost totally confined within the DES. There was evidence of a level of physical management or connectedness in knowing that the neighbourhood was a source for his shopping and social needs, and leisure activities. There was also evidence of a temporal schema to his physical knowledge of the area. Specifically, during daylight hours he spoke about being generally unrestricted in where he went within the area. However, when night time came he felt it was "best to be off the street".

The greatest source of environmental press for Mr Goodleaf appeared to be cultural differences in lifestyle. Being raised in a culture where people were connected to the land, specifically for sources of subsistence and worship, and moving to a European system, which was "money oriented" and where the land was not a source of support for food or worship, appeared to be difficult. The discontinuity he encountered between these two lifestyles appeared to be a challenge to his psychological well-being in that he continuously worried about being able to afford his rent and food, and sustain a "healthy life". Despite these challenges, Mr Goodleaf was able to cope with and manage his daily environment. His ability to do so might have been a function of two factors. The first relates to the sense of belonging or social connectedness that was provided by a large native community in the area. The second relates to his role as spiritual counsellor within the community, specifically his determination to 'heal' the street people. The activities and teachings within this community represented a central feature within the interview; through this community he might have been able to create some element of continuity or connectedness to the past that enabled a level of physical and psychological management within the present environment. Without this support, Mr Goodleaf would likely have encountered more challenges to his psychological well-being.

Emotive or sentimental connection to the DES was absent from Mr Goodleaf's discourse on the environment. Rather, the environment was perceived as a "continuous struggle" and unhealthy, and there was a lack of connection to the land and nature. The contrasting cultural perspectives perceived in the DES reinforced a sense of alienation from his cultural and spiritual past. This was contrary to the lifestyle he wished to live, and therefore worked to undermine and challenge emotive place attachment to the DES.

Although there appeared to be a lack of place attachment to the DES, there was evidence that Mr Goodleaf exhibited notions of place attachment related to the area in which he was raised as a child (that is, North West Territories). For Mr Goodleaf, that area represented a place that supports his traditional cultural values and lifestyle. The land provided nourishment, creating strong emotive and sentimental bonds that could not be met by residence in other places. Despite being absent from the area for over 40 years, it continued to influence how and present a standard by which other places were judged. He suggested that his quality of life would be better if he were able to return there to "retire and kick back". However, he felt a sense of duty to help the street people in the DES and his daughter and grandson – "I'd rather be helping my family, it's my job, it makes me happy".

A large part of the interview focused on cultural issues related to the past and "how things used to be and what has been lost". It was continuously reinforced that there was an almost urgent need for the present to have more of a connection with the past or 'tradition'. Mr Goodleaf felt that it was the environment and lack of spiritual guidance that made people sick. Being rooted in 'the past' enabled connection or reconnection to his 'traditional ways of thinking', allowing him to manage and exert some control over challenging environmental conditions. Although the past gave him strength to adapt to and cope with his present environment, it could be argued that Mr Goodleaf's past thwarted and undermined place attachment to his current area of residence and conversely that it might have increased his attachment to his childhood place.

In summary, Mr Goodleaf's case study is unlike the other interviews conducted within this research project. It illustrates differing cultural and spiritual perspectives on the psychological and physical management and negotiation of place and ageing. Despite challenging environmental demands, Mr Goodleaf is committed to staying in the DES because of his need to help his family and provide spiritual guidance for the street people. Spirituality is a way of managing the environment and was a feature in a number of other case studies, including Patricia Reilly, Felicity Parker and Roger and Gretta Graham in Manchester. These are presented in Table A1 in Appendix A and in the biographies in Appendix B.

Helen Fox – Manchester

Aged 78, Mrs Helen Fox has lived in Cheetham for over 30 years. Widowed four years before the interview, she now lives by herself in a house she and her husband bought. Despite physical health limitations and deleterious environmental change, she is determined to remain within her house and neighbourhood, and be as independent as possible.

Mrs Fox once enjoyed a very active life, working until the age of 69 and enjoying leisure activities such as dancing: "Oh I've had a very hectic life, very, very hectic life. I used to go dancing a lot me and that's what kills me … I love dancing". A stroke a couple of years previously had left Mrs Fox paralysed from the waist down and confined to a wheelchair: "I get very embarrassed being in a wheelchair". She was housebound for much of the week, which she found very frustrating:

> "Very bitter, very bitter.… Since I've had my stroke yea, I've changed a lot, gone very bitter now.… But I've not got to think about it you see. I've got to go forward. You have to do … I'm not one that's crying all the time, you know, about my health and anything like, you know. I don't think about that you see … I've got to go forward."

Rather, despite what doctors told her, she was determined to walk again:

> "They said I'd never walk again … I go to the physio … they've given me a sheet [of] the exercises.… So I push myself with that, you know. But I can walk a little bit now with my sticks, but not very far … I've helped myself really like. Very independent me you know, very."

Although having been offered a small flat by the local social services department, Mrs Fox did not wish to move from her home and neighbourhood: "I mean they [social services] wanted me, mithered me, to go in a flat, you know. But I don't want it". To enable her to stay in her home, her son helped her make a number of adjustments to her home, such as relocating her bedroom downstairs and installing a personal security alarm:

> "Well my son's made it as I've got everything down here. I mean, he'll bring all my winter clothes down and take my summer clothes upstairs and we work it that way.… And I just manage. I said I've got my little flat here … I won't give in you see."

Concern over falling precipitated the installation of a personal safety alarm to help her feel more secure when in the house: "In the last five years I've only fell twice so I think that's quite good really".

Mrs Fox appeared to have a supportive social network. Her family helped her with the household chores and shopping and on occasion she accompanied them on day trips. They also appeared to be in frequent telephone contact: "A lot of people phone me like, you know, all my family phone me". She also has a friend who comes to stay. Despite these social interactions, Mrs Fox described herself as 'lonely'. However, she commented that her loneliness did not bother her because "there's nothing you can do about it". Perhaps in an effort to counter this Mrs Fox used the phone a lot. Sometimes she made so many phone calls that she worried that she might not be able to afford the bill at the end of the month: "I'm always on the phone".

Mrs Fox took pride in trying to do things for herself: "I try and do things that I can do, you know … like tidying up … I mean I do my hoovering and I wash all my washing and ironing … I'm kept busy". But she was bitter that she couldn't do more: "I often think I'd love to walk to the bus stop, get on a bus and go up the market. But I can't, you see, so it don't bother me". This has also led to a number of frustrations with family members: "He [son] carries me about. He gets on my nerves … 'I'll get it, sit down I'll get it' … well it does get on my nerves", and with ex-daughter-in-law and granddaughter: "I'd like to go shopping on my own, you know. They take me and I've just got to sit there like an idiot.… 'Do you want this? And do you want that?' And that's what gets on my nerves now".

Living in an area of mostly boarded-up houses, Mrs Fox had little contact with neighbours. However, she appeared to greatly value the friendship she had with one of her neighbours:

> "I have a neighbour who'll come and have a little chat, you know what I mean. I don't have all the neighbours, there's one in the first house there, and I do my own cooking but occasionally she'll come and say to me 'I'm cooking tea tonight so I'll put you one out, Helen'. You know a friend like that."

There was also a sense of loss with respect to neighbours:

> "Well the old neighbours, there's only two of us now … they've all died and the lady next door 'cause I said to her the other day, like we talk to one another, she can't walk proper, you see, so we talk to one another like over the fence, you know, and I said 'there's only me and you left, Betty'."

In reference to new neighbours, she commented that they are "all right, people are nice around here … [they] don't bother me".

Since an incident when someone had come into her house under a false pretext and stolen from her, Mrs Fox has been very fearful: "I'm always frightened like when the bell rings". "I thought it was my granddaughter" so Mrs Fox opened the door:

> "She looked as if she was on drugs, you know her eyes kept rolling around. I thought how am I going to get rid of her?… She came downstairs [after supposedly using the toilet] and she had things under [jacket] I didn't ask her what she'd got, you know what I mean? I thought whatever it is she can take them. As long as she leaves me alone."

Now Mrs Fox will only open the door when she knows who is calling: "People that know me shout my name through the letterbox. Anybody that doesn't shout I don't open the door".

Although Mrs Fox recognised that her area was not a safe place to live in and was 'rough', she perceived it to be better than some of the other areas on the estate and therefore felt that she should not really complain:

> "It's a very bad estate this you know, at the top end, oh very rough I believe.… My friend's just moved from there with all the hassle she used to get … I'm all right really you know, I never complain, I never moan or anything."

Even though Mrs Fox found her present health status and environmental circumstances challenging, reminiscence appeared to provide an important source of quality of life and pleasure for her:

> "I've had a very good life, very, very good life. I get photographs to show my granddaughter when I was about 18 or 19, I have a big box of photographs. My son brought them down. He said when you get fed up, he said, I've got tapes and all. I can sit and watch the tapes ... with the children on yea 'cause he has a video camera and so I sit and watch them."

Discussion

The case study of Mrs Helen Fox represents a situation in which significant physical health limitations appear to reinforce the need to age in place despite many internal and some external environmental challenges. In this case study, Mrs Fox's dependence on her immediate space determined her interaction and perception of her external space. As will be discussed later, this might have acted as a protective factor for environmental demands present in her neighbourhood.

It can be argued that Mrs Fox's attachment to place was not so much connected to a strong sense of social or historical connectedness, but to a physical need that helped her maintain an independent self-identity and have both physical and psychological control over her environment. A level of physical connectedness can be argued to be integral to her self-identity by sustaining independence. This theme was pervasive throughout the interview. By reorganising her house, such that everything was located downstairs, she was able to physically manage her space. Although there was external pressure to move, she resisted this: "I won't give in you see". In this case, physical connectedness appeared to be the central factor in pressure not to move. She had worked out a routine in which she was able to live as independently as possible by being able to manage household chores like hoovering, washing, ironing and cooking. Her family was available to do things that she could not do, and together these appeared to work well for her, keeping her physically mobile and part of the community. A telling indication of her sense of preserving self and independence can be seen in the following quote: "He'll [son] bring all my winter clothes down and take my summer clothes upstairs and *we* work it that way". This shows that despite functional limitations she still was able to reify physical action by proxy, and therefore retain some level of perceived environmental mastery. This enabled preservation of identity and an ability to psychologically cope in the presence of physical health challenges that restrict her life.

Mrs Fox's strong sense of self-awareness and identity of 'who she was' and 'who she was not' was a pervasive theme, continuously reinforced throughout the interview. Examples of these statements are: "I'm not one that's crying all the time, I've got to go forward" (which was mentioned frequently in relation to her health), "I'm very independent me", "I never moan" and "I never complain". Her self-perception of being independent and her portrayal to others as being independent appeared important. This was particularly evident in two situations. When asked about support from social services, her response to the interviewer was: "I have a girl come on [Friday] … [but] *I've told you, I'm very independent me*". With reference to her friend/neighbours, Mrs Fox was quick to say that "*I do my own cooking*, but occasionally she'll come and say to me I'm cooking a tea tonight so I'll put you one out". There are a number of possible reasons for Mrs Fox's need to continuously reinforce the self. The first might have related to her need to have continuity with her past (physically active) self. Although staying in place, she had the ability to preserve her identity or idea of self as it once was when she was physically mobile and had a "hectic life". Despite present physical health challenges, her ability to remain in her community and her house allowed at least some continuity with a normal, familiar life before a decline in health, and perhaps enabled easier adaptation to her present health situation. It likely allowed for continuity in the reminiscence of self. Pictures and videos represented a feature that gave pleasure to her life. Sharing pictures of herself when she was a teenager with her granddaughter and looking at family videos enabled preservation of identity as it was in the past, not as it is in the present. Another possible reason for her need to continuously reinforce herself, might relate to practical issues, specifically, her need to be perceived as managing her environment for fear that she would be forced to move.

Although appearing generally content with her level of physical connectedness within her immediate surroundings, Mrs Fox was at times frustrated by not being able to negotiate certain aspects of her external environment. This was expressed in the following quotes: "I'd like to go shopping on my own … they take me and I've just got to sit there like an idiot" and "I often think I'd love to walk to the bus stop, get on a bus and go up the market. But I can't". Her external physical spatial knowledge was thwarted by her physical limitations that shifted control of the environment to others; her frustration might in part be a function of discontinuity between her ideal self as independent and a perceived image which might reflect dependency because of reliance on others.

As a consequence of her limited physical function, managing her internal environment, specifically, the immediate perimeters of her ground-level house, was the central focus of the discussion. Secondary areas in this case could be defined as the upstairs of her house and the wider external environment (that is, her neighbourhood). Beyond the immediate perimeters of her house there was little discourse on neighbourhood challenges. In this situation, spatial restriction might have served as a protective function for external environmental risks that might require a more active lifestyle to experience presses. There was evidence to suggest that there existed some external environmental demands; for example, her acknowledgement that she was living on a "bad estate" and awareness of the risk and fear of crime: "I'm always afraid when the bell rings". However, in general, external environmental issues appeared secondary, if only briefly mentioned, compared with those connected to the internal environmental challenges that she faced as a consequence of limited functional mobility.

Evidence of social support or connectedness to her neighbourhood or friends in the area appeared marginal. A sense of social support could be argued in reference to her neighbour who occasionally cooked for her, whom she affectionately called "a friend like that"; her friend down the street with whom she had frequent telephone contact; and her next-door neighbour who she occasionally chats "over the fence with". Other than this, she appeared to have little social contact with others in the area: "they don't bother me".

Mrs Fox appeared to be able to make a temporal distinction in the assessment of her quality of life. In rating her present quality of life, she felt that it was poor; however, she spoke about her overall quality of life as good: "I've had a good quality of life". The discussion of her overall quality of life was associated with her ability to reminisce by looking at old photographs of when she was young and when her children were young. This gave her great pleasure, possibly in part because it gave her a chance to escape from her present physical limitations in both space and time.

In accordance with the competence-press theoretical framework, Mrs Fox appeared to exhibit both environmental docility and environmental proactivity. On the one hand, it could be argued that Mrs Fox appeared to represent a situation of someone with low competence and high press. The external environment was unmanageable for her level of physical health, despite her desire to go shopping and walk to the bus stop by herself. On the other, her actions and ability to restructure her internal physical environment (for example, relocating her bedroom downstairs), and help provided by her family (for example, cleaning, shopping), indicated a level of environmental proactivity. Restructuring enabled the reduction of environmental press (for example, stairs, issues of personal safety), allowing for greater personal competence over her internal physical spatial environment. This was achieved in spite of very limited physical function.

In summary, Mrs Fox appeared to be able to manage internal environmental presses (for example, restructuring her home to suit her needs). However, she was overwhelmed by external environmental presses (for example, the wider neighbourhood) because of functional health limitations. Mrs Fox's competence with her immediate environment appeared to be very important in enabling continuity and retention of her past self. However, this raises the issue that if the wider environment was better able to support her level of personal competence her physical and psychological space might have not been so restricted. Spatial restriction can limit opportunities for social and physical connectedness. This case study is similar to another interview, that of Mrs Maud Brown living in Longsight. The case study was similar to a number of other case studies where environmental management was governed by functional health challenges; see Dan Sapp, Josephine Diamond and Winifred Peters in Vancouver. These are presented in Table A1 in Appendix A and in the biographies in Appendix B.

Category 3: environmental distress

There were a number of interviews conducted with older people within this research that could be categorised as representing situations of environmental distress (see Appendices A and B). In this section, the focus is on two individuals in the environmental distress category: Harold Waters in Cheetham, Manchester, and Elizabeth Laing in Grandview-Woodland, Vancouver. Mr Waters represents a situation of someone highly conscious of and distressed by the changes in his environment, and Ms Laing represents a situation of someone who used to be distressed by her environment until relocating to a new neighbourhood. Ms Laing, despite not currently living in 'environmental distress' is analysed under this category because of the dominance in focus given to her previous neighbourhood within the interview, and because of the continued impact that living in this area continued to have in her life.

Harold Waters – Manchester

Aged 69, Mr Harold Waters has lived on a council estate in Cheetham in North Manchester for over 30 years. Typical days do not appear to vary a great deal for Mr Waters. Each morning he gets up at 5 o'clock in the morning and has two pots of tea, and "cheese on toast, boiled eggs, poached egg on toast, [or] Spam butties". He never watches television in the morning: "I wait while it's time to go shopping". To keep busy and "pass the time on" he goes shopping almost everyday: "Most days I go, well if I don't go shopping there's a couple of markets up the road you know, big markets, so I go wandering round there, pass the time on". He usually returns home at lunchtime to prepare his main meal of the day, which might include meat he picked up from the butcher: "I usually get some meat two or three times a week from the butchers, you know, ready cooked like brisket and turkey and have it with new potatoes or now and again I have suet dumplings". In the afternoon, Mr Waters watches television and four nights a week travels to a pub 10 minutes away by bus outside the area, sometimes more: "[If] I get really fed up, then I go out another night, just depends how much money I've got". On these nights he usually gets in no later than 10.00 to 10.30 in the evening, and will have a "cup-a-soup or cheese buttie or owt like that". On nights that he does not go to the pub, Mr Waters goes to bed early, because he says that there is nothing to do and he gets bored. He feels that none of his days are 'special', all continually reinforcing his almost perpetual state of boredom: "They're all boring. When you live by yourself it's boring.... Just a case of oh getting up, oh another boring day".

Financially, Mr Waters felt that his occupational pension enabled him to have enough security for his present activities: "If I only had my pension I wouldn't be able to go out at night and buy things like I do. But I've got a bit of money saved up ... I can manage". Mr Waters also appeared to be in good functional health, reporting no long-standing illnesses, and boasting about the infrequency of his visits to his general practitioner: "I've not seen him for years. I don't know when I last seen him. Touch wood. I'm fortunate in that way me. I'm never ill, I never get a cold and I can walk miles, it doesn't bother me. So that's the only good thing about me".

Originally very happy with living on the estate, he now felt that the estate had declined, buildings had deteriorated and neighbours were not what they used to be:

> "It was brand new when I moved in here with my mother ... lovely ... your neighbours. No such thing as neighbours now.... Well you don't congregate like same as like on bonfire night. In the old days, all the neighbours used to be outside with chairs and what have you ... having treacle toffee and roasted potatoes and all this lot, nobody cares about you now ... it was that nice on this estate. As I say, I was the first one in this house. When I moved in here it got full up this estate because it was that nice, well kept you know. They've had to pull houses down over there because they're vandalised. But there was a waiting list for this estate. Now they can't get rid of them. They pull them down they get vandalised so much ... I mean that green out there on a summer's day we used to all be sat outside there with our sunshades and tables and you could leave them tables there all night and sunshades, go to bed, go out next morning and they'd still be there. Not now ... the general appearance of the estate has deteriorated. Broken lamp standards and empty property."

Crime and personal safety had also become an important part of managing everyday life. Recognising certain 'trouble spots' in the neighbourhood, Mr Waters travelled at certain times of the day and used one path in and out of the neighbourhood:

> "They've got a big pub over there, they're nutters, they're always fighting and the police is always raiding it for drugs ... I've got an eight-minute walk, but I avoid the pub at nights, I go out my way. Instead of coming across here I walk down the road so I don't have to go past the pub.... It just shows you though what you've got to do, doesn't it?"

Even during daylight hours, Mr Waters spoke about using one path in and out of the estate: "I never go in any other areas. I just walk across here. When I do all my shopping it's all up the road ... I've never wandered out this estate". His activities were also governed by certain time constraints; this was particularly evident on pub nights. Four nights a week, Mr Waters enjoyed meeting up with a couple of old work colleagues at a pub outside the area. However, concerns over personal safety prompted Mr Waters to return home sooner than he would like: "I get home early me. With being old I get home for half past 10. It's not very nice travelling round here by yourself at night … I go out at seven. I go out early and get back early, get locked up". Mr Waters was particularly afraid of groups of young people. When he saw a group congregate: "I do a detour, try and avoid them … I try and make sure there's none of them knocking about when I'm going out at night when it's dark because they know I live by myself and they're terrors". Mr Waters felt that he was sometimes a 'prisoner in his own home' because of this constant fear of crime. It took away from what he saw as his one pleasure in life – going to the pub – and therefore reduced his quality of life even more.

His evenings at the pub appeared to represent an important event for Mr Waters. Discussion about the pub was typically in connection to memories of the past:

> "The reason I have to get a bus is I used to live further over … I used to work further over near the pub with a load of lads. We all used to work there, and then I moved here. But that's why I still go there because I still know them … I used to live on X road.… We all used to work together, well most of us did, a big gang of us at Smith and Fields.… We all used to meet in there, that pub."

Although there were only a couple of old work colleagues left, Mr Waters still continued to go to the pub because he said that he enjoyed the company of "local neighbours who I've got to know through going in the pub itself you know, sitting with them".

Mr Waters had limited social support from family and neighbours. After years of caring for his mother and receiving no or little help from family members, Mr Waters decided to end contact with his family: "cause I told them what to do after the way they treated me and my mother … I had to do everything, put her on the toilet, change her and I never got a bit of help from them so when she died I said well that's it, I just don't want to see you again now". The only contact he had with his family was with a sister who visited him twice a week, usually on a Wednesday and Saturday. Outside this visit and his evenings at the pub with old work colleagues and 'local neighbours', Mr Waters appeared to have no other regular social contact.

Social support from neighbours was also limited: "Most of them died, there's only three of us left who moved in together … they're both elderly, one's 84, I think, the other one's as old as me, 69, so you don't see them in the winter". For Mr Waters, the loss of old neighbours and an inability to establish relationships with his present neighbours appeared to reinforce his feelings of isolation and the feeling that "nobody cares about you now". His infrequency of social contact was of great distress to him. More than anything he felt that his life lacked company and he felt powerless to do anything about it, because "it is too late".

Given the opportunity to move, Mr Waters felt certain he would, even knowing the location he wished to move to: "[move] Oh definitely.… Anglesey … it's nice there, nice and peaceful and I've got a couple of friends who've moved there as I used to work with". However, financial restrictions and recent psychological distress had prevented him from doing so: "My mother died three years ago and I'm not interested in this house at all now. I'm not interested in anything round here actually. Come to think about it, I'm not really that interested about living. If I die, I die".

Discussion

The case study of Mr Harold Waters represents a situation in which deleterious neighbourhood change and lack of informal social support have an overwhelming impact on an individual's feelings of social isolation and disillusionment. Environmental demands challenge personal competences and impact negatively on the construction of a positive self-identity and quality of life. In this situation place and ageing is perceived not to be optimal.

The environmental docility hypothesis finds support in this case study. It was evident that the perceived environmental presses overwhelmed Mr Waters' personal competences. The environmental presses identified were numerous and appeared to have a significant behavioural and psychological effect. These 'presses' were viewed as deleterious environmental changes, encompassing fear of crime and deterioration of the area and relationships with neighbours, and lack of amenities. Fear of crime governed Mr Waters' behavioural activities, such as creating a path that he could use to leave and as well as return home safely, at times preventing him from going out and continuously worrying about personal safety – when out or preparing to go out. Deterioration of the area and relationships with neighbours created a sense of loss, disconnection and the feeling that "nobody cares about you any more". Lack of amenities contributed to feelings of lack of support and a sense that "all days are the same, boring".

Although overwhelmingly stressed by his environment there was some evidence to support a certain level of environmental proactivity. Proactivity was evident from his ability to manage threats to personal safety perceived by the physical environment. Mr Waters revealed very specific patterns of neighbourhood activity; during the day he had a specific path that took him in and out of the neighbourhood, never wandering outside his immediate estate, and at night he would go out of his way to avoid the location of "the pub". Not only was he restricted by where he went, but also by the time he went. His negotiation and traversing of his geographical environment was governed by fear of crime. Although such a path is bound to have a sense of physical connectedness, or 'residential knowing', the process by which it functions, as a possible masking of impaired physical function, is unlike the process for which it was operating in the case of Mr Waters. In this situation, the impairment was not a physical but a psychological function – fear of crime. The path provided a sense of psychological comfort, which enabled him to manage his daily activities in and out of the neighbourhood. This could be equally argued for spatial restriction, where literature concepts of restriction were rooted in declines in physical health function. However, as evidenced by Mr Waters, psychological elements of fear were the restricting physical feature. Although obviously making a number of behavioural adaptations to the environment, Mr Waters showed his frustration at having to manage his life in this way: "It shows you though what you've got to do".

Mr Waters' construction of a pathway in and out of the neighbourhood and his pub visits showed at least some level of adaptation or environmental proactivity. His ability to create a path on which he felt some level of personal safety and reduced fear of crime illustrated in part an ability to manage and cope with some of his perceived environmental presses. In this case, the need to satisfy his limited personal competence for social support, and hence a sense of belonging, was stronger than the threat perceived from environmental presses.

To understand Mr Waters' geographical experience of place it is best to consider and analyse it temporally. In this way, both attachment to place and negative disruptions to place were evident. The neighbourhood of the past represented a "nice estate, well kept", with nice neighbours who "cared for you" and congregated on bonfire night "with treacle toffee and roasted potatoes". It was a place of low crime where you could leave chairs and tables out all night. For Mr Waters, living on the estate was at one point associated with a sense of pride and attachment. Analysis of the present, however, revealed disruptions to physical and social connectedness to the area. Mr Waters' dialogue associated with the neighbourhood at present revealed a contrary situation. Neighbours did not congregate in the same way on bonfire night and they did not care, crime and fear of crime had increased and the physical condition of the area had deteriorated. Although it has been suggested in the environmental science literature that the past is an important source for identity and creating well-being, this was clearly not evident in Mr Waters' situation. Rather, his past experiences established an important standard by which meaning was constructed about 'how neighbours should be' and subsequently an evaluation of 'how they have changed'. This image worked to reinforce a discontinuity between the past and the present, creating feelings of loss and disillusionment with both the place and people. Mr Waters was unable to reintegrate and form satisfactory attachments that would enable psychological well-being.

An inability to create a continued sense of social connection was likely a feature of failed historical connectedness with people in the area. The absence of old neighbours through attrition and/or relocation, and the predominance of new neighbours, likely contributed to discontinuities in social and historical connectedness and integration. Had Mr Waters been able to share these memories or create a sense of historical continuity of the neighbourhood as it was in the past, with other old neighbours, it might have helped him cope with area decline and feel less psychologically distressed and less detached from neighbours and the neighbourhood.

The lack of social contact was a significant theme in Mr Waters' life. His social awareness, in relation to neighbours, was that there was "no such thing as neighbours now" and that "nobody cares". His trips to the pub were as much about connecting to the past as seeking company for the present. When asked if there was anything that he goes without, company was mentioned, as well as his disillusionment and helplessness to change his present situation: "it's too late". In a comment he made to the researcher, he again emphasised this point: "That's why I said to you [researcher] on the phone when you said, "Can I come round?", I said it'll be somebody to talk to, pass an hour on". The lack of perceived social support for Mr Waters appeared to be a salient factor accounting for his poor demeanour. He even stated that he went "without nothing, except company", and felt defeated and unable to fix this situation because, he reasoned, "it's too late".

The ability to construct a sense of meaning and attachment to a place might be important in preserving a sense of identity, and this is argued to be evident in the case of Mr Waters. His lack of, in particular, social and autobiographical insideness presented challenges to his psychological well-being. He tried to construct some sense of social belongingness in his nightly pub visits. In some respects he managed to create a level of adaptation or internal consistency by physically and emotionally escaping the neighbourhood. However, this event appeared to be too infrequent for his personal needs. He still felt he lacked company. Breakdown of family and neighbour relationships had also undoubtedly had some negative impacts on Mr Waters' self-identity and poor psychological health functioning, continuously reinforcing the feeling he had that "nobody cares about you". Historical continuity was challenged by deleterious change of the neighbourhood and lack of neighbours to share the neighbourhood of the past with. These memories or reminiscence, rather than providing satisfaction and self-reflection on his life, worked to further disconnect Mr Waters from the present. His ability to try and capture or create some kind of internal consistency was evident in his pub visits, but this only lasted for a short period of time. The creation of attachment to place was difficult when faced with physical deterioration and acute concerns of personal crime that restricted an already limited social engagement. Breakdown in family relationships had also undoubtedly led to attachment issues and psychological distress. Most appreciably, this had translated into how Mr Waters felt about himself and his life: "I'm not interested in anything round here actually. Come to think about it, I'm not really that interested about living".

Mr Waters' visits to the pub could be understood on several levels. First, these visits could be viewed as a form of escapism from the neighbourhood. By removing himself physically and psychologically from this setting he was able to make some positive meaning out of his life; for a short time period of time he could create a sense of well-being and positive self-worth, which he appeared unable to do within his neighbourhood. Second, the pub also provided a familiar environment for him, where he was known, felt a sense of belonging and could relate to people – a few old work colleagues and/or 'local neighbours'. At the basic level, this situation enabled a level of social connection. Third, perhaps more significantly, the pub had symbolic meaning in that it provided a historical link back to his past self or life. This might be significant for two reasons. For Mr Waters, work was an important motif in talking about the reasons for going to that particular pub. Work appeared to provide a sense of belonging within a group or "gang" – "we all used to work together … a big gang of us … we all used to meet in there, that pub". In addition to work associations, the pub might have also represented a time in which he felt less loss with respect to relationships, most specifically, neighbours and family. The visits to the pub enabled a level of attachment – social and historical integration – not afforded within his area of residence.

Another significant theme within the current case study was the finding that analysis of daily or weekly units (that is, selection of activities and passing of time) provided insight into personal identity and physical and psychological well-being. In this case, Mr Waters appeared to view time and the passing of time with a certain hostility. For example, he considered none of his days 'special', "they were all boring" or "another boring day". Such activities as going to the market or even conducting the interview was a way for Mr Waters to "pass the time on" or "pass an hour on". His inability to go 'beyond the day as a meaningful unit' and his conscious reference to time, would suggest that he is not coping/managing effectively with either the loss of his mother and/or broader changes connected to physical and social changes in his environment.

In summary, the case study of Mr Waters represents a situation in which feeling a sense of place attachment is disrupted by perceived negative social and physical environmental changes and increasingly perceived presses. Mr Waters expressed a negative affective emotional state and poor psychological well-being in statements like "they're [days] all boring", "nobody cares about you any more" and "Come to think about it I'm not really that interested about living. If I die, I die". Reification of a positive personal identity appeared only possible in reference to the past and his present quality of life was felt to be very poor. This case study was similar to a number of other case studies: see Robert O'Farrell and Keppol Polanski in Vancouver, and Jay Omar and Paul Cook in Manchester. These are presented in Table A1 in Appendix A and in the biographies in Appendix B.

Elizabeth Laing – Vancouver

Aged 64, Ms Elizabeth Laing has lived in her current flat in Grandview-Woodland for just over five years. Before this she had lived in the DES for many years. Ms Laing's daily activities usually depend on her work commitments. Two to three days a week she works as a community peer support worker in the DES for people suffering from mental health problems. This work is very important to Ms Laing because for much of her life she has also had mental health problems: "I was sick, very sick for a very, very long time, and now I've got a life and it's a good life and to work with other people who are really sick and know that they can get a life again is so rewarding I mean". On days that she does not work, Ms Laing enjoys relaxing in her flat in the morning, doing some tidying up, and then visiting a couple of neighbours or meeting up with two of her close friends for a coffee or lunch. In the evening, when it gets dark, she prefers not to go out:

"I just don't go out after dark, you know. It has to be something really special". Instead she prefers to watch television, listen to the radio or read, and on occasion might have company over.

Until moving to Grandview-Woodland, housing had been a particular issue in Ms Laing's life. For many years, she lived in temporary accommodation in the DES and even experienced several months of homelessness. She described her move from the DES to her present location in Grandview-Woodland as making a "huge difference" in her quality of life:

> "I mean living in the worst part of a city is a horrible experience ... I mean down there I would not go out past four o'clock, you know. You just couldn't. If you walked a block to the corner store, you would be asked at least once if you wanted to buy drugs and several times if you could give someone a cigarette ... I mean living down there is really, it's really, really bad.... You are just a nervous wreck when you live down there, you know you go out on the street and you can't walk along normally. You are looking all around you, and looking behind you, and clutching your purse and you are always nervous if you are outside, and it's kind of not really normal to just be stuck inside ... I lived right across the street from a park [Oppenheimer] and in seven years I never once went in it. It's that bad."

Ms Laing was also quick to criticise those who appear to define the DES as a good place to live:

> "I know there are people who do not think it is a lost cause. They always talk about a sense of community, you know, but I think probably Auschwitz had a sense of community. If you are in a horrible situation, of course you tend to care for each other."

For many years, Ms Laing tried to move out of the DES and into an area she felt safe in. However, she encountered numerous problems:

> "When you live there and you apply anywhere for housing and give that as your address, no one wants to accept you. So that happened to me. So I put my name on every housing list imaginable everywhere, and one of the first ones that came available was a brand new building in the DES and no one else was accepting me at all.... So it's nearly impossible to get out of there."

After more than five years of "desperately trying to get out", Ms Laing was finally moved to another area – Grandview-Woodland.

Ms Laing does advocacy work for mental health organisations. Several times a month she speaks on issues related to mental health (that is, awareness). A particular issue important to Ms Laing was the housing of mental health patients in the DES:

> "I don't agree with housing being built down there.... A third of the people that live down there have mental health problems.... In mental health they bought three of the old hotels down there in the past few years and have redone them, moved people in. I was just exasperated. Like first of all, mental patients have a hard enough time ... they are very vulnerable to drugs ... dual diagnosis and mental illness is a growing thing."

Ms Laing has learned from her own experience that once living in the DES, it is hard to get out because of the stigma associated with the neighbourhood, and also because much of the low-cost housing is located there. Based on her experience, she found that when people recover from mental health problems "the first thing they want to do is move. But it becomes a huge thing for them to move out of the area".

Ms Laing recalled that:

> "When I first moved here, I would go down to the bus stop and people would be sitting there and I would say 'hello' and after I did this a few times, one lady said why do you say 'hello' all the time and I realised this is weird. Like you just don't speak to people at a bus stop right. But the change was so huge from a place where you don't even want to look at the people on the street to just normal people sitting there that I was saying hello to them just because they looked like nice ordinary people."

Compared with the DES, she was able to enjoy many features of the neighbourhood, which she felt were missing from the DES, such as safety, a family-oriented area and access to great services and amenities:

> "A mile away there is lots of little veggie markets which I really like in this neighbourhood. It's wonderful to have all the produce you want at reasonable prices.... The Drive is pretty well complete as far as your shopping needs."

Ms Laing's fear and worry about personal safety, particularly at night, is likely the result of being a repeated victim of crime. In the previous 10 years she had her purse stolen three times and had a bottle of coke stolen from her: "I never really lost a lot of money. It's just that horrible feeling you're left with". Her most violent incident happened when she had a bottle of coke stolen from her: "I was coming home carrying it and three men surrounded me and said give me your pop or we'll punch you and I said 'no, go away'. So they punched me, so I said 'here take the pop'". Most of theses crimes happened when she lived in the DES; however, her most recent incident happened a couple of years previously when walking to her flat in Grandview-Woodland during daylight hours.

For many years, Ms Laing's mental health problems prevented her from having a good relationship with her family: "Mental illness usually breaks families apart. In my case it definitely did". Although now recovered from her mental health problems, she preferred not to have frequent contact with her family: "If I go to one of these family occasions I will be welcomed but I will spend the first two hours kind of on show proving I am not crazy, you know, so I don't go that often". The only family contact Ms Laing actively sought was with her children. A mother of two, Ms Laing had frequent contact with her children and grandchildren. Although her children did not live close by, she appeared to have regular telephone contact and managed to see at least one of them every month. Ms Laing was married at one time but got divorced in her early twenties, citing her mental health problems as a contributing factor. Every month Ms Laing met up with a couple of her close friends and had weekly contact with some neighbours.

"Pleasant" was the descriptive word used to describe her present quality of life:

> "A good quality of life is that you feel like most things in your life are pleasant. I do think I have quality of life ... I've got a pleasant home. Most of the little things I want to buy I can. I've got loving children, loving grandchildren, you know. We have nice Christmases and Thanksgivings, and you know I can always manage to send each of them a little birthday gift. Most of the things I want in my life I have."

She compared this with her 'previous life': "I may be different than your average person in that I had such a horrible life for a while, that I really appreciate what I have".

Discussion

The case study of Ms Elizabeth Laing is unique within the current study because it provides a perspective on a single person's experience of living in both the Vancouver research localities in the study – the DES and Grandview-Woodland. The case study is illustrative of a situation in which deleterious environmental conditions have had, and continue to have, a profound effect on an individual's physical and psychological expression of place.

Ms Laing was someone who was acutely aware of her environment. The enormous challenges that she faced while living in her previous neighbourhood likely contributed to a sensitivity related to her relationship with her present environment. Of particular salience throughout this interview was the idea of 'quality of life and neighbourhood' as being connected. When describing her move from the DES to Grandview-Woodland, she referred to it as a "huge difference" in her quality of life. This idea was continuously reinforced with descriptive tales of how "horrible" life was in the DES and how "pleasant" her life and home was now.

Evidence of the existence of place attachment and/or possible disruptions to place attachment is difficult to argue in this case study. Place attachment appeared absent or weak from any discussion connected to the DES and Grandview-Woodland. The absence of, or failure to form, place attachment in the DES might have been a consequence of one or more factors evident in Ms Laing's case study: the presence of strong neighbourhood presses, negative past memories associated with the neighbourhood and/or an inability to form place attachments due to lifecourse events.

It could be argued that the environmental presses operating in the DES and her level of personal competence (for example, mental health problems) appeared to have prevented Ms Laing from forming physical and sentimental attachment. Most salient in this discussion are descriptive details of her experiences of living in the DES; specifically, a high incidence of personal crime, such as having her purse stolen three times and being assaulted for a bottle of coke. Ms Laing felt that she continuously lived in fear and was restricted from going out by fear. Her inability to develop familiarity with the environment, specifically greater physical spatial mobility, was potentially significant. Ms Laing's fear of crime and concerns about leaving her home, and avoidance of areas in her neighbourhood (for example, the park), prevented the formation of environmental familiarity leading to physical and psychological spatial connections with her neighbourhood. This lack of physical familiarity also prevented the formation of social integration or connection and hence restricted social support. This restricted physical mobility was again not a function of mobility declines but rather governed by psychological distress – fear of crime.

Past memories associated with the neighbourhood might also have been a hindrance to the formation of place attachment. The DES might have come to symbolise a time in her life that was personally very challenging. For example, while living in the DES, Ms Laing experienced a period of homelessness, had struggled with mental health problems and her ability to maintain a relationship with her children was difficult. These associations could have worked to intensify negative feelings about the neighbourhood and her "horrible" life.

Finally, there is a possibility that Ms Laing's inability to form place attachment was a function of lifecourse events. For example, much of Ms Laing's adult life – over 30 years – had been spent in transient accommodation, such as mental health hospitals and boarding houses and for nine months she experienced a period of homelessness. The lack of choice in selection of these locations and an inability to stay long enough to become familiar with these settings likely affected the ability to form attachment to these locations at that time and such instability might possibly challenge future attachments to place.

In her present neighbourhood of Grandview-Woodland, Ms Laing spoke favourably about the area and enjoyed such features as "personal safety, the family-oriented nature of the neighbourhood, and access to services and amenities". A weak sense of social connection within the area might be argued in her relationship with a couple of neighbours with whom she had coffee with on a weekly basis. However, the comfort and ease she had in her present neighbourhood was not argued by the researcher as an indication of place attachment at this time. In particular, it was not specific features of the neighbourhood of Grandview-Woodland per se that had given her a "pleasant" life or a better quality of life, but features that, if generic to other areas, would be equally embraced by Ms Laing (for example, safe, affordable housing). Although possible notions of place attachment in the future should not be discounted, Ms Laing's five years' residence might not have yet permitted familiarity or intensification of feelings about the environment, which now had the possibility of being realised by a lack of restriction on physical spatial knowledge.

In this case study, consideration of temporal dimensions – the past and the present – is significant in understanding support for both environmental docility and proactivity. As previously illustrated, the DES had numerous environmental challenges or high press and Ms Laing appeared to have low personal competence (for example, poor mental health and a lack of social support and financial resources). As predicted, this led to maladaptive affect and behaviour. Ms Laing felt that she was a nervous wreck, was always looking behind her and had a horrible life. However, at some point this began to change, likely because of increased personal competence with improvements in mental health, and she began to be more proactive. Her environmental proactivity was evident in her need to make plans to get out of the DES. She also began to be more proactive in regard to challenging city officials and health boards about placing people with mental health problems in the DES: "it's the last place they should be".

In summary, Ms Laing's case study illustrates a situation of two environmental extremes. These contrasting neighbourhoods allowed differing expressions of physical and psychological experience – one that restricted mobility and created psychological distress, and the other that enabled mobility and gave quality back to her life. This case study was unique in that it gave an account of life in both research study areas of Vancouver. Although Ms Laing is currently not living in a state of environmental distress, she is analysed within this category because the effects of living in her past neighbourhood continue to influence her behaviour in the present. An interview that paralleled some of the issues found in this case study was an interview conducted with Milton Johnson, who had recently moved from Moss Side to another neighbourhood of Manchester. This is presented in Table A1 in Appendix A and in the biographies in Appendix B.

SIX

Reconceptualising the person–environment relationship

Introduction

This chapter examines how the findings gained from researching 'place and ageing' in deprived neighbourhoods build on and progress our knowledge in the field of environmental gerontology. This chapter brings together and summarises the findings from 26 interviews in Manchester and 26 interviews in Vancouver – as expressed through eight case studies, 44 short biographies (Appendices A and B) and three participants' photographs and descriptive text. It proposes a reconceptualisation of factors important in the person–environment relationship; such as the consideration of temporal dimensions (for example, past, present and future) and intervening variables (for example, such as religion and spirituality, and lifecourse). The chapter also explores issues around comparative research, factors associated with 'place and ageing', outcome variables (for example, quality of life and identity), and methodological and analytical aspects of the research. The final section summarises the study's contribution to the advancement of knowledge on place and ageing.

Cross-national research – empirical findings

The strength and uniqueness of this study is, in part, based on the comparative analysis of older people living in deprived urban neighbourhoods in England and Canada. Although there has been a growth in comparative research in recent years, as illustrated and discussed in Chapter One, there remains a paucity of comparative research within the environmental gerontology literature. Added to this, there is a lack of research within England and Canada investigating concepts of place and ageing, particularly in deprived urban neighbourhoods. Therefore, this research is in the unique position of being able to add to scientific knowledge not only in general, but also cross-nationally and within each country.

Findings from 26 interviews in Manchester and 26 in Vancouver were compared cross-nationally in relation to three factors. These were:

- environmental categories – comfort, management and distress;
- factors underlying place and ageing;
- the relationship between place and ageing and well-being.

Analysis of the interviews across these three factors reveals significant similarity of findings within and across countries. Findings revealed similar factors underlying older people's experience of place and ageing, and in the relationship between place and ageing and reports of well-being (that is, quality of life and identity). Each of these factors will be discussed later.

Although findings with respect to the cross-national comparisons were similar, there were differences with respect to neighbourhoods. As previously highlighted, the DES differed from the other neighbourhoods on a number of sociodemographic characteristics; namely, the area had a greater proportion of men, individuals who were single and had never married, people with multiple health problems and people reporting neither good nor poor quality of life. In addition to these differences, the interview data collected with residents in the DES also reflected a differing discourse on neighbourhood. Interviewees tended to use more negative or emotive words to describe their area. 'Skid row' was used frequently to refer to or describe the area; this was used by participants in both the DES and Grandview-Woodland. Other descriptive words related to the resident population of the area, such as drug addicts, sex trade workers and mental health patients. One participant even referred to the DES as resembling a concentration camp (see Ms Laing in Chapter Five) and another as "worse than the London slums" (see Mr O'Farrell in Appendix B). In addition, almost all interviewees mentioned having to be careful about the friends they made in the area and there were frequent references to 'trust' related to people living in the area. Expression of self-identity as 'unlike' the area or residents in the area was particularly evident in interviews conducted in the DES. The need to be identified outside of the immediate context or 'out of place' was evident in a number of residents living there. This was illustrated in the case study of Mr Matthews, but was evident in a number of other interviews conducted in the DES (see Appendix B – Keppol Polanski, Robert O'Farrell, Azimoon Rahaman and Mabel Smith).

It should be clarified that these neighbourhood differences did not change the main findings associated with place and ageing. Rather, they facilitated examination of a more extreme level of urban 'deprivation'. These differences, it is argued, might make the experience of place and ageing comparatively more challenging than in other neighbourhoods. This supports some neighbourhood effects research, in that there exists a greater or lesser degree of deprivation, which might be more intensively experienced in some areas compared with others (see Krause, 1996; Atkinson and Kintrea, 2001; Buck, 2001). Despite these areas sharing similar characteristics, this research highlights the heterogeneity among these types of areas and the need to consider this in analysing findings.

Environmental experience

According to La Gory et al (1985) 'older persons sharing the same neighbourhood do not necessarily occupy the same environmental worlds' (p 405). This study supports this. Research findings revealed a diversity in the experience of place and ageing for older people in these neighbourhoods. In particular, this supports other literature findings on the individualisation of the environment (Gubrium, 1973; Lawton and Nahemow, 1973; Rowles, 1978; Kahana, 1982; Golant, 1984; Peace et al, 2003). Although recognising the diversity in experience, both literature (for example, Rowles, 1978) and the current research have found support for common themes in people's experiences of place. In this research, three common environmental themes emerged from the data. This was found across all five neighbourhoods in England and Canada; these were environmental comfort, environmental management and environmental distress.

These categories were found to apply across nations and neighbourhoods. In addition, proportionally similar numbers of participants were found in each category and in each nation. Just over one in three of those interviewed were found to be in a state of 'comfort' with respect to their neighbourhood. This was illustrated with the case studies of Mary Perkins (Manchester) and Jennifer MacDougall (Vancouver). They perceived their area as having low environmental demand or risk and they had sufficient personal resources (for example, social support, financial security) to enable a sense of environmental ease within their daily life. Within this group, the environment appeared not to present barriers or restrict the negotiation of their daily life. There was also a strong sense of place attachment to the immediate neighbourhood and there was no desire to move. Ratings of quality of life were typically good or very good. Place and ageing in this situation was supported by the environmental and/or personal situation of the older person.

Close to half of the research participants were found to be trying actively to manage their neighbourhood. This was illustrated in the case studies of Muriel Allen (Manchester), Helen Fox (Manchester), Berry Matthews (Vancouver) and Howard Adams Goodleaf (Vancouver). These participants perceived their neighbourhood as having a number of risks that presented challenges to their personal competence. Older people in this category were acutely aware of the presses in their environment, but managed to remain engaged within the neighbourhood. Issues of emotive attachment to place were evident. However, this was not necessarily located within their immediate neighbourhood. For those whose emotive connection was located in another neighbourhood, there was, not surprisingly, a desire to move, usually back to the neighbourhood they were attached to. However, for those attached to their immediate neighbourhood, there was a desire to age in place. In general, quality of life ratings appeared divided – those who wished to stay in place reported a good quality of life and those attached elsewhere reported neither a good nor a poor quality of life.

Environmental management supports the notion, originally neglected by prominent theorists such as Lawton and Nahemow (1973), that people are active agents of their environment, that despite strong environmental challenges people find the personal resources to negotiate daily life and maintain well-being. The idea of environmental proactivity, later developed by Lawton (1990), relates to this idea. This also provides support for the resilience literature related to older people (Hardy, 2004), and might also contribute to successful ageing and ageing-well literature (Baltes and Baltes, 1990; Johnson, 1995).

Almost one in five of older research participants were found to be in a state of 'distress' with respect to their neighbourhood. This was evident in the case studies of Harold Waters (Manchester) and Elizabeth Laing (Vancouver). Mr Waters appeared acutely affected by environmental presses and although Ms Laing had relocated to another neighbourhood, the DES, her previous neighbourhood, continued to present a source of distress. In this environmental distress category, significant challenges and disruptions to place and ageing were evident. Environmental presses presented the individuals with significant demands and risks for managing daily life. Personal resources, in general, were unable to cope and maladaptive behaviour and psychological distress were present. There was no evidence of current place attachment, but in some cases there was evidence of disruptions to place attachment, and there was a strong desire to relocate; however, people lacked resources and options to do so. For those who were once attached to their neighbourhood, but at present experienced disruptions to place attachment, psychological distress appeared to be more acute compared to those who had never been attached to place. This supported Lambek and Antze's (1996, p xvi) claim that memories can undermine identity 'by glimpses of a past that no longer seems to be ours'. In addition to identity, failed or disrupted attachments threaten well-being (Brown and Perkins, 1992; Rowles and Ravdal, 2002). This was evident in the poor to very poor quality of life reported by people in this group, and connected to this was their discourse on self-worth and well-being, as illustrated by Mr Waters, who felt that "nobody cares about you now".

The environmental distress category largely supports Lawton's (1980, 1982) environmental docility hypothesis. In numerous cases, environmental press overwhelmed personal competences and led to negative affect and maladaptive behaviour, for example Mr Walters stated that he was "not really interested in living. If I die, I die". However, there were a few cases that challenged the direction of this relationship. In particular, having low competences and high presses did not necessarily negatively impact on ratings of quality of life. This was supported in the case of Roberta Peterson and Millicent Taylor (see Appendix B) where religion appeared to be a protective factor against poor quality of life. This highlights the need to respect the complexity of the person–environment relationship.

The environmental categories (comfort, management and distress) found within this research have support within the literature (Lawton and Nahemow, 1973; Kahana, 1982; Lawton et al, 1982; Brown, 1995). Lawton's competence-press has been recognised as influencing – after an inductive analysis of transcripts – the discourse and basic theoretical framework around docility and proactivity used within this research. However, this is as far as the similarity extends. These categories are unique in that they are generated from qualitative data and evolved from the discourse of older people's narratives about place and ageing. These environmental categories also respect and accept the complexity of the person–environment relationship, such as the acknowledgement of life history and religion/spirituality – for an example, see the case study of Howard Adams Goodleaf in Chapter Five. This is difficult to find within many of the current conceptual models and frameworks in the environmental science literature. In particular, a critique of Lawton's and others' approach to the study of older people's environmental experience relates to the imposing of quantitative measures in the construction of these frameworks (for example, the Ecological Model of Ageing). This approach prevents the expression of other factors that might be significant in the understanding of the older person and their environment. In addition, although Lawton and others have praised the competence-press model for supporting a combination of person–environment scenarios, the relationship is unidirectional. For example, strong press and low competence equates to negative affect and maladaptive behaviour. This research challenges this straightforward relationship. There is evidence within this research to suggest that this is not necessarily the scenario; spirituality/religion and/or life history might intervene as possible protective factor(s) against negative affect (for example, see Roberta Peterson and Millicent Taylor, Appendix B). In addition, as was illustrated in the case study of Mr Waters (see Chapter Five), environmental proactivity can operate within a situation of environmental distress. These 'complexities' are accounted for in the development and design of Figure 6.1.

Figure 6.1: Person–environment relationships

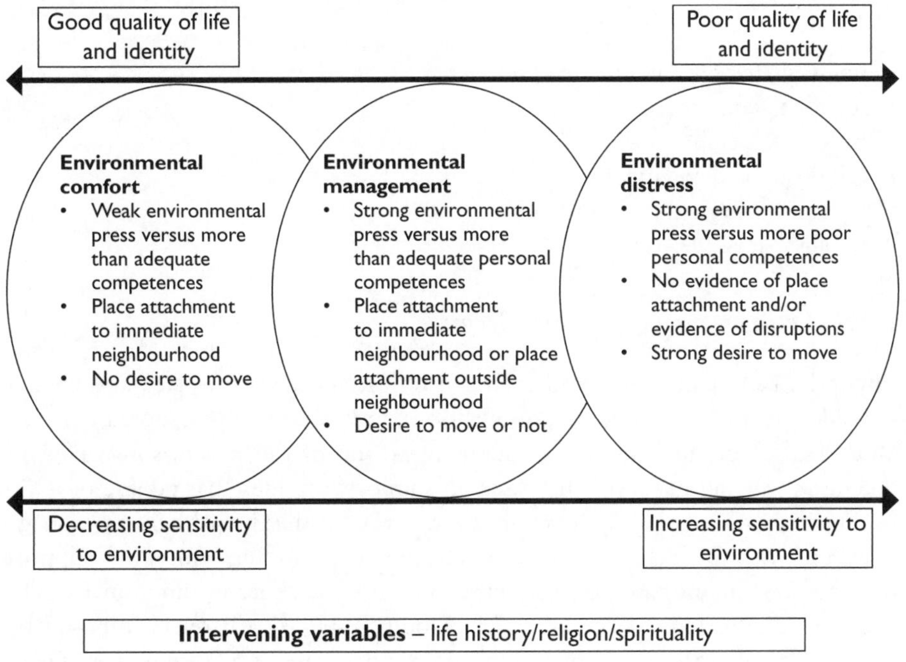

Good quality of life and identity

Poor quality of life and identity

Environmental comfort
- Weak environmental press versus more than adequate competences
- Place attachment to immediate neighbourhood
- No desire to move

Environmental management
- Strong environmental press versus more than adequate personal competences
- Place attachment to immediate neighbourhood or place attachment outside neighbourhood
- Desire to move or not

Environmental distress
- Strong environmental press versus more poor personal competences
- No evidence of place attachment and/or evidence of disruptions
- Strong desire to move

Decreasing sensitivity to environment

Increasing sensitivity to environment

Intervening variables – life history/religion/spirituality

The reliance on conceptual models such as the competence-press and its approach to data generation might in part be a major factor in criticism about the 'languishing state' and 'lack of innovativeness' associated with environmental ageing research. In addition, despite significant achievements of research in this area, Parmelee and Lawton (1990) and Wahl and Weisman (2003) both recognise that there 'remains no cure or remedy'. This research, in part, addresses solutions and presents new ideas to move the study of environmental gerontology forward.

Factors in place and ageing

This part of the discussion of findings centres around exploring the factors important in place and ageing. Specifically, why do some older people wish to remain in place, in spite of strong environmental presses, and what are the factors behind others' desire to leave their place despite the generally conceived notion within the literature that ageing in place is optimal?

The interviews and photographs revealed a number of factors important in place and ageing. Across the two nations and five neighbourhoods, participants revealed a similar discourse in their underlying accounts of place and ageing. These findings parallel and support those found by Rowles and others, but also go beyond this by suggesting the inclusion of other factors that might be relevant to the study of older people living in neighbourhoods characterised by multiple risks. These are:

- physical attachment and area knowledge;
- social attachment;
- historical attachment;
- religiosity and spirituality;
- the life history;
- public spaces.

Physical attachment and area knowledge

Physical attachment was found to be an important factor in place and ageing for older people in all five neighbourhoods, regardless of the national context. Within the literature, physical attachment is one of the key reasons given in defence of ageing in place. This research supports the idea that people develop 'intimate knowledge' of their physical environment that helps them to manage daily life despite declines in health. The research findings not only support physical attachment based on barriers imposed by declines in functional health (for example, Helen Fox, Jennifer MacDougall), but also barriers imposed by environmental presses and psychological concerns based on these presses. These are discussed in detail later.

According to Rowles (1983a, 1983b), the ability to develop intimate familiarity with an environment is important in place attachment. Physical connection presented in this research supports and is similar to Rowles' (1980, 1983a, 1990) concept of physical insideness and Lawton's (1985) 'state of residential knowing'. According to Rowles, attachment to place might, in part, be physical because of a propensity, through years of residence or adaptation, to form physical attachments. Similarly, 'Intimate knowledge of the idiosyncrasies of one's dwelling ... enhance the unit's livability' (Lawton, 1985, p 508). A significant focus and conclusion of Rowles and Lawton's research was that this physical knowledge masked declines in functional health status. Intimate knowledge or physical insideness has been found to hide declines in functional health, enabling older people to maximise their independence. Certainly, this can be argued to be evident in a number of the interviews and case studies in this research; most specifically, Mrs Jennifer MacDougall (Vancouver) and Mrs Helen Fox (Manchester). Years of residence in their neighbourhood and continuous performance of physical tasks is argued to have enabled a higher level of functional performance despite significant physical challenges. Both women were able to maintain presence within their environment or restructure it in a way that retains an acceptable level of environmental independence. For Mrs MacDougall (aged 90), the intimate knowledge she had developed of her neighbourhood enabled her to maintain a busy five-day-a-week schedule and to maintain a level of environmental comfort, despite health problems. Her interview provided particularly rich data on her physical as well as social relationship with her neighbourhood. For Mrs Fox, the restructuring of her living space to the ground floor of her house allowed her to remain active socially and physically in place despite significant mobility problems (that is, being wheelchair-bound).

Place attachment might also be an important factor in successful adaptation to spatial restriction. Having a 'history' in the development of physical knowledge might lead to intensification of emotive feelings about place. As suggested by Rowles (1978, p 202), 'constriction in the realm of action accompanied by expansion of geographical fantasy' might precipitate 'selective intensification' of feelings about place. This can be argued in relation to the case of Mrs MacDougall and Mrs Fox. Mrs Fox's physical health challenges appeared to have reinforced her need to age in place. Place attachment in this situation appeared a consequence of a strong need to be seen as independent and have a sense of continuity of a past 'busy' self, key to this remaining engaged physically and socially with the community. The recognised value of geographical fantasy and reminiscence was evident in Mrs MacDougall's case study. In her short story *A walk down memory lane* she presents a vivid illustration of past neighbourhood memories and recognised the value of memories to help her in the future, stating "good memories, in one's later life, are better than money in the bank.... And maybe, I will have some warm memories of this day years from now when I might be feeling a little bit lonely".

Spatial restriction might further feelings of place attachment by acting as a protective factor in the face of negative neighbourhood change. As suggested by La Gory et al (1985), more active lifestyles might be necessary for people to experience environmental stresses, and therefore possible disruptions to place attachment. Certainly, there is some evidence to suggest that Mrs Fox's neighbourhood has negatively changed, particularly in respect to neighbours and crime. However, as this area is peripheral to the immediate maintenance and management of her daily environment, she appears largely to be unaffected by these negative environmental changes. Rather, the emphasis is on the immediate surroundings for reification of her past self (for example, independent self) and present self (for example, still managing to be independent).

Also important in physical insideness is area knowledge. It is generally recognised in the environmental gerontology literature that area knowledge is advantageous (Rowles, 1978; Lawton, 1985). Knowing whom one can count on and where to satisfy needs has important implications for environmental control and mastery (Francis, 1989; Oswald et al, 2003a). Area knowledge is an important feature in the management of daily life and/or enables at least some level of environmental coping despite significant distress. This appeared particularly relevant to the current study. Findings revealed that physical attachment not only supported increased functional health, but was also important and sensitive in relation to alleviating psychological (for example, fear of crime) and environmental barriers (for example, trouble spots). Physical attachment and intimate area knowledge enables interaction and participation in the neighbourhood that might not be achieved in their absence. Area knowledge in the majority of the interviews, case studies and photographs appeared to be predominantly governed by a need to ease psychological fear, specifically, fear of crime, rather than a feature of functional health decline. This can be illustrated by creating a path or routine that maximises experience of place and minimises psychological distress. The case studies of Mr Waters and Mr Matthews best illustrate this point, in addition to photographs and descriptive text generated by Mr Bennett. Mr Bennett illustrated this when referring to areas that were safe during the day, areas in which people would need to 'proceed with caution', and 'no go areas'. This feature of area knowledge or physical attachment has largely been neglected within the literature, possibly in part because it is a feature associated with older people who live under these particular types of conditions and within these types of neighbourhoods.

Routines might also be evidence of physical attachment. In many of the interviews and case studies in the environmental comfort and management categories, there was evidence of a familiar physical existence of daily life; specifically, the day or week was constructed around a general routine or frequency of certain activities performed at certain times of the day or week, such as walks, housework and social engagements. For example, for Ms Allen this revolved around her twice-daily walks in the parks with her dogs. For Mrs MacDougall, being able to physically manage a complete weekly schedule was important. In the case of Mrs Perkins, this was her almost daily visits to the shops. And for Mrs Fox, routine was located in her ability to manage her immediate environment, such as doing her housework, despite her functional health problems. As suggested by Rubinstein (1986, 1988), the ability to construct a routine based on either a full day or a week is indicative of how well a person is physically and psychologically coping with their environment. This feature was certainly evident in this research. Older people who had a routine were found to be managing or comfortable within their environment, while those who did not have a routine were found to be in a distressed state. This was particularly evident in the case of Mr Waters.

Social attachment

Social attachment was found to be important in place and ageing in all five neighbourhoods. This supports a significant research literature that links social support and place attachment (Rowles, 1980, 1983a, 1983b; St. John et al, 1986; Francis, 1989; Mesch and Manor, 1998; Fried, 2000; Sugihara and Evans, 2000; Cattell, 2004). Social connection in this research parallels Rowles' (1983a) concept of social insideness. Specifically, people form social affinity with their area through social integration and participation, and thus create emotive attachment to place.

Findings revealed that formation of social connections within the neighbourhood is an important factor in place and ageing. Older people who had social support within their neighbourhood were more likely to be attached, and tended to cite friends as the reason they would not move (for example, see Alfred and Serta Williams in Appendix B). Equally, those who had social connections beyond their immediate neighbourhood frequently expressed a desire to move so that they could be closer to their family/friends (see the case study of Mr Matthews in Chapter Five). Therefore, the social integration of the older person within their neighbourhood is a key feature in place and ageing.

A range of social connections was found across the interviews, case studies and photographs. Some participants expressed a strong sense of informal social ties, which were important in relation to their need to age in place; being close to family and friends was especially significant (see Mrs Perkins). However, for some the development of formal relationships appeared to be just as significant to creating a sense of belonging. Both Ms Allen and Mrs MacDougall valued their many acquaintances. For Ms Allen, the interaction she had with people she met while walking her dogs played a significant role in her day (for example, determining whether she was out for one or two hours) and reinforced her self-identity. This was also found in the photographs and descriptive text provided by Ms Flora Clark, in which the majority of images centred around people she had met that day. This supports the idea that social integration provides a sense of belonging and possibly leads to place attachment and development.

The importance of social connection or belonging as a feature of place and ageing might best be strengthened with a look at failed social connections. Perceived failed social attachments were particularly acute in the case studies of Mr Waters and Mr Matthews. For Mr Waters, the lack of social support within his neighbourhood was inadequate for his level of need. This translated into his feelings of nobody caring and his continuous references to being bored. The inability to form social attachments in his immediate neighbourhood led Mr Waters to seek some sense of social belongingness elsewhere. This was in part satisfied, if only temporarily, by his regular visits to the pub. Lack of social attachments was also a feature in the case of Mr Matthews. Evidence suggests that Mr Matthews tried to develop some sense of social connection to the neighbourhood (for example, through volunteer work and friendships in his place of residence). However, he found this largely unsuccessful. These failed social attachments can be argued to have had two effects: first, they caused Mr Matthews to seek a sense of belongingness outside his neighbourhood, and, second, they hindered his attachment to place. This supports the idea that failed social integration within the neighbourhood, when it is sought, leads to feelings of rejection and abandonment of place attachment.

Historical attachment

The historical attachment of older people to their neighbourhood was found to be an important feature in the development or hindrance of factors associated with place and ageing. This is supported by other research findings (Rowles, 1980, 1983a, 1993; Taylor, 2001). In particular, Rowles' concept of autobiographical insideness supports notions of a historical connection to place. Historical connection in this study relates to how older people's personal history is intertwined and rooted, usually developed through years of residence within the area. This historical connection enables reminiscence and review of the lifecourse, and has been found to be important in psychological well-being (Butler, 1963; Bornat, 1994; Taylor, 2001). Indeed, according to Rowles (1980), this might represent the strongest indication of people's attachment to place.

Within the interviews, case studies and photographs of older people who had remained in place for a significant part of their lives, the presence of historical connection to place was evident. This was particularly salient in the photographs and descriptive text provided by Ms Allen (Manchester) and Mr Bennett (Vancouver), and the case study of Mrs MacDougall (Vancouver). All of these cases present rich descriptive data concerning older people's historical connection with their neighbourhood. Ageing in place has been found to be critical for intensifying place attachment; according to Rowles (1980), autobiographical insideness can rarely be created in a new setting. This was certainly supported by Mrs MacDougall's short story (see Appendix C) in which she stated: "Twice I moved to other areas of Vancouver. I was miserable. I moved back. I came back because a lot of good memories are connected to this area".

Reminiscence or memories associated with historical connection might also undermine place attachment and psychological well-being. This is certainly evident in the case study of Mr Waters. In this situation, reminiscence, unlike what is generally portrayed in the literature, is negatively perceived and life review within the context is undermined. Recollection of the neighbourhood and neighbours of the past appears to continuously produce a sense of loss and isolation, and serves to create a global feeling that nobody cares. This situation hinders and disrupts place and ageing.

Religiosity and spirituality

Religiosity and spirituality were found within this research to represent important factors in the relationship of the older person to their environment. The findings revealed two underlying factors relevant to the consideration of place and ageing: the idea that life situations are governed by 'God's will', and that individuals might have a more spiritual relationship with place. Each of these will be discussed in turn.

The idea that 'God's will' governs one's life was evident in a number of interviews, particularly among Black Caribbean residents in Moss Side (see Appendix B: Elsie Forester, Marva Collins, Patricia Reilly, Felicity Parker, Millicent Taylor, Sydney Potter and Roberta Peterson). For these older people, God was a significant feature and source of guidance in daily life, with some perhaps perceiving their daily struggles with their neighbourhood as representing a test of their faith. Certainly, this can be argued in the situations of Millicent Taylor and Roberta Peterson, both of whom were found to be in a situation of environmental distress, yet reported a good quality of life. Religion might be a significant intervening or protective factor. This is supported by Krause (1998), who established that the negative effects of living in run-down neighbourhoods were reduced for older people who used religion as a coping strategy. Therefore, religious factors associated with place and ageing need to be considered much more fully within environmental gerontology research, especially where such research encompasses the perceptions of minority ethnic older people.

Another important factor relates to individuals' spiritual relationship with place. Surprisingly, spirituality has received relatively little attention within the relevant literature. This might be attributable to the fact that a large amount of empirical research has been focused on white middle-class America, and has consequently neglected other ethnic or cultural groups' relationship with place. Within this study, the inclusion of a variety of ethnic groups allowed exploration of cross-cultural differences in the experience of place and ageing. This was certainly captured with the interview of Howard Adams Goodleaf, the First Nations man in the DES. His relationship with place was based on a spiritual connection to his ancestors, and the idea that 'place' (that is, land) was sacred and provided the means of subsistence. The inability to establish an equivalent spiritual relationship with place in his current neighbourhood caused significant stress in his daily life, which he described as being a "struggle from the time you get up in the morning". Consideration of older people's spiritual relationship with place can arguably provide a different perspective and understanding of place and ageing factors. Future research might wish to consider taking this feature into consideration.

The life history

The lifecourse or life history was found to influence factors associated with place and ageing in this study. Connected to this is the danger of romanticising place attachment; as suggested by Hummon (1986, 1992) and Western (1993), attachment to place is not a collective phenomenon. In the present study, lack of feelings of place attachment was found among a number of participants in both Manchester and Vancouver neighbourhoods. This lack of attachment, despite research suggesting that failed attachments are detrimental, did not appear to be maladaptive to psychological well-being (for example, identity and quality of life). Lack of place attachment to an area might have been a feature of the lifecourse, length of residence and absence of physical and psychological need. This was particularly evident in the DES, most likely reflecting the lifecourse mobility of many of the participants. Many interviewees had lived very transient lifestyles, moving from one job to another across the country, working away in the logging camps (in the British Columbia interior), and some had even experienced periods of homelessness. Lifecourse factors were evident in the case study of Ms Laing and in a number of other interviews (see Appendix B: Frank Lander, George Knotsberry and John Rankin). Exploring the lifecourse of the individual presents a greater depth of understanding of and insight into individual factors associated with place and ageing.

Public spaces

Public spaces appear to be important in older people's positive experience of place and ageing. Public spaces in this research related primarily to local parks. The importance of parks for psychological well-being was found in the case study of Ms Allen and Mr Matthews. However, they appeared to serve different functions. For Ms Allen, the presence of a park in her neighbourhood appeared to reinforce social and historical connectedness, and hence place attachment to the area. For Mr Matthews, on the other hand, concerns over safety connected to his neighbourhood park precipitated a connection with a park located outside his neighbourhood, providing a means of escape and a strategy for coping with environmental demands. As is highlighted in the literature, public spaces, in particular parks, are an underutilised resource primarily because of fear of personal safety (Mumford and Power, 2003). In research examining the effects of development and regeneration of community parks and gardens by local residents increased rates of civic engagement and attachment were found (Francis, 1989; Armstrong, 2000). Attention of policy makers to the social value of public spaces (for example, parks) in deprived areas might work to increase population well-being and place attachment.

Another consideration in the importance of parks to place and ageing might be connected to spirituality. As in the case study of Mr Goodleaf and his deep connection with the land, parks might provide a way for urban residents to connect with 'mother nature'. There is a lack of research exploring this particular issue. This research suggests that some individuals have a need to connect with nature in order to sustain well-being and place attachment.

Quality of life and identity

It can be argued from the findings of this study that quality of life and identity are, in part, environmentally driven. Across the three environmental categories (comfort, management, distress), quality of life and identity differ according to the categories. Older people within the environmental comfort category were, in general, found to have very good to good quality of life, compared with those within the environmental distress grouping, who, in general, expressed very poor to poor quality of life. Older people in the environmental management category tended to rate quality of life as either good or neither good nor poor. The connection between quality of life and the environment was strongly evident in a number of the case studies, for example Elizabeth Laing, Harold Waters and Robert O'Farrell (see Chapter Five and Appendix B). Ms Laing argued that her quality of life had significantly improved upon relocation from the DES, while Mr Waters suggested that his life was made poor by his environmental conditions, lack of good neighbours, fear of crime and neighbourhood decline. Mr O'Farrell simply felt he could not talk about quality of life while living in the DES. This suggests that, at least for some older people, quality of life is environmentally bound. This supports literature findings suggesting an association between the person–environment relationship and quality of life as an outcome measure (Farquhar, 1995; Raphael et al, 1999; Stevens-Ratchford and Diaz, 2003; Gabriel and Bowling, 2004; Wiggins et al, 2004). Therefore, improvements in quality of life need to be addressed through the tackling of environmental press factors that impinge on well-being. This has implications for policies on regeneration and the renewal of deprived neighbourhoods.

However, solely looking at this relationship in this way ignores the complexity of quality of life (Smith, 2000). Although the findings largely reflect a predictable relationship between place and quality of life, there were some cases in which quality of life was good despite 'distress' and 'neither good nor poor' despite 'comfort'. This possibly suggests one of two things. First, as previously stated, quality of life is complex and individualised. In this context, place might not be a salient feature in quality of life if other factors are currently the focus, such as health, family relationships or finances. Second, spirituality/religion and the lifecourse might work as protective factors against negative environmental factors and hence perceptions of well-being. This is supported by previous research that reported a connection between environmental deterioration and religious coping strategies (Krause, 1998).

Place attachment was found to be significant for quality of life and perceived identity. For Mr Waters, disruptions to place attachment in terms of his inability to reintegrate and form satisfying relationships clearly impacted on his feelings of self-worth and psychological well-being. This is supported within the literature (Cutchin, 2001; Peace et al, 2003). Harnessing and supporting place attachment in these environments has implications for the quality of life of residents and the community. In general, older people in this study who were attached to their immediate neighbourhood were found to report a better quality of life than those who were not attached (but wished to be) and/or were experiencing disruptions. It also needs to be mentioned that not everyone was found to be attached, and that those who lacked attachment did not necessarily confirm that they had a poor quality of life. A good example here would be the situation of Ms Laing. This raises the issue of romanticising place.

Connected to quality of life is self-worth or identity, which was found to be a factor influenced by place and ageing. Reification of the self within the study's context was viewed as both personally and environmentally bound. The research supports Kaufman (1986) and Brandtstädter and Greve (1994), who argue that the ageing self seeks continuity, and is resilient and resourceful in spite of personal change(s). In addition, the current research suggests possible environmental factors that challenge the self. Achieving positive or negative reification of the self might be dependent on the level of support needed and the ability of the environment to meet this level.

The self is viewed as drawing meaning from the past as a way of recreating the present self (Kaufman, 1986). This is evident in Mrs Fox's case study, where there was evidence of a connection to aspects of her former self and life, for example "I've had a very good life ... I get photographs to show my granddaughter when I was about 18 or 19". The mechanisms highlighted by Rowles (1980, 1983a) that allowed for reinforcing memories of the past were the preservation of artefacts such as pictures, and ongoing participation in a familiar setting. Reminiscence through pictures and videos represented a feature that gave pleasure to her life; sharing pictures of herself when she was a teenager with her granddaughter and looking at family videos enabled reification of the self and preservation of identity as it was in the past, not as it is in the present. The ability to remain or age in place likely enabled preservation of and continuity to her past self and life.

However, this research suggests that the ageless self is also strongly environmentally bound and constructed, in that the environment can work to support or threaten achieved continuity to the ageing self. According to Rowles (1978, 1980, 1983), people's identities are *intertwined*, *preserved* and *reinforced* by the place they live. Evidence of this was found in a number of interviews and in the case study analyses. For example, Mrs Fox's ability to retain her independence despite profound functional health challenges was, in part, environmentally determined; consider for a moment what would happen if her immediate environment became too much to manage or she was forced to relocate – this would likely create significant challenges to her 'independent self'. Certainly, a coherent and continuous sense of self would be threatened. This is connected to the work of Peace et al (2003) on place attachment and identity maintenance; their findings revealed that individuals have a comfort level for environmental connectedness, which enables maintenance of the self and mastery over the environment. This further reinforces the importance of environmental management or ageing in place in the maintenance and preservation of the self within a context of personal and/or environmental change. Similarly, Mrs MacDougall's drive to 'keep going' and retain an active weekly schedule was, in part, supported by her level of achieved environmental comfort. In this case study there was evidence to suggest that a change in environmental support might negatively influence the self.

There is, however, evidence to suggest that rejection of the immediate environment can also enable positive reification of the self. In the case study of Mr Matthews, rejection of the immediate environment (for example, the people and neighbourhood) as unlike or dissimilar to the self, enabled retention of a positive self-image and connection to his previous life – "I grew up with people with money". This was similarly found in Novak and Lerner's (1968) study, in which rejection of the self as unlike others was a protective factor for self-esteem and self-worth.

Although the environment in this situation is considered primarily as a strategy to enhance environmental coping, it should be mentioned that it can also undermine the self. Findings from interviews and case studies on reification of the self in situations of environmental distress and disruptions to place attachment suggest an inability to construct a coherent sense of self. This was evident in the case study of Mr Waters, in which he perceived his environment as unfeeling and uncaring. This appeared to translate into his personal feelings of low self-worth and the idea that no one would care if he died. This supports Golant's (2003, p 642) argument that those older people 'whose self-concepts are strongly rooted or anchored to past experiences and behaviors (the proverbial "living in the past") may experience the most difficulties'.

Summary

Comparative analysis of 26 interviews in Manchester and 26 interviews in Vancouver revealed similarities across the environmental categories of comfort, management and distress, in factors underlying place and ageing, and in the relationship between 'place and ageing' and well-being. Examination of place and ageing within the two countries has come at a time when these and other nations are focused on meeting the needs of an increasingly ageing society and on solving some of the challenges present in urban areas. Certainly, findings from this study provide support for the consideration of a more complex relationship between the older person and their environment. Despite the environmental challenges present in the areas in the study, over one in three older people interviewed was found to be comfortable within their environment, expressing in some cases strong commitment to place. There was also a significant number, almost half, who were found to manage. This illustrates the resilience of older people, and their adaptability to environmental and personal changes. In some cases, despite strong environmental presses, there was a desire to age in place. However, for others this was not the situation and these individuals might benefit from government policies aimed at tackling some of the underlying factors hindering place and ageing. For example, programmes aimed at increasing community participation such as development of local parks or gardens might aid in place attachment. However, attention also needs to be given to tackling broader issues such as crime.

The research also highlights a significant number of older people who were in distress, and did not feel that ageing in place was optimal. Nine out of the 52 research participants were acutely negatively aware of their environment and expressed a wish to move (or had moved). If this number was found to be proportionally generalisable to neighbourhoods with similar characteristics, this might present a challenge to current ageing in place policies in England and Canada, and other countries. This group might benefit most from policies aimed at tackling factors associated with environmental presses, for example, high crime, poor infrastructure and instability of resident populations. This might in turn influence personal competence, such as health and social support, and hence possibly lead to a greater sense of well-being.

England and Canada share a number of similarities. At a macro level, both countries share a similar type of political and judicial system, their social welfare systems are broadly comparable and the nations are socially and culturally similar. England and Canada also share a number of trends, such as similar population ageing projections and an increase in challenges to urban inner-city neighbourhoods. Therefore, similarities in results between the two countries should not be unexpected; the study also supports research from the US literature. This suggests that such findings might be usefully considered beyond the current study, to other countries sharing similar characteristics (for example, political, economic and social systems).

The study's contribution to knowledge

This section of the chapter highlights the study's contribution to scientific knowledge. In Chapter Two, a number of gaps in knowledge within the current literature on place and ageing were identified. These concerned lack of knowledge relating to contextual limitations (leading to a critique of a lack of innovativeness and stagnation within environmental gerontology) and a neglect of temporal dimensions in the consideration of place and ageing issues.

The first contribution made by this study concerns cross-national research in gerontology. This study was unique in that it sought to gain a cross-national perspective on place and ageing issues in deprived urban settings. The comparative element of this research enabled the expansion of scientific knowledge related to place and ageing issues in general, and, in particular, in deprived inner-city neighbourhoods of England and Canada. This enabled the redressing of Parmelee's (1998, p 179) critique of environmental gerontology, which suggested that findings would benefit from an internationalisation in order to learn how generalisable the results are, such that 'Are we observing culturally universal behaviour patterns that are intrinsic to spatial behaviour in late life or simply the effects of being old and North American?'.

The interviews and photographs in the present study revealed a shared experience of place and ageing cross-nationally. Factors found to be important in establishing place and ageing were: physical, social, historical attachment; the lifecourse; religion and spirituality; and public spaces. Some of these findings support previous environmental science research, therefore building on previous knowledge, such as physical attachment and area knowledge, and social and historical attachment. Other findings identified new knowledge that has largely been neglected or ignored: for example, the expansion of knowledge related to religiosity/spirituality and lifecourse, and the importance of public places. The research also found that physical attachment and area knowledge were important in the easing of psychological fear (that is, fear of crime) alongside the more commonly achieved masking of functional health challenges. This finding possibly reflects the type of study locality – deprived urban neighbourhoods.

The second contribution relates to the environmental categories and new conceptual model (Figure 6.1). These categories are unique in that they were generated from qualitative data that allowed the older person's discourse on place and ageing to emerge. A shortfall of current conceptual models on the person–environment relationship is that measures are imposed and narrowly focused, and therefore restricting. A key strength of this conceptual model is that the data inductively evolved. The relationship was found to be complex and not always straightforward. Specifically, high environmental press and low personal competence were not always associated with perceptions of poor quality of life. This raised the need to consider the complexity of the person–environment paradigm and to consider in particular variables such as life history and religion/spirituality. Taking this approach might aid in the advancement of environmental gerontology beyond its present 'languishing state'.

The conceptual model also recognised the importance of being temporally located in time and place. Although individual cases needed to be fixed in time and place for analysis, Figure 6.1 recognises the fluidity of an individual's relationship with their environment (for example, comfort, management and distress), such that throughout an individual's lifecourse they might move through several environment categories, possibly as circumstances in their life change, for example, health, relocation and/or neighbourhood changes. The findings and model also highlight the need to consider how the past has impacted on the present, and how the past and present might impact on the future. Within this study, consideration of these factors enabled greater understanding of place and ageing factors and the relationship between 'place and ageing' and well-being (that is, quality of life and well-being). These findings illustrated the significance of including temporal factors in the analysis of place and ageing data.

A third contribution relates to methodological limitations within the current research literature. This research aimed to redress the imbalance in research on quantitatively driven conceptual frameworks on environmental ageing (for example, the Ecological Model of Ageing). Criticisms have predominantly related to a lack of innovativeness in methodological approaches, leading, therefore, to stagnation in scientific knowledge gained in this area. Although there has been a growth in the use of qualitative data to build on the conceptual framework of Lawton (for example, Rowles, 1978, 1983; Peace et al, 2006), few have used qualitative data or a mixed-methods approach to drive forward a better conceptual model or seek new ways of exploring the person–environment relationship.

Within this study, the selection of a mixed qualitative methodological approach enabled the acquisition of data gathering from a number of perspectives, adding increased insight and validation to the findings. This produced rich knowledge on place and ageing, which builds on previous findings and conceptual frameworks, and found previously neglected or new ways of understanding some of the factors associated with place and ageing. The incorporation of participants' photographs and descriptive text provided a useful way of verifying interpretations arising from the face-to-face interviews. This exercise established participant photographs as an innovative way of data gathering and generation. This both enabled the capturing of the neighbourhood from the perspective of the resident and provided a way to engage the older person in the active construction of meaning. The approach was also sensitive to the complexities of the person–environment relationship. This enabled the development of a conceptual figure (see Figure 6.1) that appropriately represents the multidimensional and multi-variable paradigm of the older person and their relationship to their neighbourhood and well-being.

A fourth contribution is related to future research. The study, while addressing a number of current gaps in knowledge, also raised some research questions for consideration in future studies. One such question relates to the study of cross-cultural issues. With an increased trend in globalisation, national differences might become less diverse; the focus then might be one of exploring cultural issues within nations. Investigating the experience and meaning of place across different cultures has the ability to add new insight into a field that has been criticised for its 'lack of innovativeness and stagnation'. Certainly, the importance of cultural and spiritual issues was raised within this research with the analysis of a native North American perspective.

Another interesting research area would be to assess possible age, generational and period effects on place and ageing. This could be achieved in a longitudinal study investigating possible cohort differences across the lifecourse. In addition, people's future relationship with place is likely to change with increased globalisation and information and communication technology. How these changes will impact on the future of ageing and older people's relationship with place might be critical to the sustainability of communities and neighbourhoods – this is discussed in further detail in Chapter Eight.

Consideration of gender effects on the use and attachment to place would also present an interesting research topic. This was not fully explored in the current research but arose in the analysis of the photographs; differences in the use of place were revealed. For example, Mr Bennett was found to capture a wider range of images and covered a wider geographical distance compared with the more narrow focus of Ms Allen and Mrs Clarke. However, because only three participants were involved in this exercise, no conclusions can be drawn on possible gender differences. Although there is some research to suggest that differences exist (Dines et al, 2007; Holland et al, 2007), this area remains largely unexplored.

Conclusion

This chapter brought together and discussed findings presented in Chapters Four and Five. This revealed findings associated with empirical and methodological contributions to scientific knowledge. Empirical findings revealed cross-national similarities in environmental experience, in factors underlying place and ageing and in the relationship between 'place and ageing' and well-being. The research also supported previous research findings on place and ageing and enabled an expansion of knowledge related to previously neglected factors and new ways of understanding the relationship between the older person and their environment. Methodological contributions revealed the appropriateness of taking a mixed-methods approach and the importance of using multiple forms of data collection. Finally, consideration of temporal factors in data collection and analysis of findings was critical to the development of accurate insight and understanding of individuals' relationship to their environment.

Part Three
Refocusing the person–environment fit

SEVEN

The way forward – building sustainability

Introduction

Part One of this book sought to revisit our thinking and knowledge on the person–environment fit. This primarily examined the contribution of Lawton's Ecological Model of Ageing and Rowles' concepts of insideness. Part Two aimed to fill gaps in knowledge related to understanding the experiences of older people living in urban neighbourhoods – in particular deprived inner-city areas – and challenge current thinking about the relationship between the older person and their environment. Part Three aims to refocus the person–environment fit by presenting the next steps and the way forward. The focus of this chapter will be on research and policy responses that are critically needed if Western countries are going to respond appropriately, in both economic and social justice terms, to support the needs and aspirations of an ageing population. The chapter primarily draws on the policy context and agenda in England.

Background

The research findings presented in Chapters Four through Six suggest that society needs to look more closely at ways to avoid putting older people under environmental distress and better support them to manage their environment and/or ensure they enjoy a certain level of comfort. Although the majority of participants in the study desired to age in place, there were a significant minority, almost one in five, who were found to be acutely distressed by their environment. As the findings revealed, this had negative implications on their quality of life and their ability to maximise their ageing well. In economic terms, this is likely to have a profound effect on health and social care spending, in addition to challenging policy agendas around social inclusion, building sustainable and cohesive neighbourhoods, and ageing in place. The chapter now examines the current policy context and this is followed by a look ahead to more appropriate ways in which society can and must prepare to support the needs and aspirations of an ageing population.

Policy context

Starting in the last quarter of the 20th century, there has been a growing policy interest in ensuring environmental sustainability. Political initiatives aimed at building sustainable urban neighbourhoods have grown in prominence in recent years (for example, the renewed European Union Sustainable Development Strategy [2006][1]; the 2007 Sustainable Communities Act[2] in the UK). Interest in the quality of the urban environment could be argued to be in part driven by a wider interest in the environment. In recent years there has been a growth of research interest internationally relating to environmental issues in an ageing society (Andrews and Phillips, 2005). This has not only been linked to environmental protection (for example, the 1987 Montreal Protocol, the 2005 Kyoto 1 Protocol, the 2007 Kyoto 2 Protocol) but also to a focus on the impact of differing environmental qualities on the physical and emotional health of individuals. In 1989, the first *European Charter on Environment and Health* was developed, which stated that 'good health and well-being require a clean and harmonious environment in which physical, psychological, social and aesthetic factors are all given their due importance' (WHO, 1989, p 7). Currently, there is a breadth of international programmes and initiatives that focus on the environment, specifically the World Health Organization's Public Health and the Environment (PHE) initiative, the United Nations Environment Programme (UNEP), the European Regional Development Fund, the European Social Fund and the World Bank's 2001 environmental strategy. All have the aim of improving the quality of the environment that people inhabit.

In 2007, 27 European Union member states signed the Leipzig Charter on Sustainable European Cities aimed at creating a foundation for a new urban policy in Europe. The Charter sets out the vision of the European city in the 21st century such as supporting self-determination by citizens (for example, improving education and employment opportunities), mixed tenure development, social inclusion (for example, tackling inequity and deprived neighbourhoods), creating high-quality public space and investing in infrastructure (for example, urban transport). The Charter makes clear that changes in urban policy are needed to meet the challenges associated with demography, climate and global economic pressures.

In recent years, there has been growing recognition of the need to improve the quality of cities and neighbourhoods in reference to supporting an ever-increasing ageing society. The Second World Assembly on Ageing held in Madrid in 2002 adopted an International Plan of Action on Ageing 'to respond to the opportunities and challenges of population ageing in the 21st century and to promote a society for all ages' (Article 1, p 1). One of the three key priority areas raised was to create 'enabling and supportive environments'.

As previously discussed in Chapter Three, the World Health Organization (WHO, 2007), working cross-nationally with 35 cities in 22 countries, has developed guidance on 'global age-friendly cities'. This guidance has been important for raising awareness around the social and physical factors in the built environment that help support ageing well. In addition, the World Health Organization European Healthy Cities programme – consisting of a network of cities from across Europe – is committed to addressing health and sustainable development. Over the next five years (2009–13) the programme will focus on three core priority areas, all of which will support an ageing population, which are: caring and supportive environments, healthy living and healthy urban design.

In the UK, in line with the sustainable neighbourhoods agenda and with consideration of the current and future demographic profile, the government has committed to moving towards creating 'lifetime homes' and 'lifetime neighbourhoods'. Published in 2008 the report *Lifetime homes, lifetime neighbourhoods: A national strategy for housing in an ageing society* (CLG, 2008) is the first such strategy to solely recognise the impact of the environment on the process of ageing, and hence the need to '"future proof" our society so that it does not alienate or exclude' (2008, p 11). It acknowledges that built environments are rarely created with older people in mind. The overall aim of 'lifetime neighbourhoods' is to lessen the impact of disability and ill-health and promote good health, overall well-being and social, economic and civic capital. This design-for-all philosophy is slowly being incorporated, with the recognition that often small changes in the environment can help to reduce falls and accidents and improve the function and quality of life (Phillips et al, 2005). Lifetime neighbourhoods 'require an accessible and pleasant built environment in which residents of all ages are not unnecessarily excluded by age, physical or cognitive ability, and remain able to work, socialise and participate for as long as possible' (Harding, 2007, p 8). In planning for lifetime neighbourhoods Harding suggests we need to consider:

- accessibility of the built environment;
- appropriateness of housing available;
- fostering social capital;
- location and accessibility to services;
- creating aesthetic pleasing public spaces which promote a sense of place and social cohesion;
- cross-sectoral integration and planning of services;
- building intergenerational relationships by shared site usage;
- better use of information technology.

Although great gains have been made in the recognition of the importance of this agenda, there is still considerable work to be done on the ground in delivery if we are able to achieve a society built for all ages and one that is truly inclusive. The Audit Commission (2008) – an independent UK government inspection body – has found that despite awareness and knowledge of a growing ageing society, the majority of councils are ill prepared to support the demographic changes; this likely resonates with other developed and developing countries.

The following two sections discuss some of the next steps in going forward, the aim is to be challenging, reflective and create debate. This draws from the author's own empirical research presented in the previous chapters, the wider research literature and policy knowledge in the area of ageing and social exclusion.

Next steps – raising key themes

According to Lupton (2003, p 1), 'Rarely has the neighbourhood enjoyed as high a profile in public policy as it does today'. There is therefore a need to capitalise on this and make progress towards building a society better able to meet the needs and aspirations of an ageing population. There is a strong policy and research agenda focused on the benefits of ageing in place; however, creating successful or optimal ageing in place denotes or at best assumes an enabling environment. From the empirical research presented previously, environments vary in the degree to which they are enabling and of a particular quality.

The next three subsections discuss some of the gaps and oversights in policy and practice. The first and second subsections consider the integration of health, care and housing; and the need for greater attention to the built environment. The third subsection takes a critical view of current housing diversity and choice. This is followed by a section that features discussion about the way forward and how academics and policy makers might redress these issues as nations prepare for the opportunities afforded an ageing society.

Integration of health, care and housing

Health trend data show that the majority of older people enjoy good health. Figures previously presented in Chapter Three show that life expectancy in many Western countries has increased significantly over the latter part of the 20th century. In countries of the Organisation for Economic Co-operation and Development (OECD, 2008a), life expectancy from 1820 to the end of the 20th century has more than doubled; in 28 countries it now exceeds 78 years (Forette and Brieu, 2007). However, not all years gained in life expectancy are spent in good or fairly good health. Healthy and disability-free years have not kept pace with life expectancy. Healthy life expectancy and disability-free life expectancy tend to be lower; this is a pattern that is found globally but with varying degrees across countries (Mathers et al, 2004; see Chapter Three for Eurostat figures).

Given the trends in life expectancy, healthy life expectancy and disability-free years, coupled with evidence on the link between housing and the impact on health (Thomson et al, 2001; BMA, 2003), there is a need for greater integration of the two. According to Giltin (2007, p 106), 'the inextricable links between housing with healthcare delivery, supportive services, and policy decisions persist and continue to serve as a barrier to enabling older people to age in place now and into the future'. The relevance of this is further supported by the knowledge that place takes on greater significance – physically and psychologically – as one ages, particularly for the oldest-old and/or when health becomes an issue (Lawton, 1990; Rowles, 1990, 1993). Within a research and policy agenda focused around 'staying put', there needs to be greater consideration of the role that public health can play in supporting ageing in place, particularly in light of growing concerns over long-term care costs in many countries (OECD, 2005; Wanless, 2006). If health and care is increasingly going to be delivered within the places where individuals reside, it is reasonable to suggest that the home and environment must be of a certain standard and quality to support the delivery of care.

Further evidence supporting care in the home comes from examining the well-being of people living in the community compared with people living in institutions. Research finds that those living in their homes have more intimate relationships, more positive self-identity and lower rates of depression (Antonelli et al, 2000; Findlay and McLaughlin, 2005). Given these findings and the wider literature around the optimality of ageing in place, integrating healthcare delivery and the home environment might enable a greater number to age in place if this is what they choose.

Some suggest that health and social care needs to be involved in the design of built environments; if care – both formal and informal – is going to be delivered in the home, the home needs to be built to support the delivery of care and foster health and well-being (Gitlin, 2005, 2007). According to Gitlin (2007), close to 80% (US figure) of people with dementia are living at home either alone or with a family member. Given this, there needs to be a closer look at the home environment and how the delivery of care can be improved to support the individual, their carer(s) and healthcare professionals. If the home and neighbourhood is increasingly going to be the place in which care is delivered, society needs to think about how the home can be used as a therapeutic environment that fosters well-being (Wiles, 2005).

The use of assistive technologies (for example, telehealth and telecare) in the home is likely to continue to grow. Although concerns have been raised that these technologies should not be sold as a fix to service delivery and face-to-face contact (Wey 2007), they might usefully be seen as an added tool for achieving better provision and support for those people who would otherwise be unable to live independently within their home. How assistive technologies change the delivery of care, and the interface between the person and their environment, has received little empirical attention. This is possibly because assistive technologies have yet to receive significant state or public investment and be mainstreamed within health and social care provision.

In the UK there have been a number of recent programmes and initiatives which focus on health, care and housing. These are briefly discussed below:

- The Partnership for Older People Programme (POPP, 2006 to 2008) aims to shift older individuals away from institutional and emergency hospital-based admissions towards targeted earlier intervention and prevention within people's homes and communities. The pilots provided services, such as falls prevention, assistive technologies and assistance at home upon discharge from hospital, which enable people to live independently for as long as possible. The programme has demonstrated cost savings for the state, and quality of life benefits for older people (DH, 2008). This programme has since been mainstreamed in many of the pilot areas.

- There has been growing interest in the concept of 'virtual wards' (Lewis, 2006). This is currently being tested in parts of the UK, with growing international interest. Patients are admitted to virtual wards based on their 'risk' of unplanned hospital admissions; this is calculated using predictive modelling tools. Patients admitted to virtual wards remain at home but are monitored by a specialist multidisciplinary health team (for example, physiotherapists, pharmacists, social workers, mental health professionals, nurses). The specialist team holds daily teleconferences, with those with acute needs discussed every day, and those with less severe needs monitored weekly or monthly. This allows those who would otherwise be in hospital to remain at home and serves to prevent further admission to hospital or a care home.
- The Whole Systems Demonstrator (WSD) pilots aim to support individuals with long-term and complex health and social care needs to live independently at home. The demonstrator pilots use advanced assistive technologies to monitor people's conditions; biometric readings (for example, of blood pressure, oxygen, weight) are sent to a clinician to be reviewed. Readings that raise concerns (for example, high blood pressure or drop in weight) are prioritised by the health teams and patients are visited at home. This programme aims to roll out 7,000 telehealth and telecare installations in individuals' homes. The findings from these pilots are due to report in 2011 and will be the largest randomised controlled trial of telehealth and telecare in the UK (see DH, 2008).

While these initiatives are going in the right direction in terms of supporting older people to age in place, the delivery of these programmes and wider health and social care services might benefit from an environment more attuned to supporting health and well-being.

Greater attention to factors important in the built environment

As discussed earlier, there is a growing awareness and consciousness around the importance of supportive, 'age-friendly' environments. However, there are still gains to be made in thinking about and taking forward plans that aim to build environments that meet the needs and aspirations of an ageing population. There needs to be greater attention afforded to factors that foster the relationship between *individual well-being* and what makes an *enabling environment*. This subsection discusses shortfalls in current thinking regarding built environments, specifically: respecting the need to view the person and the environment as interrelated; the need to consider the power of social relationships; and the need to build for all.

Integration of the person and the environment

Policy and practice needs to move beyond the siloed thinking of a 'people' or 'place' duality, and more towards the construction of 'person–environmental fit'. One of the key findings from this research was the need to respect the complexity and multidirectionality of the individual's relationship with their environment. If we neglect this, we will have limited scope for understanding. Taylor's (2008, p 1) examination of effective strategies for regeneration found that 'Debates about whether to focus on place or people interventions impose a false divide. The social equity principles of sustainable development require effective, interlinked approaches across social, environmental and economic domains'. This duality in thinking neglects the understanding of the interaction and interface of people and place and how this works to impact on outcomes (for example, regeneration, place attachment). Understanding the person–environment interaction is critical for building sustainable communities. For Manzo and Perkins (2006, p 347), such interlinking is highly relevant when considering that:

> place attachments, place identity, sense of community and social capital are all critical parts of person–environmental transactions that foster the development of community in all of its physical, social, political, and economic aspects. In particular, affective bonds to places can help inspire action because people are motivated to seek, stay in, protect, and improve places that are meaningful to them.

Communities that work better are those where emotional ties to place are evident. A criticism from Manzo and Perkins (2006) is that place attachment does not play a part in community planning and development.

Building social insideness

There is a growing cross-disciplinary body of empirical evidence supporting the importance of social relationships (Rowles, 1980, 1984, 1990; Halpern, 2004; Helliwell and Putman, 2004; Wahl and Lang, 2006; Leadbeater, 2008). Social relationships have been found to be linked to reports of physical and psychological well-being, attachment and belonging to place, and community action. As previously discussed in Chapter Two, Rowles' (1983a) concept of 'social insideness' highlights the need for older people to be able to 'integrate with the social fabric of the community' and as a consequence foster place attachment and well-being. Evidence suggests that social relationships and networks can act as a buffer or protective factor for negative neighbourhood and individual characteristics (for example, depression, poverty) (Cattell and Evans, 1999; Taylor, 2001; Innes and Jones, 2006). Even in neighbourhoods that present multiple risks to residents, social connection to place (for example, trust of neighbours) can be a positive factor mitigating against other environmental risks.

Social relationships have also been found to be important in tackling neighbourhood issues. Innes and Jones (2006) analysed how crime, disorder, fear of crime and social control impacted on residents' perception of neighbourhood security and therefore brought about neighbourhood change. They found that managing 'insecurities' depended on levels of collective efficiency in the area – the degree to which people come together around a shared goal. Formal and informal relationships played a significant role in the ability of residents to turn around their neighbourhoods. In addition, there is increasing support for the importance of relationships in driving improvements in outcomes related to public service reform (Leadbeater, 2008) and achieving better health outcomes (Gwande, 2008).

Given these findings, there needs to be greater consideration of how we build and support 'the social' into housing and neighbourhood design. This speaks to a broader issue of supporting and fostering interdependence and intergenerational capacity in communities. As argued by Giddens (2007), community is at the heart of driving life chances.

Building for all

Although the physical environment has received comparatively more attention and debate than aspects of the 'social', there is still considerable work to be done. According to Philips et al (2005), there is evidence to support the 'designing out' of risk factors – such as uneven or slippery floors, poor lighting, lack of handrails – that might lower the incidence of falls; using US figures, between one third and a half of all falls in older people in the community are due to environmental factors (Philips et al, 2005). Increasingly, design features would benefit from a greater understanding of how people with dementia orientate and navigate their space and how we build dementia-friendly cities (see Well-being in Sustainable Environments Research Unit [WISE], www.brookes.ac.uk/schools/be/oisd/sue/wise/). This will become increasingly important as the population ages.

There is a critical need to move more aggressively towards 'designing out risk' and building supportive environments for all. Oswald et al (2007) found that older people living in more accessible housing, and who perceived their house to be meaningful and useful, were more independent and reported a better sense of well-being. The principles presented in the *Lifetime homes, lifetime neighbourhoods* report (see CLG, 2008) speak to the importance of accessibility and barrier-free factors. By 2013, the UK government wants all new housing to be built to lifetime homes standards; should this not happen, regulation will be brought in to ensure that these standards are met.

However, for the most part, 'age-friendly' environments have not been driven by regulation and legislation in most Western countries, but by an awareness of older people as consumers who are able to buy services and environments that support their ageing (Phillips et al, 2005). This excludes the participation of those unable to afford such choices. In reality, these are likely to represent some of the most vulnerable older people in society, who are possibly most in need of enabling and supportive environments to age well but are living in neighbourhoods that present multiple risks. According to O'Bryant (1983, p 29), 'Every person's environment should allow a life-style that satisfies his developmental stages and individual needs, regardless of the age of the individual'. This should not be a condition of adequate financial resources, allowing some to *elect* their lifestyle and others to be *excluded* (Phillipson, 2007).

In terms of policy and practice, academics and policy makers need to become better at supporting and implementing factors in the built environment that can drive better outcomes (for example, quality of life, falls prevention) for older people within their homes and neighbourhoods. As discussed earlier, this suggests the need for greater sensitivity to the integration and construction of the person–environment relationship, the power of social relationships in fostering community well-being and support, and building neighbourhoods for all.

Diversity in housing or segregation

There is also a need to review and evaluate policies and practices that support housing diversity. Although ideas of diversity – having options and choice – are generally valued, in this subsection the author takes a critical look at policy and practice and what they might reveal about cultural attitudes to ageing.

Some of the criticism waged against current housing policy is articulated by Laws (1993), who took a critical look at how US urban policy has constructed age relationships. She argues that urban planning has shaped built environments that have worked to hinder intergenerational relationships, such that policy can be found to be 'implicated in the production and reproduction of ageist relations' (1993, p 673). She argues that there is a feeling that we have moved from a spatial arrangement in which young and old lived and coexisted as members of the same household (for example, a model that dominated in pre-industrial, agrarian communities) to large-scale residential segregation 'in which younger and older people choose to be freed from what they see as incompatible lifestyles of others' (1993, p 688). Housing diversity is therefore creating geographical divisions, which is not compatible with mixed-generational tenure living. Laws feels that 'Intergenerational conflicts have taken on a new territorial dimension: the choice by the healthy and wealthy aged to segregate themselves spatially is very different than the turn-of-century separation of the "dependent" elderly' (1993, p 685). Although the UK and many other European countries are still dominated by intergenerational communities, the rise in age-segregated housing options speaks to some of the concerns and issues raised in Laws' paper.

Housing that seeks to create segregation (for example retirement villages) raises significant policy and practice implications. Built environments that are not designed to support ageing and older people might suggest societal acceptance that segregation is acceptable. From a critical gerontological perspective, this should raise concerns regarding the value society places on older people and their ability to retain continued participation within residential neighbourhoods. Viewed from this critical perspective, housing diversity is contrary to many Western governments' policy agendas around the need to tackle social exclusion, create community cohesion and build sustainable neighbourhoods.

To address this, Holstein and Minkler (2007, p 26) suggest that we need to build sustainable spaces and neighbourhoods not by responding to defined age cohorts but rather by encompassing intergenerational and lifecourse perspectives; such that 'we do not separate the sick from the well, the very old from the less old'. Given that there is some evidence to support the benefits associated with intergenerational relationships and neighbourhoods (Power et al, 2007), policy might benefit from consideration of intergenerational issues and how family policies can influence neighbourhood development and regeneration.

In summary, this section has sought to diagnose some of the shortfalls evident in the support of older people's relationship to their environment. It has highlighted the need for greater attention to the built environment and factors that support sociospatial sustainability and outcomes. There is a strong argument to be made for the integration of healthcare delivery with housing design, such that healthcare professionals, architects, city planners and policy makers would benefit from joint dialogue and the sharing of knowledge. Lifetime homes and lifetime neighbourhoods would help to address the criticism regarding housing diversity and segregation, and move towards a more inclusive society. The steps needed to achieve resolution of the above themes are discussed next.

Next steps – planning the way forward

This section aims to refocus, rethink and redirect the focus of research, policy and practice so that they are able to nationally and internationally meet the needs and aspirations of an ageing populace. It suggests that this can be achieved through attention to the following:

- driving forward evidence-based policy and practice;
- consideration of minimum standards;
- expanding notions of ageing;
- recognising the limits of ageing in place;
- investing in older people;
- sharing research and policy knowledge.

The contribution of each to directing thinking and action is discussed and illustrated below. The key aim is to be challenging and reflective and to spark debate.

Driving forward evidence-based policy and practice

The research and vision generated from environmental gerontology and other related disciplines have an important contribution to make within this policy agenda. However, there are still significant gains to be made in translating empirical findings to policy and practice solutions. Within environmental gerontology and the wider literature there is a breadth of knowledge and understanding of what underpins and sustains people's relationship with their environment and conversely how the environment supports this. However, academics/researchers need to be better at engaging with policy makers and city planners/architects to ensure that policy and practice are appropriate and driven by robust empirical evidence.

According to Lawton (1986, p 15), the goal of environmental gerontological research is to see a society better able to meet the needs of its ageing population:

> The vulnerability of this age group makes more compelling the search for ways of elevating behavior and experienced quality of life through environmental means. By this line of reasoning, if we could design housing with fewer barriers, neighbourhoods with more enriching resources, or institutions with higher stimulating qualities, we could improve the level of functioning of many older people more than proportionately.

This has social and economic consequences for society and governments. Ageing in place, and to some extent potentially place in ageing, implies an enabling environment, such that the 'staying put' philosophy of current social policy (Haldemann and Wister, 1993) needs to be guided by empirical and theoretical research. According to Scheidt and Windley (2006, p 105), the 'hope is that this understanding may aid in the development of preventative and ameliorative interventions targeting both individual and environmental factors to affect a better "fit" between the individuals and their environments, thus enhancing their quality of life'. As Phillips et al (2005, p 147) suggest, 'an urban environment that is friendly for older people is also likely to be suitable for other age groups too'.

However, the vision and policy drive towards an 'age-friendly' environment is not supported by any robust evidence base of its effectiveness (Bartlett and Peel, 2005). Thus, there is an urgent need for policy makers, planners, architects and academics to work together to address this gap and drive change so that we are better able to develop neighbourhoods that build on and enhance well-being and a sense of community.

Consideration of minimum standards

Within the UK, there has been a drive to improve key aspects of public services by setting minimum standards, for example, on education and the health service (for example, the 2001 National Service Framework), and more recently for new housing (for example, lifetime homes standards). This raises the possibility of the need to consider a minimum standard for neighbourhoods. Given trends previously cited in health (for example, healthy life expectancy, disability-free years), demographic ageing and a rise in urbanisation and geographic polarisation, is there a need to set a minimum standard by which neighbourhoods should be built and maintained?

Consideration of a minimum standard is supported by research on neighbourhood effects, and the findings that an area can influence health, well-being, aspirations and life chances (Atkinson and Kintrea, 2001; Marmot and Wilkinson, 2005; Stafford and McCarthy, 2005). There is also a further argument to be made for developing a minimum standard given increasing focus on ageing in place and the delivery of health and social care within people's homes and neighbourhoods. Health and social care spending and outcomes might in part be driven by the quality of environments people find themselves in.

The aim of raising this idea here is to spark discussion and debate about its feasibility, what this might look like and what society would hope to achieve. Minimum standards can work to support some of the ideas already put forward in the lifetime homes standards and lifetime neighbourhood concepts. Depending on how minimum standards are set, this might enable greater citizen participation in intergenerational community living and for some enable ageing in place for a longer period of time.

Expanding notions of ageing

There is a growing need to call for a different lexicon and dialogue that we use to describe ageing and older people. Growth in life expectancy and the numbers of older people should be celebrated as a societal achievement, rather than continuously sold as a challenge or problem. In a report by the UK policy think tank Demos, Huber and Skidmore (2003, p 9) state that 'An ageing society has long been conceived as a burden and a cost, as if the old were some kind of tax on the young' and they criticise a policy agenda that 'has come to resemble little more than a damage limitation exercise in those domains where an ageing society threatens to disrupt or undermine the stability of current arrangements' (2003, p 21); specifically pensions, work and retirement, health and long-term care. The result, they say, has been a public policy debate that has been highly negative and excessively focused on the economic and fiscal burdens of ageing.

Connected to these ideas, Giddens (2007) calls for a rethink on 'ageing society' and the discourse we use to describe older people. He suggests the dropping of the term 'pensioner': 'It suggests that when people reach a certain age they become dependent, unable to live an independent and flourishing life' (2007, p 9). And although political attention has grown with respect to interest in meeting the needs of an ageing society, it is still very much tied to ideas of pensions and health.

There is a need to reframe the perception of older people in policy terms, away from a dialogue of challenges and problems to that of opportunity. The recently published UK *Ageing strategy* (HM Government, 2009) goes some way to challenging negative notions of ageing and older people by espousing the need of society and government to support the opportunities and aspirations of an ageing population. The strategy aims to move towards a more age-friendly Britain or a Britain that is suitable for all ages by tackling age discrimination, and helping individuals to prepare for and make the most out of later life. The discourse in this strategy goes some way to tackling negative social, cultural and political notions of the problems and challenges of ageing.

Recognising the limits of ageing in place

There needs to be a better awareness of the potential hazards associated with the blanket notion that ageing in place is somehow always optimal. According to Means (2007, p 81), ageing in place should be seen as one option rather than the only option. When an environment fails to meet the expectations and needs of an individual, Peace et al (2006) found that individuals began to engage in *option recognition*. As previously discussed in Chapter Two, individuals were found to proactively preserve and protect a sense of well-being and identity by adapting their environment to maintain a level of mastery or considering their housing options, such as the possibility of relocation to a more suitable location.

Understanding the 'un-optimality' of ageing in place is equally relevant given the deleterious effects this might have on ageing. Older people need to be supported to make the best possible decision to suit their situation and maximise their fit or relationship with their environment. Given this, planning for housing suitability might warrant the same level of consideration as planning for one's financial retirement.

Investing in older people

There needs to be a change in thinking about how we view the funding or costs associated with ageing and older people. Typically, policy and practice discussions are seldom couched in terms of *investing* in older people. Investment in early years is seen as important for downstream cost savings and achieving better life chances for children and young people (PMSU, 2006). However, according to Allen (2008, p 23), 'as old age becomes increasingly long as people live for longer, there is evidence that investment in early old age will pay off in older old age. Moreover, there are compelling ethical, moral and social justice reasons for further support and investment in older age'. In recent years there has been some strong cost–benefit analysis in favour of investing in prevention programmes for older people (DH, 2008).

Sharing research and policy knowledge

The lessons and thinking drawn from Western nations on building and developing sustainable communities for all might benefit from being disseminated to developing nations as they work to build their infrastructure. According to the UNFPA (2007) report *Unleashing the potential of urban growth*, developing countries will see an unprecedented rise of an urbanised populace; Africa and Asia are set to see a doubling of their urban population between 2000 and 2030. The report calls for action, such that a pre-emptive approach is needed in developing urban areas if they are to solve the social (poverty reduction) and environmental (sustainability) challenges. In addition, much of the future growth in developing urban areas will be among poor urbanites and a growing older population. According to the United Nations (UNFPA, 2002), 'As the tempo of ageing in developing countries is more rapid than in developed countries, developing countries will have less time than the developed countries to adapt to the consequences of population ageing'.[3]

There will also be a significant growth in megacities (defined as cities that exceed a population of 10 million) in developing countries: it is estimated that by 2015 there will be 23 of these types of cities, of which the majority will be in developing countries. As a consequence, the United Nations (UN, 2007) calls for steps to be taken now, so that individuals and society can all benefit from urban living. In addition, given the breadth of knowledge gained in ageing research and in particular on environmental ageing across many Western countries, there is a need for greater reciprocal knowledge transfer between all countries (both those developed and developing) as they prepare to meet the needs of an ageing population.

Conclusion

In the last quarter of the 20th century there was a growing policy interest in building sustainable environments. This was concerned with environmental protection as well as growing awareness associated with the quality of the environment and its impact on individual health and well-being. In recent years there has been a growing consciousness and awareness around the ability of cities and neighbourhoods to support the needs of an ageing population. This has led to a discourse and discussion around 'age-friendly' environments and 'lifetime neighbourhoods'. Although great gains have been made in this agenda, there is still considerable work to be done to deliver the vision of 'age-friendly/lifetime neighbourhoods'.

This chapter has highlighted a number of shortfalls in thinking and knowledge related to the implementation of this agenda, specifically, the need to integrate healthcare and housing, pay greater attention to the built environment and design factors that foster ageing well, and critically analyse housing diversity options which work to segregate older people. The chapter has also discussed next steps in the way forward, such as the need to better link environmental gerontological research with those who make policy, and to ensure that empirical and policy knowledge is disseminated to developing countries that are undergoing rapid urbanisation and growth in the ageing of their populations. The chapter has also raised the idea of having a minimum standard for neighbourhoods, the need for a rethinking and different discourse around ageing and older people, and the need to invest in ageing.

Note

[1] http://ec.europa.eu/sustainable/welcome/index_en.htm

[2] www.communities.gov.uk/publications/localgovernment/sustainablecommunitiesact

[3] www.un.org/esa/socdev/ageing/popageing.html

EIGHT

Influences, opportunities and challenges

Introduction

This chapter considers current influences on and possible future opportunities and challenges to the person–environment relationship. The aim of the chapter is to highlight some of the externalities acting on the person–environment relationship and factors that might play a role in refocusing the way in which we have come to understand place and ageing. This will explore *current* influences and how these might impact on interpretations and perceptions of place and ageing. In addition, it will address *future* factors that might work to challenge individuals' emotive and physical attachment to place or equally present new opportunities to advance their relationship with place. These opportunities and challenges are likely to have an impact on the process and experience of ageing.

Influences, opportunities and challenges in current and future place and ageing relationship

Arising from a review of existing research, there are a number of current and future challenges to 'place and ageing' research that warrant further discussion. To recap and as previously stated in Chapter Two, place and ageing comprise two concepts – *ageing in place* and *place in ageing*. Ageing in place is concerned with understanding the process of ageing in a familiar environment, and place in ageing is interested in the meaning of place in the process of ageing; each interact to influence the other.

The discussion of *current* influences is meant to highlight some of the intervening factors present in our current understanding and analysis of the relationship between place and ageing. Here we consider the influence of:

- romanticising place;
- age, generational and period effects.

Future influences, opportunities and challenges are intended to provide further insight into and debate on how these might effect change or possibly refocus the person–environment relationship in the years to come. Here we consider the impact of:

- globalisation;
- technology and communication;
- the economic downturn.

Current influences

Current influences examine the possible role of four intervening factors in our current interpretation and understanding of the relationship between the individual and their environment. We need to consider that such factors might be underpinning the person–environment interaction and that only through longitudinal research will we come to better understand the role that they play.

Romanticising place

The ideas raised by Rowles' (1978, 1980, 1983a, 1983b, 1990) research, that people's identities are *intertwined*, *preserved* and *reinforced* by the place in which they live has been criticised for romanticising place attachment. Even Rowles (1993, p 68) cautions that not 'all older people are attached to a single place or set of places in the way described.... There is a danger of romanticism – of exaggerating the role of familiarity and emotional affiliation with place'. Attachment to place is not necessarily a collective phenomenon; this was supported by Hummon (1986, 1992) who found some people to be emotionally ambivalent or lacking place awareness. It is also important to recognise that place attachment has its limits; as previously discussed, emotive sentiment to place can also work to disrupt and undermine well-being (Fried, 2000; see also the case study of Harold Waters in Chapter Five).

This suggests a need to examine more broadly how place attachment is considered within the literature and that there might be layers to attachment that have yet to be considered, rather than a dichotomous position of attached or not attached. In addition, there is a lack of consideration within the literature of connections that might be made in places that are new and unfamiliar.

Age, generational and period effects

There is still a lack of clarity given to the influence of age, generational and period effects on the person–environment relationship. Rowles (1983a, 1983b) found that differences observed in attachment of young-old and old-old groups might be a feature of generational or cohort differences that have resulted in different expressions of attachment to place. For example, historical events (for example, the First World War or the Depression) and changes in mobility patterns have potentially altered the expression of place attachment among differing cohorts of older people. Also, it is still unclear to what extent years of residence in a single location is more or less relevant to the formation of place attachment than the need for people to maintain independence and a sense of a continued self in the face of declines in health; such that, does age or the ageing process influence the degree or intensification of feelings to place? To overcome this, future research might consider a longitudinal approach to viewing older people's lives, 'one in which relationships to people and places are viewed as an ongoing process rather than as a cut in time' (Rivlin, 1987, p 28).

Also to date there has been little research and policy focus on the experience of baby boomers (1946–64). Huber and Skidmore (2003) suggest that despite some commonalities, the baby boomer generation is the most diverse and divided generation up to this point. They suggest that this relates to differing experiences associated with age and formative influences, wealth, longevity, education, gender, ethnicity and politics. There is also evidence to suggest that baby boomers might be more disconnected from their local communities, and hence less attached to place, than earlier generations (Huber and Skidmore, 2003; Walker et al, 2006). However, little empirical research has been done on this (Findlay and McLaughlin, 2005). Yet this could potentially have important implications for policy and practice, such as how this impacts on the process of ageing and how we currently think about and build neighbourhoods that are more inclusive.

There are also period effects that might be important. If we consider period shifts or changes in how we consider ageing and older people, and the interest in environmental sustainability (previously raised in Chapter Seven) we might begin to see possible influences on the person–environment relationship, such that, according to Laws (1993, p 688), 'The topography of the land of old age is constantly reworked as the meaning of old age is renegotiated'.

Some suggest that the built environment for ageing is undergoing a shift from a modern to a postmodern lifecourse, and increasingly caters to diverse forms of ageing in place (Holdsworth and Laws, 1994). For example, built environments range from those that are age segregated to those that are not segregated: '"Land of old age" will likely be restless and chameleon-like in the decades ahead, and its landscape manifestations more varied and confused' (Holdsworth and Laws, 1994, p 181). As previously raised by Laws (1993) and discussed in Chapter Seven, these increased forms of age-segregated housing might work to create intergenerational conflicts by creating new territorial dimensions. How this will be played out and influence the relationship of people or age cohorts to place will only be known in future research. How changes in the perception of ageing and the focus on environmental sustainability will impact on the person–environment relationship is currently difficult to unpick.

This also raises the issue of age-friendly environments or lifetime neighbourhoods: will the fostering or facilitation of an enabling neighbourhood allow for a better fit between the person and their environment? And how will this impact on or change the experience and process of ageing?

Future influences, opportunities and challenges

Future influences, opportunities and challenges relate to the possible impact that globalisation, technology and communication, and the economic downturn might have on the individual's relationship with their environment. Specifically, how are these likely to change the interaction or the way we view the person–environment relationship and most importantly what will be the impact on the process of ageing.

Globalisation

Globalisation can be seen to provide both new opportunities and risks for older people and later life, some of which have been previously raised in Chapter Three. According to Phillipson (2007), globalisation has enabled the rise of new types of movement in later life through the expansion of places and lifestyles. However, the acceleration of global migration and the spread of mobile communities might have also worked to challenge older people's identity within a new uncertain global community (Phillipson, 2002, 2003). Certainly, globalisation presents a challenge to the way in which older people have typically aged in place. The trend towards increased mobility has also brought into question the very idea of place attachment within contemporary and future societies; according to Relph (1976), mobility creates placelessness. Similarly, McHugh and Mings (1996) found that retirement migration might create 'footloose' attachments to place.

Other research has suggested an expansion in place attachment (Hummon, 1986; Gustafson, 2001). Hummon (1986) reported that geographical mobility might create divided or multiple place attachments and identities. Supporting Hummon's (1986) claim, Gustafson's (2001) study of Swedish retirees to Spain found people to have developed multiple place attachments. With the trend of increased retirement migration, both in North America (Longino, 1990; McPherson, 1998) and Europe (Warnes et al, 2004), this might present a significant area of research and greater understanding of placelessness and/or multiple place attachments. This supports the idea initially raised under romanticising place, which suggests the need to broaden our understanding of place attachment away from notions that individuals can only be sentimentally connected to one single location and that the relationship is dichotomous (for example, attached or not). There is a need to better understand the complexity and layers of attachment, particularly as globalisation might work to test the way in which we have come to traditionally view place attachment.

Although globalisation might bring opportunities for multiple sentimental attachments, physical attachments or insideness might be challenged. According to Gitlin (2003, pp 629-30), 'staying in place, particularly in one's life-long residence, may be an essential optimization strategy for successful adaptation'. With increased mobility, future generations of older people might experience difficulties with masking functional health declines. This might make the design of built environments (for example, lifetime neighbourhoods and homes) even more relevant for the future of ageing well.

Phillipson (2006, p 45) also makes the point that:

> Increasingly, national sovereignty is influenced, to a greater or lesser degree, by transnational organisations and communities of different kinds. Older people themselves experience a range of global, national, regional, and local forces that influence the construction of later life.

Such factors could be argued to present both new opportunities in the construction of a 'better' relationship between the individual and their community and a risk of disruption and uncertainty.

It has also been suggested that globalisation has created similar places. The following comment from Relph (1976, p 5), although made over 30 years ago, is still relevant today: 'global culture is moving toward a situation where every place can be anyplace in an essentially placeless world ... today we may visit what is in many respects the same place, the same McDonald's in New York, Pittsburgh, Peoria, or even Moscow'. Although the idea of creating 'like places' is criticised as 'placelessness', this might equally work to create transference of sentimental attachment, if a place is seen as being familiar and evokes positive associations.

Technology and communication

The expression of place attachment and the way in which we age is changing with advances in technology and communication (Rowles, 1993; Becker, 2003). It has been suggested that technology has created an increase in what has been termed 'non-places' (Auge, 1995). According to Novak (1997, p 269), technology has altered place, such that 'a new, nonlocal urbanism is in the making'.

Technology has also contributed to changing the way in which people interact socially. For example, shopping online compared with going to a local neighbourhood store is likely to reduce individuals' physical contacts with local residents. As previously discussed in Chapter Two, access to local services and amenities is important in the facilitation of place attachment (Rivlin, 1987). As suggested by Rivlin (1987, p 14), when an 'area becomes the context for servicing the major domains of life, that area will assume a particular importance to residents, in contrast to instances where people go all over a city'. Thus, shopping online might contribute to changes in the nature of local economies and the stock of social and community capital through this alteration in transactions.

However, this might be compensated for by a growth in virtual contact. Stokols (1999) suggests that exposure to the internet has the ability to create connection(s) to remote peoples and places. For older people, advances in new technologies, such as the internet, might provide a way to sustain social ties by facilitating the maintenance of connections with the outside world. Rowles (2008) suggests that technology is changing the way we age along with our relationship with places.

Web-based social networking sites (for example, Facebook) and virtual worlds enable the construction of virtual social and built places; environments in which individuals can self-design and control their space enable them to have mastery over their world. In addition, technology is likely to have a profound impact on social relationships. Clark (2000) and Giddens (2007) also make a similar point about the impact of telecommunications on the transformation of social relationships and networks. The social has lost the connection with a specific place, and people, location and lifestyles are transported or transportable.

The internet and the availability of global communications have also altered proximal and distal features of the environment: a 'much broader array of remote places and events can now be brought squarely into the individual's consciousness ... seemingly [creating] unlimited opportunities to experience those places' (Stokols, 1999, p 342), such that technology might be a mechanism by which people can sustain ties and place attachment. This is supported by a case study by Peace et al (2006) in which an older Indian man living in Britain most of his adult life was able to live in 'limbo' between his country of birth and his country of residence by watching Asian television: "I've got two Indian channels on my television which are directly from India so I get the news and entertainment and everything – what they get, I get ... it's like being in India when you are watching that" (2006, p 147).

Technology might also change the way in which people physically interact and manage their environment in the future. Better use of assistive technologies, such as telecare and telehealth, will aid in people's ability to remain independent within their home and communities. This might work to create differing types of lived experience and connections to place, and might promote a deeper sense of attachment as more people are able to stay put. These technologies will increasingly position healthcare within a home context, and change the relationship individuals might have with their environment in sickness and health, in addition to changing the experience and process of ageing.

Economic downturn

Although still early days, there has been much speculation as to how the recent global economic downturn will shape and impact on society. With fears of a deepening recession there is a need to discuss what this might mean for governments' response to and ability to prepare for an increasingly ageing population, specifically what risks and/or opportunities this might bring to older people and ageing and their relationship with the environment.

What risks might this bring?

To date there has been comparatively little debate and discussion on the impact of the economic downturn on older people (see the Institute for Public Policy Research's 2009 programme on Tomorrow's Capitalism). Most of the current focus seeks to understand and mitigate against unemployment and impacts on already vulnerable groups (for example, families with children in poverty). The current neglect and absence of older people from this discussion might work to increase the risk and vulnerability of this group by resources and interest being targeted elsewhere to those individuals/groups deemed more in need.

A recession could see a slowdown in the preparation and planning for an ageing society, most specifically in relation to innovation in housing and neighbourhood design and investment in public services. In the UK this might present specific challenges to the lifetime neighbourhoods agenda; there is a risk that the gains made in moving to mainstream this within planning and development will be lost, and that housing and neighbourhood development will move back to building for numbers and targets, rather than long-term planning for individual and community well-being (Harding, 2009). This could further drive geographical inequalities and hence influence the process of ageing. There is a risk that greater disparity will be created between those able to afford a supportive environment in which to age, and those struggling to manage the daily risks within their neighbourhood.

There is also a concern that public services will come under increasing pressure and be cut. This might result in a continued policy and service focus on acute and crisis interventions, rather than a move to an agenda around prevention and investing in older people (Allen, 2008). According to Harding (2009, p 7): 'This spending squeeze will undoubtedly become a "double whammy" when coupled with a likely increased demand for services caused by economic deprivation'.

The downturn possibly presents most challenges for those countries with new or emerging economies; it is important to remember that such nations also have advanced ageing profiles. Thus, sharing knowledge and lessons learnt – between and among policy makers, academics, health and social care professionals, architects and planners – will be of critical importance now and in the immediate future.

What opportunities might this bring?

The economic downturn might also present nations with opportunities to address longer-term challenges. In a recent discussion paper by Leadbeater and Meadway (2008), they suggest that a way of attacking the recession is by making gains and investing in sectors that will help meet some of the longer-term challenges: green energy, environmental services, biotechnology and *services for an ageing society*. In regard to services for an ageing society, they propose that the recession could be a vehicle by which better efficiency and innovation in public services are driven forward. One way of achieving this might be through more integrated strategies and joint working (for example, housing and healthcare delivery) (Harding, 2009). In addition, concerns raised previously around the delivery of the lifetime neighbourhoods agenda might benefit from aligning with the green agenda as both are underpinned by the need to create sustainable environments. This would ensure that societies and governments are at least in part interested and prepared to support the health and well-being of older people.

The recession and efforts to combat the economic downturn might also result in a change in attitude around ageing and older people; as governments and the public/private sectors look for new ways to stimulate movement, this might precipitate the development and promotion of new economic and social opportunities to engage with an ageing society, 'For example, to provide new forms of work and participation, new kinds of social and leisure activities, new kinds of social housing and shared transport' (Leadbeater and Meadway, 2008, p 18). However, this raises some concern that such opportunities might not be equally distributed, with those lacking the resources unable to adapt to new forms of opportunities. It is too soon to say how the restructuring of society around new forms of opportunity will interplay and influence the relationship between people and their neighbourhoods and the wider environment, and subsequently how this will impact on ageing. The risks or challenges and opportunities presented here were only meant as a way of provoking further discussion and debate. However, rather than wait to see the effects and impacts of the economic downturn on older people and societies' preparedness for an ageing population, academics, practitioners and policy makers have a role to play in shaping the opportunities and mitigating the risks.

Conclusion

This chapter briefly discussed some of the influences on, opportunities for and challenges to the person–environment relationship. It considered some of the possible intervening factors acting on our current understanding of place and ageing, such as the danger of over-romanticising place, and the effects of age, generational and period influences. It suggested that place attachment might not be a universal or collective phenomenon and that people might be capable of multiple attachments or ambivalence. The view that people are attached to a single location and that they are either attached or not attached might be inappropriate and might lead to misinterpretation as to how we analyse individuals' connection with place.

The impact of age, generational and period effects is still difficult to differentiate in the absence of longitudinal data. For example, what is having the greatest influence on the person–environment relationship: an individual's years of residence in a single location or the need to maintain independence and well-being when health declines threaten the individual's relationship to place and space? In addition, what will be the influence of the baby boomer population and how will 'shifts from modern to postmodern lifecourse' shape our understanding of the person–environment relationship?

The impact of globalisation, technology and communication are likely to have a growing influence on older people's relationship with place. Globalisation appears to bring opportunities for those who have the resources to adapt to new lifestyles but presents risks as far as acceleration in global migration and increasingly mobile communities are concerned. Technology presents both challenges and opportunities to connect to people and places. While shopping online might restrict the opportunities individuals have for physical contact with people, it can also work to expand social relationships through networking sites. Also, advances in technology, specifically assistive technologies, might help to support individuals who would otherwise be unable to manage to have greater control over their environment. This is likely to influence people's experience of their environment and the process by which they age.

The economic downturn, although in its early days, presents both risks and opportunities for nations preparing for an ageing population. Areas most at risk of slowdown or cuts are innovation in housing and neighbourhood development, and public services. This might present considerable risks for the older person's relationship with their environment. Policy makers, practitioners and academics have a critical role to play in turning these risks into opportunities in order to advance nations' preparedness for an ageing society.

The influences, challenges and opportunities presented here support a refocusing of and rethinking about the person–environment relationship. What appears to be evident is that the relationship between place and the ageing person will continue to be dynamic and complex, evolving at the individual, societal and now global level across time and space. Understanding this will be critical to building social and physical environments that are appropriate and responsive to the needs of older people and support ageing.

NINE

Conclusion

The goal of this book was to progress our understanding of the older person's relationship with their neighbourhood and see a society – government – that is better able to meet the needs and support the aspirations of an ageing population. Given that ageing is malleable and that environment can have an enabling or disabling impact, there is a need to ensure that the agenda around ageing in place considers the importance of supportive environments in which we commit people to ageing.

This last chapter summarises the main points raised in the book under each of the key overarching parts – *revisiting*, *rethinking* and *refocusing* the person–environment relationship. The chapter will bring together the key findings and points of learning from the book. It will argue that given new empirical findings there is a need to rethink and refocus the person–environment fit to better support ageing now and in the future.

Revisiting the person–environment fit

Part One aimed to take stock of the empirical data and knowledge gained within environmental gerontology over the last 40 years. Lawton's Ecological Model of Ageing (1980, 1982, 1986, 1990), often referred to as a 'pivotal' (Golant, 2003) or 'landmark' (Wahl and Weisman, 2003) theory, was examined as to the contribution of this model to our understanding of the individual's relationship with their environment. Key concepts and hypotheses evolved: *personal competence* and *environmental press* revealed the factors that interact in the person–environment relationship and the two hypotheses – *environmental docility hypothesis* and *environmental proactivity hypothesis* – explain the direction of the relationship. Lawton (1982, p 43) envisaged the framework to function in the following way:

> Behavior is a function of the competence of the individual and the environmental press of the situation ... a behavior (or affective response) is seen as the result of a combination of a press of a given magnitude acting on, or perceived by, or utilized by, an individual of a given level of competence.

The literature around ageing in place and place in ageing was also revisited as to its contribution to our understanding of older people and their environment. The literature overwhelmingly supports the idea of older people ageing in place. The reasons stated for this are financial benefits and familiarity. From the perspective of the state and the older individual, ageing in place appears economically viable.

In addition, place is believed to become a physical necessity for some older people as they age. Ageing in place was found to be important in the successful adaptation to increased spatial restriction. Rowles (1978) suggests that as older people's physical orientation with neighbourhood changes there is an expansion in the role of fantasy in which people reflect on past selves and places. In this situation, place can take on a greater intensification of feelings. However, this can only really happen when the person ages in place.

Connected to ageing in place is the idea that place is also important in the process of ageing – place in ageing. Place is believed to hold emotive and sentimental connections. This has been found to be particularly true for older people for the following reasons: place attachment is believed to be gained through the lifecourse and is important in the maintenance of self-identity and in the process of life review. The literature has found a number of factors to affect place in ageing. Of particular relevance for the present research is location (Fried, 2000; Corcoran, 2002; Parkes et al, 2002; Airey, 2003; Helliwell and Putnam, 2004; Burholt and Naylor, 2005). Research on rural environments suggests that characteristics present in these settings support place attachment (Rowles, 1980, 1990), whereas urban areas present challenges to attachment. However, research in this area is equivocal. Some research suggests that disadvantaged inner-city areas support place attachment because marginalisation and lack of opportunities work to unite residents and create a sense of belonging (Fried, 2000; Taylor, 2001). Yet other research finds that people living in deprived areas have less place attachment because of characteristics present in these areas, for example, high crime, high turnover in population and poor health (Corcoran, 2002; Stafford et al, 2003; Brown et al, 2004). There is also evidence to support the existence of both, referring back to Corcoran's (2002) research, where some research participants expressed 'placelessness' and a desire to move, while others were found to be defiant and resistant to marginalisation.

In summary, the literature associated with ageing in place and place in ageing suggests that ageing is made easier if individuals remain in place; the reasons for this are related to physical and psychological factors:

- 'Physical insideness' or intimate physical knowledge is argued to facilitate management of increasing functional health decline. This allows independence, a stable level of environmental control or mastery, psychological well-being by continuity in perceived self and knowing what to expect.
- Coping with 'spatial restriction' was found to be made easier if one remained in place. Having intimate physical knowledge of the environment enables people to gain control of their physical and/or psychological 'deficits', and by doing this influence their environmental use, perception, attachment and psychological well-being (Francis, 1989).
- Place attachment is considered an emotive bond between the person and the environment (both physical and psychological). Place attachment can be

positive or negative, and not being attached to place does not always denote maladaptive behaviour.
- Place and ageing were found to be important for a number of reasons. Reification of identity, lifecourse or life review, and quality of life might only be achieved when the individual ages in place. For older people this might be particularly significant. For those who have remained in place for a significant length of time, place provides a backdrop from which to reify past selves and enable life review.
- Place attachment has been found to be influenced by a number of factors, including length of residency, social integration, environmental barriers and geographical locality. Such characteristics have been found to be particularly challenged in deprived inner-city areas, raising the prospect that living in these areas might challenge place attachment.

Despite significant gains in knowledge over the past 40 years in relation to our understanding of the person–environment relationship, there remain a number of shortfalls. These relate to contextual and temporal limitations. Parmelee (1998), in a critique of American environmental ageing, suggests that better understanding would benefit from an 'internationalisation' and testing of the generalisability of the findings. Although there has been some recent work to correct this (see, for example, Peace et al, 2006, for a UK context), there still remains a dearth of understanding around cross-cultural and national issues and the testing of place and ageing in challenging environmental settings. In particular, is environmental context important? Do the multiple risks present in deprived inner-city neighbourhoods challenge the literature and hence notions of the optimality of ageing in place? And what does this mean for the agenda around ageing in place and building sustainable age-friendly neighbourhoods.

Understanding and being able to answer these questions is important given the rise in population ageing and urbanisation. For the first time in history, more people are living in urban centres than ever before (UNFPA, 2007). We also know that urban areas present extremes such as congestion, crime, social polarisation, access to public transport, world-class medical centres, museums and theatres (Rodwin et al, 2006). Such factors can work to hinder as well as support ageing well. However, the growth in geographical polarisation coupled with population ageing, and an agenda around ageing in place, should raise concern among academics and policy makers around the appropriateness of some neighbourhoods to support this – such as some deprived and marginalised neighbourhoods.

Rethinking the person–environment fit

Part Two sought to test the generalisability of the findings and redress the shortfalls in knowledge. The study sought to investigate issues related to ageing in place and place in ageing in deprived urban neighbourhoods. Of particular interest was what is important in place and ageing. Areas selected for research in England

and Canada were those characterised as among the most deprived within their respective countries.

Descriptive profiles on each of these neighbourhoods presented the historical changes and present-day characteristics. Historical accounts supported the literature surrounding the downgrading of neighbourhoods (Downs, 1981). Most were at one time affluent or middle-class areas that through time experienced downgrading due to local or international changes in economic activities and social structure. Today these areas are characterised by poor housing, low educational attainment, poor health, high rates of unemployment, poverty, drugs and prostitution. The profiles drew on data from historical references, government reports and statistics, and media images. Missing from these descriptive profiles was the voice of older people. Older people's perceptions of their neighbourhood were captured with the use of participant-led photography and descriptive text. This enabled the construction of area knowledge through the 'eyes' of the older person. The photographs and text revealed older people's use of and connection to place. These findings enabled further contextualisation of the area profiles, and enabled the validation of factors important in place and ageing.

Fifty-two semi-structured interviews revealed older people as belonging to one of three categories – environmental comfort, environmental management or environmental distress. *Environmental comfort* was characterised by people reporting an absence of negative environmental features, an attachment to area and hence no wish to move, and good overall well-being. *Environmental management* was characterised by people reporting a presence of negative environmental features that they had to manage on a daily basis, some attachment issues, or, for some, a desire to move, and either good or neither good nor poor quality of life. *Environmental distress* was characterised by persons reporting difficulty managing daily life, disruptions to place attachment or a lack of formed attachments, in general a strong desire to move, and in general a poor quality of life.

Case studies presented the main focus of in-depth analysis and discussion. The 44 biographies and participant photographs and text were used to provide further validation and support for analysis of the eight case studies. The key empirical findings were:

- *Cross-national versus cross-cultural:* an important finding was the similarity revealed in the experience and expression of place and ageing of older people in deprived neighbourhoods of England and Canada. When evaluated across the environmental categories, factors underlying place and ageing and influences on well-being were comparable in both countries. In addition, similar numbers of participants across the two countries and five neighbourhoods were found across the three environmental categories of comfort, management and distress. What appeared more relevant in the research and, in particular, the relationship an individual had with their environment was cross-cultural factors (for example, spirituality and religiosity; see the case study of Mr Howard Adams Goodleaf in Chapter Five).

- *Factors underpinning the person–environment relationship in deprived urban areas:* the in-depth interviews and photographs revealed some shared underlying experiences of place and ageing – three of which were comparable to those previously found within the literature: specifically, a *physical*, *social* and *historical* connection. In addition, three factors that have received relatively little attention in the literature were found to be relevant: *the lifecourse*, *religiosity and spirituality*, and *public spaces*. The research also highlighted the importance of physical insideness and, in particular, area knowledge in the easing of psychological fear (for example, fear of crime). This extends our understanding of the physical insideness concept to include a psychological dimension.
- *Understanding the interaction between the person and the environment – 'respecting complexity':* the outcome variables of quality of life and identity showed, in general, a predictable direction; specifically, those older people in 'comfort' reported positive well-being and those in 'distress' reported negative well-being. However, findings also revealed that the relationship is not straightforward. Rather, religion/spirituality and lifecourse factors, and possibly access to public spaces (for example, parks), might play a protective role in connection with deleterious neighbourhood change. Such 'complexity' has been accounted for in Figure 6.1.
- *Temporal considerations – past, present and future:* the importance of temporal – past, present and future – dimensions was also highlighted within the research. The findings revealed that data gathering and analysis need to consider the fluidity of the older person's experiences of place. Consideration of the past and the future provides useful insight into and understanding of current place and ageing issues. The research made clear that without consideration of temporal dimensions, significant understanding could be lost and issues surrounding scientific rigour challenged (for example, see the case study of Mrs MacDougall in Chapter Five).

The similarity in findings across the two countries in relation to environmental categorisation and factors underpinning the relationship between the person and the environment (for example, social, physical and historical) suggest that these results might be extrapolated to other countries sharing similar characteristics. This is significant because the rise in the number of older people coupled with increasing urbanisation and geographical popularisation has created a need to better understand the person–environment relationship and meet future demands. Meeting these needs and demands will have to be driven by empirical, theoretical and innovative methodological research that generates greater understanding of the relationship between the ageing person, the process of ageing and their impact on the environment, and the environment's impact on the ageing adult. The present research goes some way towards addressing these issues. It comes at a pivotal time in gerontological research and social policy. Understanding the relationship between place and ageing and how this leads to a desire or rejection of ageing in place and place in ageing has important implications for national housing and neighbourhood policies and fits with current international discourse and concern around environmental sustainability.

Refocusing the person–environment fit

Part Three aimed to refocus the person–environment fit by presenting the next steps. The main objective of this part was to spark wider debate and present a forward look for academic research, policy makers and practitioners. If society is to keep pace with preparing for an increasingly ageing society and supporting agendas around environmental sustainability, critical steps with regard to social inclusion and ageing in place have to be taken now.

Chapter Seven highlighted the growing policy interest in building sustainable neighbourhoods. Emerging from this has been an increasing questioning of the appropriateness of the current environment to maximise individuals' ability to age well. There has been a growing international discourse and consciousness around 'age-friendly' cities (for example, WHO, 2007) or within the UK context 'lifetime neighbourhoods' and what makes a supportive environment in which people are committed to ageing. Chapter Seven argued that while great gains have been made in illustrating the vision of 'age-friendly' cities, little has been done with regard to delivery on the ground.

This led onto a discussion of a number of shortfalls in thinking related to the implementation of this agenda. This highlighted the need to integrate healthcare and housing, to pay greater attention to the built environment and the designing in of factors that foster ageing well, and to critically analyse increases in housing diversity options. The chapter also discussed next steps in the way forward for research, policy and practice, such as the need to better link environmental gerontological research with those who make policy, and to ensure that empirical and policy knowledge is disseminated to developing countries that are undergoing rapid urbanisation and ageing of the population. The chapter also raised the idea of having a minimum standard for neighbourhoods, the need for a rethinking and different discourse around ageing and older people, and called for an investment in ageing.

Part Three also discussed and speculated on some of the *current* and *future* influences on, opportunities for and challenges to the person–environment relationship (Chapter Eight). Some of the current issues related to such factors as romanticising the role of place in ageing, and unpicking some of the possible influences of age, generational or period effects on the interface between the individual and their environment. Furthermore, there is research evidence to suggest that not everyone experiences attachment to place and that people may have multiple attachments. Thus, place attachment might be more diverse and complex than what has been considered within the current literature. The impact of these effects is difficult to differentiate in the absence of longitudinal data.

Future influences, opportunities and challenges with regard to research and policy were also highlighted. Our future understanding of older people's relationship with their environment is increasingly likely to be shaped by globalisation (Phillipson, 2003, 2006), technology and communications (Auge, 1995; Novak, 1997; Stokols, 1999) and the recent economic downturn (Leadbeater et al, 2008; Harding, 2009). How we currently experience place and the process of ageing is changing. We are likely to experience more diversity (for example, virtual place or uncertainty created by the economic downturn) in the relationship between people and their physical, social or virtual environment.

The influences, challenges and opportunities presented in this book support a refocusing and rethinking about the person–environment relationship. What is overwhelmingly evident is that the relationship between place and the ageing person will continue to be dynamic and complex, interacting and evolving at an individual, societal and now global level across time and space. Our respect of this complexity will be critical to building social and physical environments that are appropriate and responsive to the needs and aspirations of an ageing society.

Trends data, the findings presented in this book and the wider literature support a focus on enabling environments for older people. However, this will come down to how we – specifically academics and policy makers – use what we know to drive change and enable the creation of more inclusive neighbourhoods. If we are to support an agenda around *ageing in place* and the outcome is greater well-being and independence, we need to move to address basic standards that 'enable' rather than hinder *all* members of society to participate equally.

APPENDIX A

Summary of participant characteristics

Table A1: Summary of participant characteristics

Name	Gender	Area	Age	Marital status	Health problems	Limits activity	Ethnicity	Years in area	Tenure	Desire to move	Place attached	Quality of life
Environmental comfort												
Sydney Potter	M	Moss Side	67	Widowed	Yes	Yes	Black Caribbean	40	Rent	No	Yes	Very good
Joan Schofield	F	Moss Side	70	Married	Yes	No	White	45	Own	No	Yes	Good
Arnold Conway	M	Moss Side	87	Widowed	Yes	Yes	White	87	Rent	No	Yes	Neither
Marva Collins	F	Moss Side	63	Widowed	Yes	Yes	Black Caribbean	40	Rent	No	Yes	Good
Edna Fields	F	Cheetham	64	Married	Yes	No	White	64	Rent	No	Yes	Neither
John Witter	M	Longsight	72	Single	No	No	White	65	Rent	No	Yes	Very good
Leslie Johnson	M	Longsight	75	Married	Yes	Yes	White	30	Rent	No	Yes	Very good
Jean Gauche	M	DES	75	Single	Yes	Yes	White	50	Rent	No	Yes	Good
Frank Lander	M	DES	69	Single	Yes	Yes	White	4	Rent	No	Yes	Neither
George Knotsberry	M	DES	68	Widowed	Yes	Yes	White	1	Rent	No	Yes	Good
Dorothy Dobson	F	DES	72	Married	Yes	Yes	White	32	Rent	No	Yes	Very good
Theresa Blackbird	F	DES	68	Separated	Yes	Yes	First Nations	25	Rent	No	Yes	Neither

Name	Gender	Area	Age	Marital status	Health problems	Limits activity	Ethnicity	Years in area	Tenure	Desire to move	Place attached	Quality of life
Kenneth Wong	M	DES	72	Married	Yes	Yes	Chinese	17	Rent	No	Yes	Very good
Albert Crowshoe	M	DES	64	Divorced/living with partner	Yes	Yes	First Nations	60	Rent	No	Yes	Neither
Doug Leyland	M	DES	92	Single	Yes	Yes	White	6	Rent	No	Yes	Good
John Rankin	M	DES	70	Divorced	Yes	Yes	White	*	Rent	No	Yes	Good
Alistair O'Connor	M	Grandview-Woodland	76	Married	No	No	White	50	Own	No	Yes	Good
Joe Dawson	M	Grandview-Woodland	68	Single	Yes	Yes	White	60	Rent	No	Yes	Very good
Mary Perkins	*F*	*Moss Side*	*69*	*Married*	*Yes*	*No*	*Black Caribbean*	*40*	*Buying*	*No*	*Yes*	*Good*
Jennifer MacDougall	*F*	*Grandview-Woodland*	*90*	*Widowed*	*Yes*	*Yes*	*White*	*40*	*Rent*	*No*	*Yes*	*Good*
Environmental management												
Angela Walkins	F	Longsight	69	Widowed	Yes	Yes	Black Caribbean	20	Rent	No	Yes	Good
Roger and Gretta Graham	M/F	Moss Side	65/62	Married	No	No	White	15	Own	No	Yes	Good
Alfred and Serta Williams	M/F	Cheetham	65	Married	No/Yes	No	Black Caribbean	40	Buying	No	Yes	Neither
Ruby Owane	F	Moss Side	63	Separated	Yes	Yes	Black Caribbean	40	Rent	No	Yes	Neither
Maud Brown	F	Longsight	78	Widowed	Yes	Yes	White	45	Own	No	Yes	Good
Betty Wilson	F	Cheetham	64	Widowed – living with partner	Yes	No	White	30	Own	No	Yes	Very good

Name	Gender	Area	Age	Marital status	Health problems	Limits activity	Ethnicity	Years in area	Tenure	Desire to move	Place attached	Quality of life
Felicity Parker	F	Longsight	60	Married	Yes	Yes	Black Caribbean	30	Rent	No	Yes	Good
Elsie Forester	F	Moss Side	74	Widowed	Yes	No	Black Caribbean	40	Own	No	Yes	Good
David Metcalf	M	Cheetham	80	Single	Yes	Yes	White	25	Rent	No	No	Good
Patricia Reilly	F	Cheetham	66	Widowed	Yes	Yes	White	32	Own	Yes	No	Poor
William Chivers	M	DES	67	Single	No	No	White	9	Rent	No	No	Very poor
Mabel Smith	F	DES	77	Divorced	No	No	White	14	Rent	No	Yes	Neither
Azimoon Rahaman	F	DES	79	Widowed	Yes	Yes	Guyana	13	Rent	Yes	No	Neither
Anna Brooklyn	F	Grandview-Woodland	88	Widowed	Yes	Yes	White	8	Rent	No	Yes	Good
Patrick and Doreen Elliot	M/F	Grandview-Woodland	81/89	Married	Yes/No	No	White	50	Own	No	Yes	Very good
Josephine Diamond	F	DES	76	Divorced	Yes	Yes	First Nations	13	Rent	No	Yes	Good
Dan Sapp	M	DES	60	Single	Yes	Yes	First Nations	25	Rent	No	Yes	**
Winifred Peter	F	DES	66	Single – living with partner	Yes	Yes	White	58	Rent	No	Yes	Neither
Peter Furkin	M	DES	77	Single	Yes	Yes	White	10	Rent	No	No	Neither
Muriel Allen	*F*	Moss Side	69	Divorced	No	No	White	30	Rent	No	Yes	Good
Berry Matthews	*M*	*DES*	*61*	*Single*	*Yes*	*Yes*	*White*	*7*	*Rent*	*Yes*	*No*	*Neither*
Howard Adams Goodleaf	*M*	*DES*	*70*	*Divorced*	*Yes*	*Yes*	*First Nations*	*40*	*Rent*	*Yes*	*No*	*Neither*
Helen Fox	*F*	*Cheetham*	*78*	*Widowed*	*Yes*	*Yes*	*White*	*30*	*Rent*	*No*	*Yes*	*Poor*

Name	Gender	Area	Age	Marital status	Health problems	Limits activity	Ethnicity	Years in area	Tenure	Desire to move	Place attached	Quality of life
Environmental distress												
Jay Omar	M	Moss Side	80	Widowed	Yes	Yes	Black Caribbean	15	Rent	Yes	No	Poor
Millicent Taylor	F	Moss Side	80	Widowed	No	No	Black Caribbean	40	Own	No	No	Good
Roberta Peterson	F	Moss Side	72	Single	Yes	No	White	65	Rent	Yes	Yes	Good
Paul Cook	M	Longsight	60	Single – living with partner	Yes	Yes	White	3	Rent	Yes	No	Poor
Milton Johnson	M	Moss Side***	75	Single	Yes	Yes	White	65	Own	Yes	Yes	Good
Robert O'Farrell	M	DES	75	Widowed	Yes	Yes	White	1	Rent	Yes	No	Very poor
Keppol Polanski	M	DES	78	Married	Yes	No	White	1.5	Rent	Yes	No	Neither
Harold Waters	*M*	*Cheetham*	*69*	*Single*	*No*	*No*	*White*	*30*	*Rent*	*Yes*	*No*	*Poor*
Elizabeth Laing	*F*	*Grandview-Woodland*	*64*	*Divorced*	*No*	*No*	*White*	*5*	*Rent*	*No*	*No*	*Good*

Notes: All names have been anonymised. Italics shows in-depth case studies. *Did not know. **Question not asked. ***Recently moved out of area.

APPENDIX B

Short biographies of participants in Manchester and Vancouver

Environmental comfort (20 participants in total)

Sydney Potter – Manchester

Aged 67, and recently widowed, Mr Sydney Potter lives in a terraced house in Moss Side. Black Caribbean in origin, Mr Potter has lived in the area for over 40 years and very much enjoys living there, "I don't fancy another area for living". His daily activities usually involve a number of walks; the first one takes place shortly after he wakes up and before breakfast, just after 4 o'clock. After breakfast Mr Potter goes on his longest walk of the day, usually around 3 hours: "[I walk] various places, sometimes I go around Moss Side then I go into Salford". He returns home for lunch, then in the afternoon, "I go for my next walk, go to the next town, visit my sister and do things for her". A father of four, he has frequent contact with a son and his grandson; his other children live elsewhere in England and visit every couple of months. Although staying in most evenings, he attends weekly bible studies and meetings of the residents' association every month. For Mr Potter the ability to remain independent is very important to him, "I like to do things for myself, put no burden on anyone". Mr Potter reported having a very good quality of life.

Joan Schofield – Manchester

Aged 70, Mrs Joan Schofield lives in a terraced house with her husband and son. She has lived in Moss Side for over 45 years and has been witness to a number of, what she feels are, negative changes, the most significant for her is the increase in crime. At one time her wish "was to retire to Blackpool", but feels "it's too late now". Mrs Schofield has regular contact with her brother and a daughter; both usually visiting on the weekends. Although recently suffering from a very bad fall for which she now needs crutches, Mrs Schofield likes to go out every day for a walk and to pick up a few groceries. A resident of the area for a long time, she is always seeing people she knows, "there is always somebody who says 'hi' and everybody knows me … I'm a chatter person, you see". She enjoys a good relationship with some of the neighbours, feeling they look out for each other. Once a week she meets up with friends for line dancing; although unable to do it herself, she says she greatly enjoys the company. Mrs Schofield felt that she enjoyed a good quality of life.

Arnold Conway – Manchester

Aged 87, Mr Arnold Conway was born in Moss Side, just two doors down from where he presently lives. He recalled a time when all he could see around him were farms. Although satisfied with living in his neighbourhood, he feels that it has deteriorated. Widowed five years ago, Mr Conway lives by himself in a terraced house. Although not having any children, or any other family close by, he appears to be very socially connected to extended family who live in other parts of England: "twice a week we phone each other and saying what's going on and what's not going on". Only recently have health problems prevented him from visiting, "when you go there is a big family … it lasts for days … but I'm not grumbling, I've had a life". Mr Conway also appears to have a number of close friendships. Every week he shares a 'Sunday roast' with a friend and then on Fridays he helps out at a friend's car dealership, occasionally answering the phone and chatting to customers: "Friday is my best day. I'm tired but happy cause I've seen more people". Mr Conway felt that his quality of life was neither good nor poor.

Edna Fields – Manchester

Aged 64, Mrs Edna Fields lives in a local authority maisonette in Cheetham with her husband and son. Born and having lived her whole life in Cheetham, Mrs Fields has been witness to a lot of what she views as negative changes in the area, such as increases in crime, but this does not prevent her from going out. Her daily activities include going out every morning for a paper, grocery shopping, tidying the house and reading. She describes herself as an "avid reader". A couple of times a week she also enjoys a visit to the arcade to play the fruit machines, referring to it as her "one vice". Mrs Fields has only limited contact with family – all her sisters and brothers are now dead – but appears to enjoy good relationships with a couple of cousins who call frequently and visit occasionally. Mrs Fields and her husband have few financial worries, they are able to buy what they need and also enjoy supporting a number of different charities. Mrs Field rated her quality of life as neither good nor poor.

John Witter – Manchester

Aged 72, Mr John Witter lives in a maisonette in Longsight. He has lived at this same address for 65 years. Although he feels some aspects of the neighbourhood have declined, he enjoys living in this area. Mr Witter has limited contact with family, he never married and has no children, and his brothers and sister are now dead; however, he does have weekly contact with a cousin who lives locally. On a Sunday "if the weather's decent I've got a cousin, she lives about 10 minutes' walk away, I usually go up to her about seven o'clock … come back at half past nine". Most of Mr Witter's friends are old work colleagues; however, many have recently died, "I've got occasional ones that come round but it's very seldom and I look forward to things like that". He also greatly enjoys his daily 'quarter-hour' chats with his neighbour. A great pastime of Mr Witter's is watching WWF, "I have never missed WWF in my life, I think it's great", and 'Who Wants To Be a Millionaire', "I phoned up a few times you know to try and get on … I think it's the easiest quiz in the world". Mr Witter felt that he had a very good quality of life.

Leslie Johnson – Manchester

Aged 75, Mr Leslie Johnson lives in a terrace house in Longsight with his wife Betty. They have lived in the area for over 30 years. He is father to nine children and a grandfather to 18 grandchildren, almost all of whom live within walking or a short driving distance: "everyday we have somebody here and sometimes we have three or four of them here". He describes them as having "a very very good family" and, because of this, feels "we have a good life". However, with the current state of his wife's health Mr Johnson is relied on to collect the daily shopping needs and do the chores, such as pay the bills. He usually combines this with his daily long walk and social visit with various shopkeepers, "I get a cup of tea and sit and talk"; "I love to walk in shops, I say I love to see things". When at home Mr Johnson entertains himself on his computer: "I use it, I say mainly now, for history, geography, arithmetic, and all the things that I think I know so much about and I find out that I don't". Mr Johnson rated his quality of life as very good.

Marva Collins – Manchester

Aged 63, Mrs Marva Collins is Black Caribbean in origin. She has lived in her neighbourhood of Moss Side for over 40 years. Recently widowed, she now shares her terraced house with her youngest child. A mother of seven, four of whom live in other parts of England and two live abroad, she is in frequent contact with them. She enjoys a physically and socially active life. Twice weekly, with her neighbour, she goes to a keep-fit class at the local gym, and the rest of the week she goes for walks around her neighbourhood. Additionally, she enjoys attending computer and aromatherapy classes at the adult education centre, which is a five-minute walk away. An integral member of her church group, she hosts weekly prayer meetings at her house and is engaged in a number of charitable activities associated with the church (for example, visiting people in hospital). Mrs Collins spoke of having numerous friends, whom she tries to see weekly. One of the great pleasures in her life is attending to her allotment on which she grows many kinds of vegetables and flowers. "I've got a lovely area which I tend to …

it's just fascinating to know that I can plant something and reap it. You know it feels really, really good". Settled in Moss Side, she does not wish to move. Mrs Collins felt that she enjoyed a good quality of life.

Jean Gauche – Vancouver

Aged 75, Mr Jean Gauche has lived in the Downtown Eastside for over 50 years. He lives in a one-room apartment, which he described as '10 by 12', on Hastings Street. For most of his 44 years of working life, he worked as a roofer until poor health – asbestosis – caused him to retire early. Originally from Montreal, Mr Gauche has no known family; at the age of five his mother died and he was put into care by the state and lost all contact with his family. He never married and has no children. Until recently, he had two close friends; however, one died and the other moved away and has subsequently lost contact. Mr Gauche enjoys taking on new projects such as learning how to use the internet and email, and has constructed a small workshop in his apartment. He is a very religious man, starting his morning off with watching '100 Huntley Street'.[1] However, poor health has recently prevented him from going to church. He likes living in the Downtown Eastside and would not wish to move, "I am so comfortable, I got a nice apartment … I have nothing to complain about". Mr Gauche reported having a good quality of life.

Frank Lander – Vancouver

Aged 69, Mr Frank Lander has lived in a purpose-built seniors housing complex in the DES for four years, following a long period of homelessness. Born in Ottawa, he initially came to Vancouver in the 1950s before spending the next 40 years moving back and forth between Ontario and Vancouver. For much of his working life Mr Lander took on numerous odd jobs before suffering almost 20 years without work. This was followed by almost 35 years of homelessness. Mr Lander never married and has no children. He has a sister in Chilliwack who visits him frequently and a brother in Ottawa with whom he is in contact. His daily routine usually involves a visit to a local pub on Hastings Street. He talks about having one close friend that he usually goes out drinking with or has over to his room for a drink, but the rest of his friends he described as all "bums and … no good". He has no concerns over safety and goes out when he pleases. He appears to like living in the Downtown Eastside and does not wish to move. He felt that his quality of life was neither good nor poor.

[1] '100 Huntley Street' is a Canadian Christian television programme, aired in the morning for one hour, Monday through Friday.

George Knotsberry – Vancouver

Aged 68, Mr George Knotsberry has lived in a purpose-built seniors housing complex in the DES for one year. Born in Toronto, Mr Knotsberry's life is best described as nomadic. He spent much of his adult years working in the United States, initially for the US Army – stationed in Korea, Vietnam and Cuba (Bay of Pigs invasion). Following that he took on numerous odd jobs and aliases over that period in order to avoid US law enforcement. In 2000 he was deported from the US and returned to Toronto. A year later he travelled out West to Vancouver. Married twice and now widowed, Mr Knotsberry has two children, but has no contact with either of them. Socially, he appears to be very isolated, having no family or friends. The only contact he had had with his family was his brother, who had recently died. He also spoke about having no friends. Mr Knotsberry feels settled in the area and does not wish to move. "I've done all my travel, I've had enough of it." He felt that his quality of life was good, because he felt more settled than at any other time of his life.

Dorothy Dobson – Vancouver

Aged 72, Mrs Dorothy Dobson lives with her husband in a one-bedroom flat a few blocks north of Hastings Street towards the Burrard Inlet in the Downtown Eastside. She has lived in the area for over 32 years. For many of those years, Mrs Dobson and her husband managed a boarding house on Hastings Street before retiring 13 years ago. Socially, they appear to know a number of people in the area and spoke about having many "very good friends" that visit daily. Usually, once a week, as a treat, they meet up with some of their friends at a local bingo hall. Mrs Dobson and her husband have almost no contact with their six children or any other members of their family. Financially, they find it very difficult to manage on their monthly federal pension, with some months having only $5 left. A long-time resident, Mrs Dobson spoke about how the Downtown Eastside had declined in the last 30 years, primarily seeing the decline of the area related to the drug problem. Although disliking what is going on in the neighbourhood, she felt that the Downtown Eastside was home and would not want to move now. She felt that her quality of life was very good.

Theresa Blackbird – Vancouver

Aged 68, Mrs Theresa Blackbird is a member of the First Nations community. She has lived in the Downtown Eastside for a total of 25 years, and for most of those years has resided in a one-room flat opposite Oppenheimer Park. For much of her working life she was employed as a cook. Currently separated from her husband, Mrs Blackbird has four children, two of whom live locally and visit frequently. Most days, Monday through Saturday, she volunteers as a cook at churches and community centres in the area that cater to feeding the "homeless, sex trade workers and senior citizens". She also helps host a coffee morning in her apartment block for residents to get together and socialise. She spoke about having a lot of work friends but no friends outside of work, saying "you can't trust anyone". Financially, Mrs Blackbird has a difficult time making ends meet, often having nothing left at the end of the month. She does not feel moving is an option; fearing "you might be worse off". Mrs Blackbird felt a bit indifferent about her quality of life, rating it as neither good nor poor.

Kenneth Wong – Vancouver

Aged 72, Mr Kenneth Wong was born in China and immigrated to Canada in 1949. He has been a resident of the Downtown Eastside for 17 years. For the first four years he lived in a run-down hotel on Hastings Street, then was rehoused to a new subsidised housing complex bordering the Downtown Eastside and Chinatown. He does not like the drug problem and crime in the area, but in general feels this does not impact on his activities. For many years Mr Wong suffered from clinical depression that had an impact on both his work and family life. Mr Wong is married and is a father to seven children, all of whom live in Vancouver. One son visits weekly and the other children less often. He has no brothers or sisters but has a cousin who he sees every week. Twice a month he meets a friend for coffee and occasionally socialises with neighbours. His daily activities involve a visit to the Chinese Cultural Centre to get a newspaper and listen to the Chinese news, morning and afternoon walks and grocery shopping. Living in very poor accommodation prior to moving into his present apartment, Mr Wong feels thankful to be living in his present accommodation and enjoys the proximity to Chinatown. Mr Wong felt that with improvements in his health and accommodation, his quality of life was very good.

Albert Crowshoe – Vancouver

Aged 64, Mr Albert Crowshoe was born into a First Nations community somewhere in British Columbia. Having moved to the Downtown Eastside as a small child and then working as a fisherman and logger, Mr Crowshoe has lived in the area on and off for almost all of his life. Now retired he is the main carer for a friend he lives with, Ms Peters. Although troubled by numerous health complaints himself, such as heart and prostrate problems, he takes care of their daily needs. Mr Crowshoe feels he is indebted to Ms Peters for helping him to stop drinking: "she helped me quit drinking, I would not be alive today if it was not for her, because I am a chronic alcoholic" and referred to her as being his only friend. Married once, Mr Crowshoe has one child. However, on account of his alcoholism, his daughter was put into state care and he has never had any further contact with her. The only family he talks to is a brother who calls once a month. To cope financially, Mr Crowshoe and Ms Peters have pooled their money together. Both feel that they could not manage financially without each other. Mr Crowshoe reported his quality of life as neither good nor poor.

Alistair O'Connor – Vancouver

Aged 76, Mr Alistair O'Connor has lived in the Grandview-Woodland area for over 50 years. Mr O'Connor and his wife own a house in a historic area just off Commercial Drive. He enjoys the vibrancy of the area, saying "there is always something going on and something to look at"; however, he felt the area does have a problem with crime, "there has been a lot of break-ins in this area ... [my] van was broken into three times and my car broken into once". Morning and early afternoon he can be found on his computer trading stocks and shares on the internet. In the afternoon he goes for a walk or a bike ride, or reads the financial newspapers. He has two children, a daughter who lives in Greater Vancouver and visits a couple of times a month, and a son who lives elsewhere in British Columbia and visits every couple of months. Mr O'Connor and his wife have a number of good friends who they meet socially, usually for dinner, every couple of months. Financially secure, Mr O'Connor does not have any money worries, feeling they could afford what they needed. He reported that his quality of life was good.

Joe Dawson – Vancouver

Aged 68, Mr Joe Dawson has lived in the Grandview-Woodland area periodically for over 60 years. Enjoying a varied employment career, Mr Dawson took on numerous types of work. On leaving the army he worked as a cook and administrator in the logging camps; he also worked in construction and lived in remote areas of British Columbia working as a fire watch warden. The onset of emphysema forced him to take early retirement in his late 50s. A very vibrant and friendly personality, Mr Dawson is socially active. Although never married nor having any children, he has close contact with family and has numerous friends who visit. Having lived for a number of years in run-down accommodation, Mr Dawson had recently moved into an independent seniors housing complex, which he feels has improved his life. He very much enjoys the proximity to Commercial Drive, saying "it is very mixed and cosmopolitan; everything you need for shopping is on the Drive or centrally located for Downtown, Metro town, Lougheed Mall". In addition to improvements in his health, he now feels he has "a terrific quality of life".

Doug Leyland – Vancouver[2]

Aged 92, Mr Doug Leyland lives in a seniors housing complex in the Downtown Eastside. He has been a resident in the area since 1996. Mr Leyland has a number of health problems, most pronounced were visual and mobility problems, and, possibly, mental health challenges. Orphaned as a child he has no contact with family and has never been married nor had any children. He appears to have a number of friends whom he visits daily, both within and outside the neighbourhood. Mr Leyland's night-time activities have created a problem between him and the management of the seniors housing complex he is staying in. Referred to as a 'dumpster diver',[3] he spends his nights and early hours of the morning collecting garbage from the dumpsters in the DES and brings it back to his room. Issues over health and safety prompt the management to clean his room frequently, often discarding what Mr Leyland considers his 'treasures'. He enjoys living in the DES and has no fears about going out at night, or concerns about personal safety.

John Rankin – Vancouver

Aged 70, Mr John Rankin has lived in the Downtown Eastside for many years, apparently living for much of this time in very dilapidated boarding houses until recently moving into a purpose-built seniors housing complex. Mr Rankin suffers from several physical and psychological health problems and has spent a number of years in a mental health facility. He is divorced and has no children. However, he has some contact with a sister in Manitoba. Mr Rankin spoke about having no friends in the Downtown Eastside, feeling you could not trust people, but felt that he had a couple of friends in his Orchestra group. Once a week he plays fiddle with a group of young musicians in bars and restaurants in the Downtown area. They appear to provide some social support for Mr Rankin, recently helping him to move into his current accommodation. In his free time he was studying Egyptology until recent mental health problems have 'postponed' it. Mr Rankin spoke about being very dissatisfied with life, and how, if he could, he would like to "go back 50 years and start over again". He enjoys living in the area and says he has no worries about personal safety. However, he avoids what he calls the "slum" areas. Mr Rankin felt that his quality of life was good.

[2] Because of Mr Leyland's 'possible' mental health problems, his understanding of quality of life was very difficult to assess, and therefore a rating of quality of life was difficult to obtain.

[3] A term used by a community worker in the DES to describe Mr Leyland's activities. A dumpster is also know as a skip in England.

Environmental management (23 participants in total)

Angela Walkins – Manchester

Aged 69 and widowed five years ago, Mrs Angela Walkins lives alone in a terraced house in Longsight. Black Caribbean in origin, she has lived in the neighbourhood for over 20 years. Mrs Walkins appears to have a very close-knit and supportive family; her one granddaughter comes over daily to cook and clean for her, and her two children visit twice a week and call almost daily. Her one brother lives across the road and pops in to see her every day. Although having frequent contact with family, Mrs Walkins was saddened by the recent departure of her close friend back home in Jamaica as she felt she lacked having good friends close by. Suffering with severe arthritis, Mrs Walkins is sometimes restricted in the activities she can do but enjoys taking walks around the neighbourhood when she can. Although generally satisfied with living in Longsight, she feels that drugs and "all the thieving going on" has become a significant problem in the area, imposing limits, out of fear, on her going out at night for a walk. She felt that her quality of life was good.

Roger and Gretta Graham – Manchester

Aged 65 and 62, Mr and Mrs Graham have been residents of Moss Side for over 15 years. Although Mrs Graham is still working part time, Mr Graham has just recently retired from paid work. Both in their second marriage, they have four children between them: two live locally and the other two live elsewhere in England. They see the children who live locally every week, usually for dinner. Mrs Graham also has her mother living with them, and a brother and niece who live just around the corner, and whom they see frequently. Mr and Mrs Graham are presently providing full-time care to her mother, which they are finding increasing physically and emotionally difficult as her health deteriorates. Despite some restrictions placed on them by caring duties, "we can only be out two hours maybe three hours", they enjoy a relatively active social life. Committed Jehovah's Witnesses, they attend a number of evening bible study groups and meetings at the Kingdom Hall. Originally describing their area as "absolutely brilliant", they now feel that "it has really deteriorated" and there are a number of areas which you need to avoid. They feel that they are able to go out at night because they have a car; without a car this might present a problem. Despite having to manage concerns over crime, they feel generally "fortunate to enjoy a good relationship with neighbours". They felt that they enjoyed a good quality of life.

Alfred and Serta Williams – Manchester

In their mid-60s, Mr Alfred and Mrs Serta Williams have lived in Cheetham Hill for about 40 years. Black Caribbean in origin, they live in a semi-detached terraced house that they are currently in the process of buying. They have frequent contact with family. All four of their children live in Manchester, with the nearest living only five minutes away. They visit frequently, either popping in after work and/or visiting on the weekend. Mrs Williams also has a brother who lives close by and visits most days. Outside the family, they have a number of friends with whom they socialise. Residents of the neighbourhood for most of their lives they feel the area has deteriorated; their biggest concern is the increase in crime, so much so that Mrs Williams will not leave her house for fear of someone breaking in. Despite this, they feel they would have mixed feelings about moving, saying they would "miss their friends" and the proximity to the shops, "you see, just across the road, the Post Office". Additionally, they are finding it very difficult to manage financially on their income, Mrs Williams feels they can afford no luxuries, "nice clothes, we have to buy the cheap ones", so consideration of moving would be out of the question. They felt that their quality of life was neither good nor poor.

Ruby Owane – Manchester

Aged 63, Ms Ruby Owane lives by herself in a new terraced house. Black Caribbean in origin, she has lived in Moss Side for over 40 years. Separated from her husband, Ms Owane has six children, all of whom live in Manchester, and at least one out of the six will visit daily. Although having reduced mobility and hearing problems, Ms Owane likes to keep busy. A great pastime is cooking, "if there is something to cook, I will cook. It is something to keep me going, you know, so I do it". She cooks frequently for a friend living just around the corner and recently cared for a friend and neighbour who was recovering from a bad fall. She explains, "I like to be busy … a lot of people like myself who retire sit down at home and have lost the ability to walk". She has a number of very close friends in the area and very much enjoys the community spirit in Moss Side. However, the increase in crime has made her frightened to go out and socialise at night. "I don't go out much in the evening … like after five, I won't go because I am alright here." She rated her quality of life as neither good nor poor.

Maud Brown – Manchester

Aged 78, Mrs Maud Brown has lived in Longsight for over 45 years. Widowed almost 10 years ago she lives alone in a terraced house. A central issue in Mrs Brown's life of late has been her health. Physically fit and socially active until recently, Mrs Brown feels greatly frustrated by her present health condition, saying she feels she has "lost confidence" in going out by herself and now feels dependent on others to take her out. Mrs Brown appears to have a very close and supportive family. She has two children, one of whom lives locally and she sees a couple of times a week, "he'll take me out and take me shopping, he's smashing". Her other son lives further away but he still manages to visit weekly; her grandchildren also visit frequently. Mrs Brown spoke about having numerous friends whom she enjoys visiting but spoke most affectionately about the relationship she has with her neighbour, "we've been friends more than neighbours". A long-time resident of the area, she feels that the neighbourhood has declined, "it's a rough area to what it was … there's a lot of drugs". Despite this, Mrs Brown has never wished to move. She felt that her quality of life was good.

Betty Wilson – Manchester

Aged 64, Mrs Betty Wilson lives with her partner and her mother of 91 on a council estate on the edge of Cheetham. She is a mother of two; one child lives locally and the other elsewhere in England. Family contact appears to be an important aspect of Mrs Wilson's life. "We're a very close family … because my mum's here I've been the lynchpin, so everybody congregates here … my family is very, very important to me." Concerned with the decline of her estate and neighbourhood, Mrs Wilson decided to take an active part in changing things. A civically engaged member of her community, Mrs Wilson sits on numerous committees – the local tenants' association and a couple of neighbourhood forums on regeneration. "I love doing it because I like being involved." She has been integral in changing run-down areas of her neighbourhood into green spaces or parks, and is editor of a local community newspaper. Not only actively engaged with these activities, she is doing a diploma at college that keeps her busy three days a week from 9 a.m. to 3 p.m., and with the help of her partner is full-time carer to her mother. She rated her quality of life as very good.

Felicity Parker – Manchester

Aged 60, Mrs Felicity Parker and her husband live in a semi-detached house in Longsight. Black Caribbean, they have lived in the neighbourhood for close to 30 years. Taking early retirement on account of poor health, Mrs Parker occupies much of her day with church activities, either reading the bible, visiting people in hospital and/or attending church and bible study groups. Mrs Parker and her husband appear to have frequent contact with their only child, a daughter, who visits and helps with the shopping at least once a week. They also appear to have a good relationship with their grandchildren, "they visit me all the time". Financially, Mrs Parker and her husband have concerns over their ability to pay monthly bills, sometimes relying on their godson to "put ends together". The relationship with their neighbours appears to be very positive, "I know all my neighbours". Worried about neighbourhood crime, Mrs Parker is comforted by the fact that she can rely on her neighbours, "we look out for one another". She felt that she enjoyed a good quality of life.

Elsie Forester – Manchester

Aged 74, Mrs Elsie Forester lives in an end-of-terrace house in Moss Side. Black Caribbean in origin, she has lived in the neighbourhood for over 40 years.

Widowed 10 years ago, she still greatly misses and mourns the loss of her husband. A mother of two, she has frequent contact with her children and grandchildren. Her son lives with her, and her daughter lives in the area. Daily activities usually involve taking her grandson to the school bus stop, household duties, shopping and, if time, a walk around the neighbourhood, "I keep myself busy during the day". Some evenings she goes to church and attends the local residents' association meeting monthly. Although enjoying the social contact from these meetings, she feels she lacks quality in her relationships and has no close friends; "I don't really go to them with my problems ... we talk about the weather and talk about our arthritis". Crime was a particular area of concern, fearing retaliation for reported crimes based on previous experience, Mrs Forester and her neighbours appeared to manage problems related to crime on their street by themselves without involving the police, feeling "it just works best that way". Mrs Forester feels that she has a good quality of life because she is able to manage life independently and get out and meet people.

David Metcalf – Manchester

Aged 80, Mr David Metcalf has been a resident of Cheetham for over 25 years. Very dissatisfied with where he was living Mr Metcalf recently moved into housing and an area that was better suited to his needs. Increasing problems of reduced mobility, deterioration of the neighbourhood and trouble with neighbours prompted Mr Metcalf to move. Never having married and having no children, and with the death and poor health of his brothers, Mr Metcalf has limited contact with family. Financially the move has been very difficult and as a consequence has been a great source of stress. He is finding it very hard to manage, with "over half of [his] pension going on rent and council tax, little is left over for luxuries". For Mr. Metcalf this means he has to "cut down on ... well, fish and chips, it's a luxury". He also feels his limited income restricts his social activities, and worries greatly about the cost of rent going up. He has sought help and advice from the Citizens Advice Bureau but feels he is not getting the proper help and feels frustrated by the process. Although he is stressed by his current financial state, he feels that his quality of life has improved from where he was living before.

Patricia Reilly – Manchester

Aged 66, Mrs Patricia Reilly has lived in Cheetham for over 30 years. Widowed, she has two children, a daughter who lives with her and a son who lives elsewhere in England. She appears to have a good relationship with both her children, and despite her son living further away she see him every month. Mrs Reilly enjoys being both physically and socially active. She goes out every day for a walk and enjoys taking on new projects, "I do a wee project around the house like trying a bit of decorating or the garden or something like that you know". Twice a week, in the afternoon, she plays bridge, "I find it very, very relaxing". Part of the day is also taken up with a visit to church and/or charity work; as a member of The Daughters of Charity she visits "the sick in hospital". Dissatisfied with her neighbourhood but not wishing to move, she feels that her activities, specifically "being about to go out and meet people" help her to cope with living in her area. She felt that her quality of life was poor.

William Chivers – Vancouver

Aged 67, Mr William Chivers has lived in the Downtown Eastside for nine years following the break-up of his relationship. He lives in what was described as "one of the better hotels" on Hastings Street. Mr Chivers' daily activities include numerous visits to the pub and more than likely a visit to the Exhibition Park to put a bet on a horse. He admitted to suffering from a drink and gambling problem, which he blames on boredom, caused, he said, by his inability to continue working: "there is nothing to do around here but walk and drink". Socially, he is in contact with a step-son who he sees every few months, and is in telephone contact with brothers and sisters living in other provinces. Feeling he can trust very few people living in the Downtown Eastside, Mr Chivers claims to only have one friend that he sees daily, usually in the pub for a drink. Despite purporting to have adequate financial resources and a dislike for living in the Downtown Eastside, "it is very cut-throat and nobody cares about you, you really have to watch yourself ", he has no desire to move. Mr Chivers feels that his quality of life is very poor.

Mabel Smith – Vancouver

Aged 77, Ms Smith was born in Rochdale, England, and migrated to Canada in her late 40s. Initially settling in the West End, financial problems, brought about by a gambling addiction, forced her to relocate to the Downtown Eastside where she has been living for 14 years. Although divorced and having lost her only child in a car accident, she is very close to her sister's children, who pay for her to spend the winter months with them in California. Ms Smith's escape during the winter months and her active civic engagement enable her to manage life in the DES. Ms Smith sits on numerous boards and committees in the Downtown Eastside. "Not one to sit about", Ms Smith is very socially active, meeting up with friends for a meal and/or shopping and a couple of times a week she enjoys travelling on the bus to visit other areas of Vancouver or the lower mainland. "I do a lot of bus riding … you can get some beautiful rides". Though recognising that the Downtown Eastside is not a "good neighbourhood", in part because she has been a victim of crime, she feels that at her age it would be difficult to move. She feels that because she lives where she does, her quality of life is neither good nor poor.

Azimoon Rahaman – Vancouver

Aged 79, Mrs Azimoon Rahaman was born in Georgetown, Guyana, and migrated to Canada 20 years ago. For 13 of those years she has lived in a one-bedroom apartment on Main Street in the Downtown Eastside. A widow and mother of 12, she has four children living locally and the rest living elsewhere in Canada and the United States. She appears to have a very close and supportive family, telephoning her most days and visiting every weekend. Mrs Rahaman is a very socially and physically active person. Her weekdays involve swimming, carpet bowling, and playing darts at a number of community and seniors centres outside the area. "I like to go to community and do activity[ies], socialise and things like that." A competitive carpet bowler, she has won many championships. She enjoys the convenience of the Downtown Eastside for her activities; however, she is troubled by the drug problem in the area and would prefer to live closer to her children. Mrs Rahaman feels that she manages to cope with living in the area by largely ignoring what goes on around her. "I can't look at them, if you look at them they can throw their needle at you." She feels that her quality of life is neither good nor poor, mostly on account of her recent health problems.

Anna Brooklyn – Vancouver

Aged 88, Mrs Anna Brooklyn moved to Grandview-Woodland after migrating to Canada from the United States in 1992 to be closer to her son. Widowed a year after settling in Vancouver, Mrs Brooklyn moved into her present accommodation, a two-bedroom flat, off Commercial Drive and just a couple of blocks away from her son's house. She enjoys many aspects of her neighbourhood, such as the locality, variety of shops and the ethnic mix of the area; however, she dislikes the crime, drugs and prostitution. She feels that some of her acquaintances and friends look down on her for living there. Financially secure, Mrs Brooklyn feels she is not limited in any way by money. Despite mobility problems, Mrs Brooklyn swims a couple of times a week and visits the lunch club at the seniors centre two or three times a week. While busy during the week with her activities she finds the weekends quite lonely, wishing to have more contact with her son and his family or to have her good friends from back home closer by. She feels that in general she has a good quality of life.

Patrick and Doreen Elliot – Vancouver

Aged 81 and 89 (respectively), Mr Patrick and Mrs Doreen Elliot live in a converted shop on Commercial Drive. Originally the site of their carpentry business, a series of costly break-ins prompted them to take early retirement and convert the shop to a one-bedroom bungalow. Residents of the area for over 50 years, they enjoy living in Grandview-Woodland, but feel the neighbourhood has deteriorated – neighbours are not what they once were and crime is a particular concern. When leaving on road trips in their motor home, they take extreme measures in securing their house from break-ins, in particular, boarding up all the windows. For most of her life, Mrs Elliot was actively involved in volunteer work within her community, winning the Governor General's[4] medal for volunteer work. During the winter months they spoke about being lonely because they did not have any of their "own children nor grandchildren running around", but take comfort and support from their relationship with their niece, "she is like a daughter to us". They both felt that they had a very good quality of life, because they could manage financially, were healthy and still had each other.

Josephine Diamond – Vancouver

Aged 76, Mrs Diamond has lived in a purpose-built First Nations complex a couple of blocks from Commercial Drive[5] for just over 13 years. Mrs Diamond has a number of health complaints, the most debilitating being functional mobility. For many years she was involved in numerous volunteer activities until poor health prevented her from continuing. Though restricted from doing her volunteer work, she still appears to lead a very active life, participating in the social activities of two seniors centres, one in her area and one in Downtown. Also every week she meets with friends to play bingo and occasionally meets up with her neighbour Mrs MacDougall to play bridge. She has two daughters who live in British Columbia, but only sees them occasionally. She appears close to one of her grandsons who visits regularly. Mrs Diamond has a large family back in Edmonton with whom she is in frequent telephone contact. She is very much settled living in Grandview-Woodland, particularly liking the proximity to numerous services and amenities, but is worried about the increase in crime. She feels that in general she has a good quality of life.

Dan Sapp – Vancouver[6]

Aged 60, Mr Sapp originated from a First Nations community somewhere in central British Columbia. He has lived in the Downtown Eastside for over 25 years, currently living in a small (10 by 10) room in a subsidised housing complex overlooking Oppenheimer Park. Suffering from major health problems, primarily due to an accident that left the right side of his body paralysed at the age of 11 years, he has spent much of his life in and out of hospital and has been unable to work. He felt that he managed to live in the area fairly well as "it is close to

[4] Canada's representative of the Queen of England.

[5] This is the same complex that Mrs Jennifer MacDougall lives in.

[6] This interview was a particularly difficult one. Mr Sapp's physical limitations were a great sources of distress for him. At times I felt that some of the questions I was asking produced a certain amount of unhappiness and distress, and as a consequence I did not ask him questions concerning his quality of life.

everything", which was important because of his limited mobility, and because he had been in the area for a long time found "people around here are friendly, more than other areas". Although immobile, one evening a week he uses his motorised scooter to drive down to the bingo hall where he meets up with friends. Other than this he appears to have very little social contact with friends. He has never been married and has no children but has two brothers and two sisters who he speaks to on the telephone every month. When asked about safety, he said that it is safe "around here if you were careful to mind your own business".

Winifred Peters – Vancouver

Aged 66, Ms Winifred Peters has lived in the Downtown Eastside for most of her life. Currently, Ms Peters is living with her friend and carer, Mr Crowshoe, in a two-bedroom flat in a high-rise building bordering the Downtown Eastside and Strathcona. Ms Peters has suffered from a number of serious health problems for most of her adult life. A vicious attack 30 years ago left her with her back broken in two places. This has left her largely immobile. Additionally, she suffers from throat cancer and asthma, and years ago also had tuberculosis. Very frail she is mostly housebound. Home help services are supplied to her three times a week. However, Mr Crowshoe provides most of the main care duties. Once married, Ms Peters had no children and has no contact with any family members. Other than Mr Crowshoe, the only other person she has contact with is an old friend, who does weekly grocery shopping for them. She felt that her quality of life was neither good nor poor.

Peter Furkin – Vancouver

Aged 77, Mr Peter Furkin was born on Prince Edward Island. A resident of a seniors housing complex for over 10 years he lives in a small one-room apartment on the ground floor. Mr Furkin is physically very frail and generally immobile, seldom leaving his residence. He has never been married and has a daughter with whom he has no contact. The only family member he has contact with is a half-brother who lives in Ontario and who visits him occasionally. He spoke about a friend who comes to visit every once in a while and they go for a drink, but other than that he did not have any friends. He mentioned not "caring to make friends" ,and "loneliness" not bothering him. He has little structure to his day, and appears to spend most of his time in his room, seldom going out in the neighbourhood. Financially, he felt he had more than enough money, seldom spending what his budget allowed. On account of his health and age, he felt moving is no longer an option. He felt that his quality of life was neither good nor poor.

Environmental distress (9 participants in total)

Jay Omar – Manchester

Aged 80, Mr Jay Omar was born in Jamaica and came to England in 1960, living for years in a terraced house in Moss Side with his wife. The death of his wife 13 years ago has had a significant impact on Mr Omar's life. He mentioned having difficulty coping and that life would "never get better". A number of recent health problems precipitated a period of hospitalisation, which has had a significant psychological impact on Mr Omar. Although his health has improved he feels less independent and is not able to do many of the church activities he previously did. Being a repeat victim of crime has also not helped Mr Omar's mental state, having had his house broken into a total of 12 times. "Every time that they break in it's always harder … it [has] always been a depressive condition, you [will] never be the same." Mr Omar's only child lives in Greater Manchester and appears to visit and/or have frequent telephone contact with his father. Having few friends, Mr Omar feels people have changed and that they are not as friendly as they used to be. Feeling lonely, Mr Omar took on a small part-time job as a cleaner; although only for an hour and a half a day, he felt "it got me out". Mr Omar felt that his quality of life was poor.

Millicent Taylor – Manchester

Aged 80, Mrs Millicent Taylor has lived in Moss Side for over 40 years. Widowed 15 years ago she lives by herself in a terraced house close to the Manchester City Stadium. Family support appears to be very limited. Mrs Taylor has a brother who lives close by whom she sees frequently, but her only child lives some distance away and therefore can only visit occasionally. She has one close friend who she visits most days and enjoys some social interaction at church. However, recent eyesight problems have reduced the frequency with which she goes to church. Mrs Taylor also appears to feel isolated from her neighbours, "you don't see nobody" and feels they could not be relied on to help her in an emergency. Mrs Taylor made a number of references to her "lonely state". "I am a lonely woman, my husband died … and me alone in here." Financially she feels that she manages; as long as she can pay her bills and buy food she feels she is satisfied, "I don't want them catching up with me". She feels that because of this she has a good quality of life.

Roberta Peterson – Manchester

Aged 72, Ms Roberta Peterson has lived in Moss Side for most of her life. Never married, Ms Peterson lives by herself in a rented terraced house that she has lived in since the age of seven. The condition of the house is extremely poor. Ms Peterson lacks adequate heating facilities and the house is in a general state of dilapidation, with numerous broken windows and a boarded-up front door. She is frustrated by the state of the house and has complained to the landlord, who has done nothing to help her. Her daily activities usually involve a visit to the lunch club at her local church, and then if needed she stays for the afternoon to help out. She appears to be actively involved with her local church. Ms Peterson appears to have no contact with family, but has a close friend who lives across the road. Taking early retirement to care for her parents and unable to find work after their deaths, Ms Peterson has continuous difficulty making ends meet. In reflecting on the state of her life she commented that, "I never intended life to end up like this". Despite this Ms Peterson felt that her quality of life was good.

Paul Cook – Manchester

Aged 60, Mr Paul Cook and his partner moved to a council house in Longsight three years ago. The move was prompted by the inability to afford where they were previously living. Mr Cook greatly dislikes the area but feels he can do little about it, saying the only good thing about the area is the proximity to the city centre, "you're literally just 10 minutes from the town centre". He has daily contact with his neighbours either side but other than that, "I see nobody". Family support appears to be very limited; the only contact he has is with a cousin with whom he has weekly telephone conversations. For a number of years Mr Cook tried to find work, "I lost track of the number of jobs I applied for", but was told he was over-qualified, and now with his poor health he feels he will never work again. Financially, Mr Cook and his partner struggle to keep up with monthly bills and food, and consequently they have no money for any extras like going out. For them a 'special day' would be "to be able to have enough to get out and afford to go somewhere socially". Mr Cook feels he has a poor quality of life.

Milton Johnson[7] – Manchester

Aged 75, Mr Milton Johnson recently sold his house in Moss Side to move to a small flat in a neighbouring part of Manchester. Mr Johnson had been a resident of Moss Side for 65 years. Although having tried to sell his house several times in that time period he was unsuccessful until recently. While he was given a chance to move within the area, Mr Johnson chose to move outside of the neighbourhood. Initially finding it hard to uproot at the age of 75, Mr Johnson is now very happy with his decision to move. He enjoys the many trees in the area, "I've never had this seeing leaves falling, I mean this is something", and the access to many services and amenities, "within 10 minutes from here either way … I can be amongst the shops". Never married and having no children, the move has also brought him

[7] Mr Johnson was interviewed for comparative environmental purposes. Interest was focused on how life had changed since moving.

in closer proximity to his remaining family. The move, and downsizing from a house to a flat, has also allowed him to feel more financially secure.

Robert O'Farrell – Vancouver

Aged 75, Mr Robert O'Farrell was born in Belfast and migrated to Canada in the late 1960s. A grocer by trade in Ireland, he took up work in the logging camps in northern British Columbia before retiring and settling in Vancouver. Following a long period of hospitalisation for a stroke a year ago, Mr O'Farrell was rehoused from his previous accommodation on Granville Street to Veterans Manor in the Downtown Eastside. Greatly distressed and bitter about being rehoused to such a "dangerous environment", he is desperate to get out. Mr O'Farrell is in the process of trying to sort out his finances and move back to Granville Street, closer to where his friends live. Married at one time, his wife died of tuberculosis and he never remarried; he has one son living in London, England, with whom he has very little communication. Every two to three months he is in contact with his sister in Scotland and brothers in England and Germany. When asked about his quality of life Mr O'Farrell felt "that you could not talk about quality of life while living in the DES [...] it was worse than the London slums"; for him it was beyond poor it was "double double poor".

Keppol Polanski – Vancouver

Aged 78, Mr Keppol Polanski was born in Poland and migrated to Canada a couple of years after the end of the Second World War. Current problems facing Mr Polanski were issues over housing and the ill health of his wife. The Downtown Eastside has been home to Mr Polanski for just over a year. He was rehoused from the Mount Pleasant area to a seniors housing complex in the Downtown Eastside following the ill health of his wife and what he felt was his inability to cope mentally or financially without her. Mr Polanski has very little social support. During the Second World War he lost all his family members in labour camps and is currently separated from his wife because of her poor health. Greatly distressed by this separation he tries to visit her at least three times a week, "now she is my family ... she is all I have". He has no friends, only what he calls acquaintances. Mr Polanski greatly dislikes the area and is very unhappy living there, but at the moment feels he has little choice. He feels that his quality of life at the moment is neither good nor poor, because he worries a lot about the health of his wife and is distressed about his living conditions.

APPENDIX C

Mrs MacDougall's short story

A walk down Memory Lane

For more than 40 years I have lived next door to the Drive – Commercial Drive, that is. Twice I moved to other areas of Vancouver. I was miserable. I moved back. I came back because a lot of my good memories are connected to this area. I firmly believe that good memories, in one's later life, are better than money in the bank.

Looking back over 40 years, I see some differences on the Drive: a few shops gone, others opened up, some buildings demolished, others built. One building in particular I remember, off the Drive on the corner of Broadway and Victoria just where the Grandview Highway makes a triangle. A lovely, stately mansion occupied this spot for many years. I made a point of walking past this corner whenever I went for a walk. The front yard had many flowerbeds, bushes and ornamental trees. I remember a rowan tree with its shiny leaves and bright red berries. The backyard had many fruit trees.

Time passed, the old folks who owned the house died and it was demolished. In its place was built a modern cement structure which housed a restaurant. The first operator was White Spot; after that, for a while, it was a Hungarian Goulash House and eventually a Chinese restaurant. Time passed and this structure was demolished and in its place was erected a Buddhist Temple. Through all these upheavals the lovely rowan tree was spared, though it didn't look so lovely anymore. Deprived of the shelter of the other trees and shrubs, it got the full blast of the traffic fumes and dust from the busy street. With the arrival of the temple the rowan tree went. There is nothing left of that beautiful garden, but I still have my memories of it firmly implanted in my memory bank.

I had an extremely busy day last week. In the space of three hours I had to change my library books, go for my bi-weekly swim, have a tooth replaced in my dentures, visit the podiatrist, stand in line at the bank to pay my bills and meet my friends for lunch. All this I accomplished in the 12 blocks of Commercial Drive in the allotted time span. Of course, I had to dodge and hop around the other people on the Drive while I accomplished these chores.

There are a lot of people shopping, talking, sipping coffee, playing billiards, and just strolling on the Drive everyday: thin people, fat people, tall people, short people, people of many races, colours, and convictions. Some young ones are dressed way out in the hopes of shocking the sedate older ones. Some are in their traditional costumes, some in rags and some in high fashion.

One thing I can be very sure of, I will never be bored when I walk down Commercial Drive. And just maybe, I will have some warm memories of this day years from now when I might be feeling a little bit lonely.

References

Airey, L. (2003) '"Nae as nice a scheme as it used to be": lay accounts of neighbourhood incivilities and well-being', *Health and Place*, vol 9, pp 129-37.

Albert, S.M. (2000) 'Time and function', in R.L. Rubinstein, M. Moss and M.H. Kleban (eds) *The many dimensions of aging*, New York: Springer Publishing Company, pp 57-67.

Allen, J. (2008) *Older people and well-being*, London: Institute for Public Policy Research.

Altman, I. and Zube, E.H. (eds) (1989) *Public places and spaces*, New York: Plenum Press.

Andrews, G.J. and Phillips, D.R. (2005) 'Geographical studies in ageing', in G.J. Andrews and D.R. Phillips (eds) *Ageing and place: Perspectives, policy, practice*, New York: Routledge, pp 7-12.

Antonelli, E., Rubini, V. and Fassone, C. (2000) 'Self-concept in institutionalized and non-institutionalized elderly people', *Journal of Environmental Psychology*, vol 20, pp 151-64.

Armstrong, D. (2000) 'A survey of community gardens in upstate New York: implications for health promotion and community development', *Health and Place*, vol 6, pp 319-27.

Aron, B. (1979) 'A disappearing community', in J. Wagner (ed) *Images of information: Still photography in the social sciences*, Beverly Hills, CA: Sage Publications.

Atkinson, R. and Kintrea, K. (2001) 'Disentangling area effects: evidence from deprived and non-deprived neighbourhoods', *Urban Studies*, vol 38, no 12, pp 2277-98.

Audit Commission (2008) *Don't stop me now: Preparing for an ageing population*, Trident Publishing, Exeter.

Auge, M. (1995) *Non-places: Introduction to an anthropology of supermodernity*, London: Verso Press.

Baltes, P.B. and Baltes, M.M. (1990) *Successful aging: Perspectives from the behavioral sciences*, Cambridge: Cambridge University Press.

Barnes, M., Blom, A., Cox, K., Lessof, C. and Walker, A. (2006) *The social exclusion of older people: Evidence from the first wave of the English Longitudinal Study of Ageing (ELSA): Final report*, London: Social Exclusion Unit, Office of the Deputy Prime Minister.

Barnes, M., Heady, C., Middleton, S., Millar, J. and Tsakloglou, P. (2003) *Poverty and social exclusion in Europe*, Aldershot: Edward Elgar.

Bartlett, H.P. and Peel, N.M. (2005) 'Healthy ageing in the community', in G.J. Andrews and D.R. Phillips (eds) *Ageing in Place*, New York, Routledge, pp 98-109.

Becker, G. (2003) 'Meanings of place and displacement in three groups of older immigrants', *Journal of Aging Studies*, vol 17, pp 129-49.

Bernard, M., Bartlam, B., Sim, J. and Biggs, S. (2007) 'Housing and care for older people: life in an English purpose-built retirement village', *Ageing and Society*, vol 27, no 4, pp 555-78.

Blane, D., Higgs, P.F.D., Hyde, M. and Wiggins, R.D. (2004) 'Life course influences on quality of life in early old age', *Social Science and Medicine*, vol 58, pp 2171-9.

BMA (British Medical Association) (2003) *Housing and health: building for the future*, London: Board of Science and Education, British Medical Association publications unit (last accessed May 2009: www.bma.org.uk/images/Housinghealth_tcm41-146809.pdf).

Boardman, D. (2003) *Longsight memories*. (last accessed May 2009: http://manchesterhistory.net/LONGSIGHT/homeopen.html).

Booth, C. (1886-1903) *Life and labour of the people*, London: London School of Economics and Political Science, www.booth.lse.ac.uk/

Borglin, G., Edberg, A.-K. and Hallberg, I.R. (2005) 'The experience of quality of life among older people', *Journal of Aging Studies*, vol 19, pp 201-20.

Bornat, J. (ed) (1994) *Reminiscence reviewed: Perspectives, evaluations, achievements*, Buckingham: Open University Press.

Bourne, L.S. (1989) 'Are new urban forms emerging? Empirical tests for Canadian urban areas', *The Canadian Geographer*, vol 33, no 4, pp 312-28.

Bourne, L.S. (1993) 'The myth and reality of gentrification: a commentary on emerging urban forms', *Urban Studies*, vol 30, no 1, pp 183-9.

Bourne, L.S. and Bunting, T. (1993) 'Housing markets, community development, and neighbourhood change', in L.S. Bourne and D.F. Ley (eds) *The changing social geography of Canadian cities*, Montreal: McGill-Queen's University Press, pp 175-95.

Bowling, A. (1995) 'What things are important in people's lives: a survey of the public's judgements to inform scales of health related quality of life', *Social Science and Medicine*, vol 41, no 10, pp 1447-62.

Bramham, D. (2003) 'Crystal meth is a recipe for mayhem', *Vancouver Sun*, 3 October.

Brandtstädter, J. and Greve, W. (1994) 'The aging self: stabilizing and protective processes', *Developmental Review*, vol 14, pp 52-80.

Broadway, M. (1989) 'A comparison of patterns of urban deprivation between Canadian and US cities', *Social Indicators Research*, vol 21, pp 531-51.

Broadway, M. (1992) 'Differences in inner-city deprivation: an analysis of seven Canadian cities', *The Canadian Geographer*, vol 36, no 2, pp 189-96.

Broadway, M. (1995) 'The Canadian inner city 1971-1991: regeneration and decline', *Canadian Journal of Urban Research*, vol 4, no 1, pp 1-19.

Broadway, M. and Jesty, G. (1998) 'Are Canadian inner cities becoming more dissimilar? An analysis of urban deprivation indicators', *Urban Studies*, vol 35, no 6, pp 1423-38.

Brook, I. (2003) 'Making here like there: place attachment, displacement and the urge to garden', *Ethics, Place and Environment*, vol 6, no 3, pp 227-34.

Brown, B.B. and Perkins, D.D. (1992) 'Disruptions in place attachment', in I. Altman and S.M. Low (eds) *Place attachment*, New York: Plenum Press, pp 279-304.

Brown, B.B., Perkins, D.D. and Brown, G. (2004) 'Incivilities, place attachment and crime: block and individual effects', *Journal of Environmental Psychology*, vol 24, pp 359-71.

Brown, V. (1995) 'The effects of poverty environments on elders' subjective well-being: a conceptual model', *The Gerontologist*, vol 35, no 4, pp 541-7.

Buck, N. (2001) 'Identifying neighbourhood effects on social exclusion', *Urban Studies*, vol 38, no 12, pp 2251-75.

Buck, D.S., Rochon, D., Davidson, H. and McCurdy, S. (2004) 'Involving homeless persons in the leadership of a health care organization', *Qualitative Health Research*, vol 14, no 4, pp 513-25.

Bula, F. (2003) 'Vancouver negotiating to buy Woodward's building: the project could revitalize seedy downtown core', *Vancouver Sun*, 24 January.

Burholt, V. and Naylor, D. (2005) 'The relationship between rural community type and attachment to place for older people living in North Wales, UK', *European Journal on Ageing*, vol 2, no 2, pp 109-19.

Butler, R.N. (1963) 'The life review', *Psychiatry*, vol 26, pp 65-76.

Calkins, M.P. (2003) 'Powell Lawton's contributions to long-term care settings', in R.J. Scheidt and P.G. Windley (eds) *Physical environments and aging: Critical contributions of M. Powell Lawton to theory and practice*, New York: Haworth Press, pp 67-84.

Cattell, V. (2004) 'Social networks as mediators between the harsh circumstances of people's lives, and their lived experience of health and well-being', in C. Phillipson, G. Allan and D. Morgan (eds) *Social networks and social exclusion*, Farnham: Ashgate, pp 142-61.

Cattell, V. and Evans, M. (1999) 'Neighbourhood images in East London', *Findings*, April, Ref 499, York: Joseph Rowntree Foundation.

Chawla, L. (1992) 'Childhood place attachments', in I. Altman and S.M. Low (eds) *Place attachment*, New York: Plenum Press, pp 63-86.

Clark, D. (2000) 'World urban development: processes and patterns at the end of the twentieth century', *Geography*, vol 85, no 1, pp 15-23.

CLG (Communities and Local Government) (2008) *Lifetime homes, lifetime neighbourhoods: A national strategy for housing in an ageing society*, London: Department of Communities and Local Government.

Cocks, M. and Møller, V. (2002) 'Use of indigenous and indigenised medicines to enhance personal well-being: a South African case study', *Social Science and Medicine*, vol 54, no 3, pp 387-97.

Cohen, D.A., Farley, T.A. and Mason, K. (2003) 'Why is poverty unhealthy? Social and physical mediators', *Social Science and Medicine*, vol 57, pp 1631-41.

Cooper Marcus, C. (1992) 'Environmental memories', in I. Altman and S.M. Low (eds) *Place attachment*, New York: Plenum Press, pp 87-112.

Commercial-Drive (2003) *On the Drive: An urban adventure!*, www.thedrive.net/sub-index.html

Corcoran, M.P. (2002) 'Place attachment and community sentiment in marginalised neighbourhoods: a European case study', *Canadian Journal of Urban Research*, vol 11, no 1, pp 47-67.

Coupland, D (2000) *City of glass*, Vancouver, Douglas and McIntyre.

Croucher, K. (2006) *Making the case for retirement villages*, York: Joseph Rowntree Foundation.

Croucher, K., Hicks, L. and Jackson, K. (2006) *Housing with care for later life: A literature review*, York: Joseph Rowntree Foundation.

Cutchin, M.P. (2001) 'Deweyan integration: moving beyond place attachment in elderly migration theory', *International Journal of Aging and Human Development*, vol 52, no 1, pp 29-44.

Cutchin, M.P. (2003) 'The process of mediated aging-in-place: a theoretically and empirically based model', *Social Science and Medicine*, vol 57, pp 1077-90.

Cutchin, M.P. (2005) 'Spaces for inquiry into the role of place for older people's care', *Journal of Clinical Nursing*, vol 14, no S2, pp 121-129.

DH (Department of Health) (2008) *National evaluation of the POPP programme*, London: DH.

Dines, N., Cattell, V., Gesler, W. and Curtis, S. (2007) *Public spaces and social relations in East London*, Bristol: The Policy Press.

Dobkin, M. (1984) 'Broughton and Cheetham Hill in Regency and Victorian times', Manchester: Neil Richardson.

Downs, A. (1981) *Neighborhoods and urban development*, Washington, DC: Brookings Institution.

Dunn, J.R. and Hayes, M.V. (2000) 'Social inequality, population health, housing: a study of two Vancouver neighbourhoods', *Social Science and Medicine*, vol 51, no 4, pp 563-87.

EC (European Commission) (1997) *Towards an urban agenda in the European Union*, Brussels: EC.

EC (1999) *Survey on the current status of research into 'ageing' in Europe*, by the Ad Hoc Advisory Committee on Coordination of RTD Policies, Biomedical and Health Research Programme, Brussels: EC.

Engels, F. (1892) *The condition of the working-class in England in 1844*, London: Swan Sonnenschein and Co.

EU (European Union) (2004) *Communication from the Commission to the Council, the European Parliament, the European Economic and Social Committee and the Committee of the Regions*, Brussels: EU, Commission of the European Communities.

Eurostat (2007) 'Healthy life years at age 65, by gender, 1995–2006', Eurostat tables, Luxembourg: Eurostat.

Eurostat (2008) *Ageing characteristics: The demographic perspective of European countries*, Luxembourg: Eurostat Statistics in focus.

Evans, G.W. (1999) 'Measurement of the physical environment as a stressor', in S.L. Friedman and T.D. Wachs (eds) *Measuring environment across the life span: Emerging methods and concepts*, Washington, DC: American Psychological Association, pp 249-77.

Farquhar, M. (1995) 'Elderly people's definitions of quality of life', *Social Science and Medicine*, vol 41, no 10, pp 1439-46.

Fellegi, I.P. (1997) *On poverty and low income*, Ottawa: Statistics Canada.

Findlay, R. and McLaughlin, D. (2005) 'Environment and psychological responses to ageing', in G.J. Andrews and D.R. Phillips (eds) *Ageing and place*, London: Routledge, pp 118-32.

Fischer, L.R. (1994) 'Qualitative research as art and science', in J.F. Gubrium and A. Sanker (eds) *Qualitative methods in aging research*, Thousand Oaks, CA: Sage Publications, pp 3-14.

Forette, F. and Brieu, M.-A. (2007) *Challenges of longevity: ILC-France perspective*, Paris, International Longevity Centre.

Francis, M. (1989) 'Control as a dimension of public-space quality', in I. Altman and E.H. Zube (eds) *Public places and spaces*, New York: Plenum Press, pp 147-72.

Frantz, D. and Collins, C. (1999) *Celebration, USA: Living in Disney's Brave New Town*, New York, Henry Holt and Company, LLC.

Fried, M. (2000) 'Continuities and discontinuities of place', *Journal of Environmental Psychology*, vol 20, pp 193-205.

Gabriel, Z. and Bowling, A. (2004) 'Quality of life from the perspective of older people', *Ageing and Society*, vol 24, no 5, pp 675-92.

Gawande, A. (2008) *Better: A surgeon's notes on performance*, London: Profile Books.

Giddens, A. (1990) *The consequences of modernity*, Cambridge, Polity Press.

Giddens, A. (2007) *Over to you, Mr. Brown: How Labour can win again*, Cambridge: Polity Press.

Gitlin, L.N. (2003) 'Conducting research on home environments: lessons learned and new directions', *The Gerontologist*, vol 43, no 5, pp 628-37.

Gitlin, L.N. (2007) 'The impact of housing on quality of life: does the home environment matter now and into the future?', in H.-W. Wahl, C. Tesch-Römer and A. Hoff (eds), *New dynamics in old age: Individual environmental and societal perspectives*, New York, Baywood Publishing Company, Inc, pp 105-25.

Glennerster, H., Lupton, R., Noden, P. and Power, A. (1999) *Poverty, social exclusion and neighbourhood: Studying the area bases of social exclusion*, London: Centre for Analysis of Social Exclusion.

Godfrey, M., Townsend, J. and Denby, T. (2004) *Building a good life for older people in local communities*, York: Joseph Rowntree Foundation (findings summary accessed at www.jrf.org.uk/knowledge/findings/socialcare/014.asp).

Golant, S.M. (1984) *A place to grow old: The meaning of environment in old age*, New York: Columbia University Press.

Golant, S.M. (1998) 'Changing an older person's shelter and care setting: a model to explain personal and environmental outcomes', in R.J. Scheidt and P.G. Windley (eds) *Environment and aging theory: A focus on housing*, Westport, CT: Greenwood Press.

Golant, S.M. (2003) 'Conceptualizing time and behavior in environmental gerontology: a pair of old issues deserving new thought', *The Gerontologist*, vol 43, no 5, pp 638-48.

Gordon, D. (2006) 'The concept and measurement of poverty', in C. Pantazis, D. Gordon and R. Levitas (eds) *Poverty and social exclusion in Britain: The Millennium Survey*, Bristol, The Policy Press, pp 29-63.

Gordon, D. and Pantazis, C. (1997) *Breadline Britain in the 1990s*, Farnham: Ashgate.

Gordon, D. and Townsend, P. (eds) (2000) *Breadline Europe: The measurement of poverty*, Bristol: The Policy Press.

Gordon, D., Levitas, R., Pantazis, C., Payne, S., Townsend, P., Bradshaw, J., Middleton, S., Bramley, G., Bridgwood, A., Maher, J. and Rowlands, O. (1999) *Millennium poverty and social exclusion*, Survey Questionnaire: Townsend Centre for International Poverty Research, Bristol: University of Bristol.

Gordon, D., Adelman, L., Ashworth, K., Bradshaw, J., Levitas, R., Middleton, S., Pantazis, C., Patsios, D., Payne, S., Townsend, P. and Williams, J. (2000) *Poverty and social exclusion in Britain*, York: Joseph Rowntree Foundation.

Graham, B.J. and Kenealy, P.M. (2004) 'Quality of life perceptions and social comparisons in healthy old age', *Ageing and Society*, vol 24, no 5, pp 755-70.

Green, G., Grimsley, M. and Stafford, B. (2005) *The dynamics of neighbourhood sustainability*, York: Joseph Rowntree Foundation.

Gubrium, J.F. (1973) *The myth of the golden years: A socio-environmental theory of aging*, Springfied, ILL: Charles C. Thomas Publisher.

Gustafson, P. (2001) 'Roots and routes: exploring the relationship between place attachment and mobility', *Environment and Behavior*, vol 33, no 5, pp 667-86.

GVRD (Greater Vancouver Regional District) (2003a) *Greater Vancouver migration component 1976–2001*, Vancouver: GVRD.

GVRD (2003b) *Immigrant landings in the Vancouver areas 1993–2002*, Vancouver: GVRD.

Hajnal, Z.L. (1995) 'The nature of concentrated urban poverty in Canada and the United States', *Canadian Journal of Sociology*, vol 20, pp 497-528.

Haldemann, V. and Wister, A. (1993) 'Environment and aging', *Journal of Canadian Studies*, vol 28, no 1, pp 30-44.

Halpern, D. (2004) *Social capital*, Cambridge: Polity Press.

Hannan (2001) *The Hannan study of older adults in Detroit's Central City*, Detroit, MI: Hannan Memorial Foundation.

Harding, E. (2007) *Towards lifetime neighbourhoods: Designing sustainable communities for all: A discussion paper*, London: International Longevity Centre UK and Communities and Local Government.

Harding, E (2009) 'Crunch time – so what's next?', in E. Harding (ed) *Weathering the downturn: What is the future for lifetime neighbourhoods?*, Discussion paper, London: ILC-UK, pp 5-10.

Hardy, S.E. (2004) 'Resilience of community-dwelling older people', *Journal of the American Geriatrics Society*, vol 52, no 2, pp 257-62.

Harvey, F. and Greenwell, O. (1988) 'Housing for inner-city, hard-to-house veterans: the Veterans Memorial Manor', in G. Gutman and N.K. Blackie (eds) *Housing the very old*, Vancouver: Gerontology Research Centre, Simon Fraser University, pp 119-35.

Hatfield, M. (1997) *Concentrations of poverty and distressed neighbourhoods in Canada*, Hull, Quebec: Human Resources Development Canada.

Health Canada (2003) *Health Canada to fund evaluation component of Vancouver's pilot supervised injection site research project*, Health Canada (online).

Health Canada (2008) *Vancouver's INSITE service and other supervised injection sites: What has been learned from research?*, Final report of the Expert Advisory Committee, Prepared for the Hon. Tony Clement, Minister of Health, Government of Canada, 31 March (accessed at www.hc-sc.gc.ca/ahc-asc/pubs/_sites-lieux/insite/index-eng.php#ex).

Heaney, P. and Wainwright, M. (2000) 'Killings put "Gunchester" back on crime map', *The Guardian*, 14 January.

Helliwell, J.F. and Putnam, R.D. (2004) 'The social context of well-being', *Philosophical transactions of the Royal Society of London*, vol 359, no 1449, pp 1435-46.

HM Government (2009) *Building a society for all ages*, London, HM Government.

Holdsworth, D.W. and Laws, G. (1994) 'Landscapes of old age in coastal British Columbia', *Canadian Geographer*, vol 38, no 2, pp 174-82.

Holland, C., Clark, A., Katz, J. and Peace, S. (2007) *Social interactions in urban public places*, York: Joseph Rowntree Foundation.

Holloway, I. (1997) *Basic concepts for qualitative research*, London: Blackwell Science.

Holstein, M.B. and Minkler, M. (2007) 'Critical gerontology: reflections for the 21st century', in M. Bernard and T. Scharf (eds), *Critical perspectives on ageing*, Bristol: The Policy Press, pp 13-26.

Holt, C. (2002) 'The Downtown Eastside', Vancouver: University of British Columbia (last accessed May 2009: www.geog.ubc.ca/courses/klink/g448/cary.html).

Hoover, E.M. and R., Vernon (1959) *Anatomy of a metropolis*, Cambridge, MA, Harvard University Press.

House of Lords Science and Technology Committee (2005) *Ageing: Scientific aspects*, London: The Stationery Office.

Howell, S.C. (1983) 'The meaning of place in old age', in G. Rowles and R.J. Ohta (eds) *Aging and milieu: Environmental perspectives on growing old*, New York: Academic Press, pp 97-106.

HRD (Human Resources Development) (2000) *High risk factors behind poverty and exclusion*, Canada: HRD.

Huber, J. and Skidmore, P. (2003) *The new old: Why baby boomers won't be pensioned off*, London, DEMOS.

Hummon, D.M. (1986) 'City mouse, country mouse: the persistence of community identity', *Qualitative Sociology*, vol 9, no 1, pp 3-23.

Hummon, D.M. (1992) 'Community attachment', in I. Altman and S.M. Low (eds) *Place attachment*, New York: Plenum Press, pp 253-78.

Hutton, T.A. (1998) *The transformation of Canada's pacific metropolis: A study of Vancouver*, Montreal: Institute for Research on Public Policy.

Innes, M. and Jones, V. (2006) *Neighbourhood security and urban change: Risk, resilience and recovery*, York: Joseph Rowntree Foundation.

Jenson, J. and de Castell, S. (2000) *Health and home literature review*, Vancouver: Simon Fraser University.

Johnson, D., Headey, B. and Jensen, B. (2005) *Communities, social capital and public policy: A literature review*, Policy Research Paper No 26, Canberra: Department of Family and Community Services, Australian Government.

Johnson, T.F. (1995) 'Aging well in contemporary society: introduction', *American Behavioral Scientist*, vol 39, no 2, pp 120-30.

Joseph, A.E. and Cloutier-Fisher, D. (2005) 'Ageing in rural communities: vulnerable people in vulnerable places', in G.J. Andrews and D.R. Phillips (eds) *Ageing and place*, London: Routledge, pp 133-46.

Kahana, E. (1982) 'A congruence model of person–environment interaction', in M.P. Lawton, P.G. Windley and T.O. Byerts (eds) *Aging and the environment: Theoretical approaches*, New York: Springer Publishing, pp 97-121.

Kasarda, J.D. and Janowitz, M. (1974) 'Community attachments in mass society', *American Sociological Review*, vol 39, pp 328-39.

Kaufman, S.R. (1986) *The ageless self*, Wisconsin: University of Wisconsin Press.

Kazempiur, A. and Halli, S.S. (2000) 'Neighbourhood poverty in Canadian cities', *Canadian Journal of Sociology*, vol 25, no 3, pp 369-81.

Kellaher, L., Peace, S. and Holland, C. (2004) 'Environment, identity and old age – quality of life or a life of quality?', in A. Walker and C. Hagan-Hennessey (eds) *Growing older: Quality of life in old age*, Maidenhead: Open University Press, pp 60-80.

Kendig, H. (2003) 'Directions in environmental gerontology: a multidisciplinary field', *The Gerontologist*, vol 43, no 5, pp 611-15.

Kluckner, M. (1982) *Vancouver: The way it was*, Vancouver: Whitecap.

Krause, N. (1996) 'Neighborhood deterioration and self-rated health in later life', *Psychology and Aging*, vol 11, no 2, pp 342-52.

Krause, N. (1998) 'Neighborhood deterioration, religious coping, and changes in health during late life', *Gerontologist*, vol 38, no 6, pp 653-64.

Kunzmann, U., Little, T.D. and Smith, J. (2000) 'Is age-related stability of subjective well-being a paradox? Cross-sectional and longitudinal evidence from the Berlin Aging Study', *Psychology and Aging*, vol 15, no 3, pp 511-26.

La Gory, M., Ward, R. and Sherman, S. (1985) 'The ecology of aging: neighbourhood satisfaction in an older population', *The Sociological Quarterly*, vol 26, no 3, pp 405-17.

Lambek, M. and Antze, P. (1996) 'Introduction: forecasting memory', in P. Antze and M. Lambek (eds) *Tense past: Cultural essays in trauma and memory*, New York: Routledge.

Langlois, A. and Kitchen, P. (2001) 'Identifying and measuring dimensions of urban deprivation in Montreal: an analysis of the 1996 Census data', *Urban Studies*, vol 38, no 1, pp 119-39.

Laverack, G.R. and Brown, K.M. (2003) 'Qualitative research in a cross-cultural context: Fijian experience', *Qualitative Health Research*, vol 13, no 3, pp 333-42.

Laws, G. (1993) '"The land of old age": society's changing attitudes toward urban built environments for elderly people', *Annals of the Association of American Geographers*, vol 83, no 4, pp 672-93.

Lawton, M.P. (1975) *Planning and managing housing for the elderly*, New York: John Wiley.

Lawton, M.P. (1980) *Environment and ageing*, Pacific Grove, CA: Brooks/Cole Publishing.

Lawton, M.P. (1982) 'Competence, environmental press, and the adaptation of older people', in M.P. Lawton, P.G. Windley and T.O. Byerts (eds) *Aging and the environment: Theoretical approaches*, New York: Springer, pp 33-59.

Lawton, M.P. (1983) 'Environment and other determinants of well-being in older people', *The Gerontologist*, vol 23, no 4, pp 349-57.

Lawton, M.P. (1985) 'The elderly in context: perspectives from environmental psychology and gerontology', *Environment and Behavior*, vol 17, no 4, pp 501-19.

Lawton, M.P. (1986) *Environment and aging*, Albany, NY: Center for the Study of Aging.

Lawton, M.P. (1990) 'An environmental psychologist ages', in I. Altman and K. Christensen (eds) *Environmental and behavior studies: Emergence of intellectual traditions*, New York: Plenum Press, pp 339-63.

Lawton, M.P. (1998) 'Environment and ageing: theory revisited', in R.J. Scheidt and P.G. Windley (eds), *Environment and aging theory*, Westport, CT: Greenwood Press, pp 1-32.

Lawton, M.P. (1999) 'Environmental taxonomy: generalizations from research with older adults', in S.L. Friedman and T.D. Wachs (eds) *Measuring environment across the life span: Emerging methods and concepts*, Washington, DC: American Psychological Association, pp 91-124.

Lawton, M.P. and Nahemow, L. (1973) 'Ecology of the aging process', in C. Eisdorfer and M.P. Lawton (eds) *Psychology of adult development and aging*, Washington, DC: American Psychology Association, pp 619-24.

Lawton, M.P., Windley, P.G. and Byerts, T.O. (1982) *Aging and the environment*, New York: Springer.

Leadbeater, C. (2008) 'Public services – the importance of relationships', Presentation to the Prime Minister's Strategy Unit, London (last accessed May 2009: www.cabinetoffice.gov.uk/strategy/seminars/public_service_relationships.aspx).

Leadbeater, C., and Meadway, J. (2008) *Attaching the recession: How innovation can fight the downturn*, Discussion paper, London:National Endowment for Science, Technology and the Arts.

Lee, K.K. (2000) *Urban poverty in Canada: A statistical profile*, Ottawa: Canadian Council on Social Development.

Lees, L. (2003) 'Visions of "urban renaissance": the Urban Task Force report and the Urban White Paper', in R. Imrie and M. Raco (eds) *Urban renaissance? New Labour, community and urban policy*, Bristol: The Policy Press, pp 61-82.

Levitas, R. (2005) *The inclusive society? Social exclusion and New Labour* (2nd edition), Basingstoke: Palgrave Macmillan.

Levitas, R., Pantazis, C., Fahmy, E., Gordon, D., Lloyd, E. and Patsios, D. (2007) *The multi-dimensional analysis of social exclusion: A research report for the Social Exclusion Task Force*, London: Cabinet Office.

Lewis, G.H. (2006) *Combined predictive model case study: Virtual wards*, London: King's Fund (accessed at www.kingsfund.org.uk/current_projects/predictive_risk/combined_1.html).

Ley, D. (1993) 'Gentrification in recession: social change in six Canadian inner cities, 1981-1986', *Urban Geography*, vol 13, no 3, pp 230-56.

Ley, D. and Smith, H. (2000) 'Relations between deprivation and immigrant groups in large Canadian cities', *Urban Studies*, vol 37, no 1, pp 37-62.

Leyland, A.H. (2004) 'Increasing inequalities in premature mortality in Great Britain', *Journal of Epidemiology and Community Health*, vol 58, no 4, pp 296-302.

Longino, C.F. (1990) 'Geographical distribution and migration', in R.H. Binstock and L.K. George (eds) *Handbook of aging and the social sciences*, San Diego, CA: Academic Press, pp 103-24.

Low, S.M. and Altman, I. (1992) 'Place attachment: a conceptual inquiry', in I. Altman and S.M. Low (eds) *Place attachment*, New York: Plenum Press, pp 1-12.

Lupton, R. (2003) *'Neighbourhood effects': Can we measure them and does it matter?*, CASEPaper 73, London, Centre for Analysis on Social Exclusion (last accessed May 2009: http://sticerd.lse.ac.uk/dps/case/cp/CASEpaper73.pdf).

Lupton, R. and Power, A. (2002) 'Social exclusion and neighbourhoods', in J. Hill, J. Le Grand and D. Piachaud (eds) *Understanding social exclusion*, Oxford: Oxford University Press, pp 118-40.

Lynch, M. (2000) 'Against reflexivity as an academic virtue and source of privileged knowledge', *Theory, Culture & Society*, vol 17, no 3, pp 26-54.

McAuley, W.J. (1998) 'History, race, and attachment to place among elders in rural all-black towns of Oklahoma', *Journals of Gerontology*, vol 53B, no 1, pp S35-S45.

McHugh, K.E. and Mings, R.C. (1996) 'The circle of migration: Attachment to place in aging', *Annals of the Association of American Geographers*, vol 86, no 3, pp 530-50.

MacIntyre, S., Maciver, S. and Sooman, A. (1993) 'Area, class and health: should we be focusing on places or people?', *Journal of Social Policy*, vol 22, no 2, pp 213-34.

McPherson, B.D. (1998) *Aging as a social process: An introduction to individual and population aging*, Toronto: Harcourt Brace.

Magilvy, J.K., Congdon, J.G., Nelson, J.P. and Craig, C. (1992) 'Visions of rural aging: use of photographic method in gerontological research', *The Gerontologist*, vol 32, no 2, pp 253-57.

Makepeace, C. (1995) *Looking back at Hulme: Moss Side, Cholton, Medlock and Ardwick*, Manchester: Willow Publishing.

Manchester (1999) *Urban regeneration: City of Manchester*, Manchester: City of Manchester, pp 1-39.

Manchester (2003a) *Manchester in modern times: 20th century history of Manchester*, Manchester: City of Manchester.

Manchester (2003b) *Districts and suburbs of Manchester (Cheetham, Longsight and Moss Side)*, Manchester: Papillon Graphics' Virtual Encyclopaedia of Greater Manchester.

Manchester (2003c) *Manchester: Economic facts*, Manchester: Manchester City Council.

Manchester (2003d) *The City of Manchester: Profile and vision*, Manchester: Manchester City Council.

Manzo, L.C. and Perkins, D.D. (2006) 'Finding common ground: the importance of place attachment to community participation and planning', *Journal of Planning Literature*, vol 20, no 4, pp 335-59.

Marmot, M. and Wilkinson, R. (2005) *Social determinants of health* (2nd edition), Oxford: Oxford University Press.

Massey, D.S. (1996) 'The age of extremes: concentrated affluence and poverty in the twenty-first century', *Demography*, vol 33, no 4, pp 395-412.

Mathers, C.D., Iburg, K.M., Salomon, J.A., Tandon, A., Chatterji, S., Ustün, B., and Murray, C.J. (2004) 'Global patterns of healthy life expectancy in the year 2002', *BMC Public Health*, vol 24, no 2, pp 66-78 (last accessed May 2009: www.biomedcentral.com/content/pdf/1471-2458-4-66.pdf).

Means, R (2007) 'Safe as houses? Ageing in place and vulnerable older people in the UK', *Social Policy and Administration* vol 41, no 1, pp 65-85.

Mesch, G.S. and Manor, O. (1998) 'Social ties, environmental perception, and local attachment', *Environment and Behavior*, vol 30, no 4, pp 504-19.

Milligan, C., Gatrell, A. and Bingley, A. (2004) '"Cultivating health": therapeutic landscapes and older people in northern England', *Social Science & Medicine*, vol 58, no 9, pp 1781-93.

Mowl, G., Pain, R. and Talbort, C. (2000) 'Ageing body and the homespace', *Area*, vol 32, no 2, pp 189-97.

Muirhead, B.W. (1992) *The development of postwar Canadian trade policy: The failure of the Anglo-European option*, Montreal: McGill-Queens.
Mumford, K. and Power, A. (2003) *East Enders: Family and community in East London*, Bristol: The Policy Press.
Murphy, J.W. and Longino, C.F. (1992) 'What is the justification for a qualitative approach to ageing studies?', *Ageing and Society*, vol 12, pp 143-56.
Murray, H.A. (1938) *Explorations in personality*, New York: Oxford University Press.
Nahemow, L. (2000) 'The ecological theory of aging: Powell Lawton's legacy', in R.L. Rubinstein, M. Moss and M.H. Kleban (eds) *The many dimensions of aging*, New York: Springer Publishing, pp 23-40.
Novak, D.W. and Lerner, M.J. (1968) 'Rejection as a consequence of perceived similarity', *Journal of Personality and Social Psychology*, vol 9, no 2, pp 147-52.
Novak, M. (1997) 'Media archaeology', in A. Kroker and M. Kroker (eds) *Digital delirium*, New York: St. Martin's Press.
O'Bryant, S. (1983) 'The subjective value of "home" to older homeowners', *Journal of Housing for the Elderly*, vol 1, no 1, pp 29-43.
OECD (Organisation for Economic Co-operation and Development) (2003) *Ageing, housing and urban development*, Paris: OECD Publishing.
OECD (2007) *OECD population pyramids in 2000 and 2050* (last accessed May 2009: www.oecd.org/dataoecd/52/31/38123085.xls).
OECD (2008a) 'Ageing OECD societies', in *Trends shaping education*, Paris: OECD Publishing, ch 1.
OECD (2008b) *Growing unequal? Income distribution and poverty in OECD countries*, Paris: OECD Publishing.
ONS (Office for National Statistics) (2002) *Manchester population: Facts & figures*, Manchester: Papillon Graphics' Virtual Encyclopaedia of Greater Manchester – using ONS 2002 statistics (last accessed May 2009:www.manchester2002-uk.com/whatsnew.html).
ONS (2003) *2001 Census*, Newport: ONS.
Osberg, L. (2000) 'Poverty in Canada and the United States: measurement, trends, and implications', *Canadian Journal of Economics*, vol 33, no 4, pp 847-77.
Oswald, F., Wahl, H.W., Martin, M. and Mollenkopf, H. (2003a) 'Toward measuring proactivity person–environment transactions in late adulthood: the Housing-Related Control Beliefs Questionnaire', in R.J. Scheidt and P.G. Windley (eds) *Physical environments and aging*, New York: Haworth Press, pp 135-52.
Oswald, F., Wahl, H.W., Mollenkopf, H. and Schilling, O. (2003b) 'Housing and life satisfaction of older adults in two rural regions in Germany', *Research on Aging*, vol 25, no 2, pp 122-43.
Oswald, F., Wahl, H.W., Schilling, O., Nygren, C., Fange, A., Sixsmith, A., Sixsmith, J., Széman, Z., Tomsone, S. and Iwarsson, S. (2007) 'Relationship between housing and healthy ageing in very old age', *The Gerontologist*, vol 47, pp 96-107.
Parker, G. (2000) 'Blessing in disguise?', *FX Magazine*, October.

Parkes, A., Kearns, A. and Atkinson, R. (2002) 'What makes people dissatisfied with their neighbourhood?', *Urban Studies*, vol 39, no 13, pp 2413-38.

Parmelee, P.A. (1998) 'Theory and research on housing for the elderly: the legacy of Kurt Lewin', in R.J. Scheidt and P.G. Windley (eds) *Environment and aging theory: A focus on housing*, Westport, CT: Greenwood Press, pp 161-85.

Parmelee, P.A. and Lawton, M.P. (1990) 'The design of special environment for the aged', in J.E. Birren and K.W. Schaie (eds) *Handbook of the psychology of aging*, New York: Academic Press, pp 465-89.

Paterson, B.L., Gregory, D. and Thorne, S. (1999) 'A protocol for research safety', *Qualitative Health Research*, vol 9, no 2, pp 259-69.

Peace, S. (1988) 'Promoting the "right" institutional environment', in N. Wells and C. Freer (eds) *The ageing population: Burden or challenge?*, Basingstoke: Macmillan, pp 217-34.

Peace, S. (ed) (1990) *Researching social gerontology: Concepts, methods and issues*, London: Sage Publications.

Peace, S., Holland, C. and Kellaher, L. (2003) 'Environment and identity in later life: a cross-setting study', Report to the Economics and Social Research Council (last accessed May 2009: www.esrcsocietytoday.ac.uk/ESRCInfoCentre/Plain_English_Summaries/LLH/health_wellbeing/index144.aspx).

Peace, S., Holland, C. and Kellaher, L. (2005) 'Making space for identity', in G.J. Andrews and D.R. Phillips (eds) *Ageing and place: Perspectives, policy, practice*, New York: Routledge, pp 188-204.

Peace, S., Holland, C. and Kellaher, L. (2006) *Environment and identity in later life*, Maidenhead: Open University Press.

Pellow, D. (1992) 'Spaces that teach: attachment to the African compound', in I. Altman and S.M. Low (eds) *Place attachment*, New York: Plenum Press, pp 187-210.

Phillips, D.R., Siu, O., Yeh, A. and Cheng, K. (2005) 'Ageing and the urban environment', in G.J. Andrews and D.R. Phillips (eds) *Ageing and place: Perspectives, policy, practice*, New York: Routledge, pp 147-63.

Phillipson, C. (2002) 'Globalization and the future of ageing: economic, social and policy implications, plenary paper', Valencia Forum, International Association of Gerontology Preparatory Conference for the Second World Assembly on Ageing, Valencia, Spain.

Phillipson, C. (2003) 'Globalization and the reconstruction of old age: new challenges for critical gerontology', in S. Biggs, A. Lowenstein and J. Hendricks (eds) *The need for theory: Critical approaches to social gerontology*, New York: Baywood Publishing Company, pp 163-79.

Phillipson, C. (2006) 'Aging and globalization: issues for critical gerontology and political economy', in J. Baars, D. Dannefer and A. Walker (eds) *Aging, globalization and inequality*, New York: Baywood Publishing Company, pp 43-58.

Phillipson, C. (2007) 'The "elected" and the "excluded": sociological perspectives on the experience of place and community in old age', *Ageing & Society*, vol 27, pp 321-42.

Phillipson, C. and Scharf, T. (2004) *The impact of government policy on social exclusion of older people: A review of the literature*, London: Social Exclusion Unit, Office of the Deputy Prime Minister.

Phillipson, C., Bernard, M., Phillips, J. and Ogg, J. (2001) *The family and community life of older people: Social networks and social support in three urban areas*, London: Routledge.

Pillow, W.S. (2003) 'Confession, catharsis, or cure? Rethinking the uses of reflexivity as methodological power in qualitative research', *Qualitative Studies in Education*, vol 16, no 2, pp 175-96.

Platt, J. (1988) 'What can case studies do?', in R.G. Burgess (ed) *Studies in qualitative methodology*, London: JAI Press, pp 1-23.

Power, A. (2009) 'New Labour and unequal neighbourhoods', in J. Hills, T. Sefton and K. Stewart (eds) *Towards a more equal society: Poverty, inequality and policy since 1997*, Bristol: The Policy Press, pp 115-34.

Power, A. and Mumford, K. (1999) *The slow death of great cities? Urban abandonment or urban renaissance*, York: York Publishing Services/Joseph Rowntree Foundation.

Power, M.B., Eheart, B.K., Racine, D. and Karnik, N.S. (2007) 'Aging well in an intentional intergenerational community: meaningful relationships and purposeful engagement', *Journal of Intergenerational Relationships*, vol 5, no 2, pp 7-25.

PMSU (Prime Minister's Strategy Unit) (2006) *Reaching out: An action plan on social exclusion*, London: HM Government.

Radley, A. and Chamberlain, K. (2001) 'Health psychology and the study of the case: from method to analytic concern', *Social Science and Medicine*, vol 53, no 3, pp 321-32.

Ransford, B. (2003) 'Sorry, but the Downtown Eastside is a ghetto, and here's the reason why', *Vancouver Sun*, 22 March.

Raphael, D., Steinmetz, B. and Renwick, R. (1999) *The people, places, and priorities of Lawerence Heights: Conclusions from the Community Quality of Life Project*, Toronto: University of Toronto.

Rapoport, A. (1982) *The meaning of the built environment: A nonverbal communications approach*, Beverly Hills, CA: Sage Publications.

Relph, E. (1976) *Place and placelessness*, London: Pion.

Riley, R.B. (1992) 'Attachment to the ordinary landscapes', in I. Altman and S. Low (eds) *Place attachment*, New York, Plenum Press, pp 13-35.

Rivlin, L.G. (1987) 'The neighborhood, personal identity, and group affiliations', in I. Altman and A. Wandersman (eds) *Neighbourhood and community environments*, New York: Plenum Press, pp 1-34.

Rodwin, V.G, and Gusmano, M.K (eds) (2006) *Growing older in world cities: New York, London, Paris, and Tokyo*, Nashville, TN: Vanderbilt University Press.

Rodwin, V.G, Gusmano, M.K and R.N. Butler (2006) 'Growing older in world cities: implications for health and long-term care policy', in V.G. Rodwin and M.K. Gusmano (eds) *Growing older in world cities: New York, London, Paris, and Tokyo*, Nashville, TN: Vanderbilt University Press, pp 1-16.

Ross, D.P., Scott, K.J. and Smith, P.J. (2000) *Canadian fact book on poverty*, Ottawa: Canadian Council on Social Development.

Rowles, G.D. (1978) *Prisoners of space?: Exploring the geographical experience of older people*, Boulder, CO: Westview Press.

Rowles, G.D. (1980) 'Growing old "inside": aging and attachment to place in an Appalachian community', in N. Datan and N. Lohmann (eds) *Transitions of aging*, New York: Academic Press, pp 153-70.

Rowles, G.D. (1983a) 'Place and personal identity in old age: observations from Appalachia', *Journal of Environmental Psychology*, vol 3, pp 299-313.

Rowles, G.D. (1983b) 'Geographical dimensions of social support in rural Appalachia', in G.D. Rowles and R.J. Ohta (eds) *Aging and milieu: Environmental perspectives on growing old*, New York: Academic Press, pp 111-30.

Rowles, G.D. (1984) 'Aging in rural environments', in I. Altman, M.P. Lawton and J.F. Wohlwill (eds) *Elderly people and the environment*, New York: Plenum Press, pp 129-57.

Rowles, G.D. (1990) 'Place attachment among the small town elderly', *Journal of Rural Community Psychology*, vol 11, no 1, pp 103-20.

Rowles, G.D. (1993) 'Evolving images of place in aging and "aging in place"', *Generations*, vol 17, no 2, pp 65-70.

Rowles, G.D. (2002) 'Introduction', in G.D. Rowles and N.E. Schoenberg (eds) *Qualitative gerontology: A contemporary perspective*, New York: Springer Publishing Company, pp 234-39.

Rowles, G.D. *Making and re-making place*, Plenary presentation to the British Society of Gerontology conference, Bristol, 4–6 September.

Rowles, G.D. and Ravdal, H. (2002) 'Aging, place, and meaning in the face of changing circumstances', in R.S. Weiss and S.A. Bass (eds) *Challenges of the Third Age: Meaning and purpose in later life*, Oxford: Oxford University Press, pp 81-114.

Rubinstein, R.L. (1986) 'The construction of a day by elderly widowers', *International Journal of Aging and Human Development*, vol 23, no 3, pp 161-73.

Rubinstein, R.L. (1988) 'Stories told: in-depth interviewing and the structure of its insights', in G.D. Rowles and S. Reinharz (eds) *Qualitative gerontology*, New York: Springer Publishing Company, pp 128-46.

Rubinstein, R.L. (1990) 'Personal identity and environmental meaning in later life', *Journal of Aging Studies*, vol 4, no 2, pp 131-47.

Rubinstein, R.L. (2002) 'The qualitative interview with older informants: some key questions', in G.D. Rowles and N.E. Schoenberg (eds) *Qualitative gerontology: A contemporary perspective*, New York: Springer Publishing Company, pp 137-53.

Rubinstein, R.L. and Parmelee, P.A. (1992) 'Attachment to place and the representation of life course by the elderly', in I. Altman and S.M. Low (eds) *Place attachment*, New York: Plenum Press, pp 139-63.

Ryan, G.W. and Bernard, H.R. (2000) 'Data management and analysis methods', in N.K. Denzin and Y.S. Lincoln (eds) *The handbook of qualitative research*, Thousand Oaks, CA: Sage Publications, pp 769-93.

Sarlo, C.A. (1992) *Poverty in Canada*, Vancouver: The Fraser Institute.

Savage, M., Warde, A. and K. Ward (2002) *Urban sociology, capitalism and modernity*, Basingstoke: Palgrave MacMillan,

Scharf, T. (2005) 'Recruiting older research participants: lessons from deprived neighbourhoods', in C. Holland (ed) *Recruitment and sampling: Qualitative research with older people*, London: Centre for Policy on Ageing, pp 29-43.

Scharf, T. and Smith, A.E. (2004) 'Older people in urban neighbourhoods: addressing the risk of social exclusion in later life', in C. Phillipson, G. Allan and D. Morgan (eds), *Social networks and social exclusion*. Aldershot: Ashgate, pp 162-79.

Scharf, T. and Wenger, G.C. (2000) 'Cross-national empirical research in gerontology: the OPERA experience', *Education and Ageing*, vol 15, no 3, pp 379-97.

Scharf, T., Phillipson, C. and Smith, A.E. (2003) 'Older people's perceptions of the neighbourhood: evidence from socially deprived urban areas', *Sociological Research Online*, vol 8, no 4.

Scharf, T., Phillipson, C. and and Smith, A.E. (2004) 'Poverty and social exclusion: growing older in deprived urban neighbourhoods', in A. Walker and C. Hagan-Hennessey (eds) *Growing older: Quality of life in old age*, Maidenhead: Open University Press, pp 81-106.

Scharf, T., Phillipson, C. and Smith, A.E. (2005) *Multiple exclusion and quality of life amongst excluded older people in disadvantaged neighbourhoods*, London: Social Exclusion Unit, Office of the Deputy Prime Minister.

Scharf, T., Phillipson, C., Kingston, P. and Smith, A.E. (2001) 'Social exclusion and older people: exploring the connections', *Education and Ageing*, vol 16, no 3, pp 303-20.

Scharf, T., Phillipson, C., Smith, A.E. and Kingston, P. (2002a) 'Older people in deprived areas: perceptions of the neighbourhood', *Quality in Ageing*, vol 3, no 2, pp 11-21.

Scharf, T., Phillipson, C., Smith, A.E. and Kingston, P. (2002b) *Growing older in socially deprived areas*, London: Help the Aged.

Scharf, T., Phillipson, C., Smith, A.E. and Kingston, P. (2002c) 'Age-old problems', *Community Care*, 31 October.

Scheidt, R.J. and Norris-Baker, C. (1990) 'A transactional approach to environmental stress among older residents of rural communities: introduction to a special issue', *Journal of Rural Community Psychology*, vol 11, no 1, pp 5-30.

Scheidt, R.J. and Norris-Baker, C. (2004) 'The general ecological model revisited: Evolution, current status, continuing challenges', in H.-W. Wahl, R.J. Scheidt and P.G. Windley (eds), *Annual review of gerontology and geriatric: Aging in context: Socio-physical environments*, New York: Springer, pp 34-54.

Scheidt, R.J., and Windley, P.G. (2006) 'Environmental gerontology: progress in the post-Lawton era', in J.E. Birren and K.W. Schaie (eds) *Handbook of the psychology of aging* (6th edition), Amsterdam: Elsevier, pp 105-25.

Schwarz, B. (2003) 'M. Powell Lawton's three dilemmas in the field of environment and aging', in R.J. Scheidt and P.G. Windley (eds) *Physical environments and aging*, New York: Haworth Press, pp 5-22.

SEU (Social Exclusion Unit) (1998) *Bringing Britain together: A national strategy for neighbourhood renewal*, London: SEU.

SEU (1998–2000) Policy Action Team reports, London: SEU (all 18 reports accessed at www.neighbourhood.gov.uk/page.asp?id=737).

SEU (2001a) *A new commitment to neighbourhood renewal: National strategy action plan*, London: SEU.

SEU (2001b) *Preventing social exclusion*, London: SEU.

SEU (2004) *Tackling social exclusion: Taking stock and looking to the future: Emerging findings*, London: SEU.

Shakespeare, N. (2002) *The dancer upstairs*, J. Malkovich (film).

Sheridan, M.J. (1996) *Statistics Canada's experience with low income cutoffs*, Ottawa: Expert Group on Household Income Statistics, Household Surveys Division, Statistics Canada.

Shumaker, S.A. and Taylor, R.B. (1983) 'Toward a clarification of people–place relationships: a model of attachment to place', in N.R. Feimer and E.S. Geller (eds) *Environmental psychology: Directions and perspectives*, New York: Praeger, pp 219-51.

Smith, A.E. (2000) 'Quality of life: a review', *Education and Ageing*, vol 15, no 3, pp 419-35.

Smith, J. and Freund, A.M. (2002) 'Dynamics of possible selves in old age', *Journals of Gerontology: Series B: Psychological Sciences and Social Sciences*, vol 57B, no 6, pp 492-500.

Smith, M., Edgar, C. and Groom, G. (2008) 'Report: Health expectancies in the United Kingdom, 2004–06', *Health Statistics Quarterly 40*, Winter 2008, Newport, Office of National Statistics (last accessed May 2009: www.statistics.gov.uk/downloads/theme_health/Health-expect-UK-2004-06.pdf)

Smith, S.J. and McCann, L. (1981) 'Residential land use change in inner Edmonton', *Annals of the Association of American Geographers*, vol 71, no 4, pp 536-51.

St. Hilaire, F. (1998) *The transformation of Canada's pacific metropolis: A study of Vancouver*, Montreal: Institute for Research on Public Policy.

St. John, C., Austin, D.M. and Baba, Y. (1986) 'The question of community attachment revisited', *Sociological Spectrum*, vol 6, pp 411-31.

Stafford, M., Bartley, M., Sacker, A., Marmot, M., Wilkinson, R., Boreham, R. and Thomas, R. (2003) 'Measuring the social environment: social cohesion and material deprivation in England and Scottish neighbourhoods', *Environment and Planning A*, vol 35, no 8, pp 1459-76.

Stafford, M. and McCarthy, M. (2005) 'Neighbourhoods, housing, and health', in M. Marmot and R.G. Wilkinson (eds), *Social Determinants of Health* (2nd edition), Oxford: Oxford University Press, pp 297-317

Statistics Canada (2003) City of Vancouver Statistics (2001 Census Data): Statistics Canada (last accessed June 2009: http://vancouver.ca/commsvcs/Census2001/index.htm).

Stedman, R., Beckley, T., Wallace, S. and Ambard, M. (2004) 'A picture and 1000 words: using resident-employed photography to understand attachment to high amenity places', *Journal of Leisure Research*, vol 36, no 4, pp 580-606.

Stevens-Ratchford, R. and Diaz, T. (2003) 'Promoting successful aging through occupation: an examination of engagement in life: a look at aging in place, occupation and successful aging', *Activities, Adaptation and Aging*, vol 27, no 3-4, pp 19-37.

Stokols, D. (1999) 'Human development in the age of the internet: conceptual and methodological horizons', in S.L. Friedman and T.D. Wachs (eds) *Measuring environment across the life span*, Washington, DC: American Psychological Association, pp 327-56.

Sugihara, S. and Evans, G.W. (2000) 'Place attachment and social support at continuing care retirement communities', *Environment and Behavior*, vol 32, no 3, pp 400-9.

Sussex, G. (1983) *Longsight: Past and present*, Manchester: Manchester Free Press.

Synders, T. and O'Rourke, J. (2001) *Namely Vancouver: Hidden history of Vancouver place names*, Vancouver: Arsenal Pulp Press.

Taylor, M. (2008) *Transforming disadvantaged places: Effective strategies for places and people*, Summary report, York, Joseph Rowntree Foundation, (last accessed June 2009: www.jrf.org.uk/sites/files/jrf/2255.pdf).

Taylor, P.J. and Lang, R.E. (2004) 'The shock of the new: 100 concepts describing recent urban change shocking social science', *Environment & Planning A*, vol 36, no 6, pp 951-58.

Taylor, S.A. (2001) 'Place identification and positive realities of aging', *Journal of Cross-Cultural Gerontology*, vol 16, no 5, pp 5-20.

Thompson, T. (2002) 'Gang warfare in Games City', *The Observer*, 28 July (last accessed May 2009: www.guardian.co.uk/uk/2002/jul/28/ukcrime).

Thomson, H., Petticrew, M. and Morrison, D. (2001) 'Health effects of housing improvement: systematic review of intervention studies', *British Medical Journal*, vol 323, pp 187-90.

Tinker, A. and Biggs, S. (2008) 'Age friendly cities: WHO research', Presentation at the British Society of Gerontology, Bristol, September.

Townsend, P. (1957) *The family life of old people*, London: Routledge and Kegan Paul.

UN (United Nations) (2002) *Research agenda on ageing for the 21st century*, Valencia Forum, United Nations and International Association of Gerontology (last accessed June 2009 http://www.un.org/esa/socdev/ageing/researchagenda.html).

UN (2003) *The ageing of the world's population*, Population Division, Department of Economic and Social Affairs, UN Secretariat, New York: UN (last accessed 2009: www.un.org/ageing/popageing.html).

UNFPA (United Nations Population Fund) (2007) *Unleashing the potential of urban growth: UNFPA's State of World Population 2007*, New York: UN (accessed at www.unfpa.org/swp/).

Vancouver (1965) *Downtown Eastside: A preliminary study*, Vancouver: City of Vancouver.

Vancouver (2000) *The Vancouver Agreement: An urban development agreement*, Vancouver: City of Vancouver.

Vancouver (2001) *Vancouver 2001 report*, Vancouver: City of Vancouver.

Vancouver (2002a) *Community profiles*, Vancouver: Statistics Canada.

Vancouver (2002b) *Insights into population and housing*, Vancouver: City of Vancouver, Planning Department.

Vancouver (2005) *Grandview-Woodland: A community profile*, Vancouver: City of Vancouver Planning Department (last accessed May 2009: http://vancouver.ca/community_profiles/grandview_woodland/history.htm).

Vindorai, T. (2001) *A tale of three cities: The dynamics of manufacturing in Toronto, Montreal and Vancouver 1976–1997*, Ottawa: Micro-Economic Analysis Division, Statistics Canada.

Wachs, T.D. (1999) 'Celebrating complexity: conceptualization and assessment of the environment', in S.L. Friedman and T.D. Wachs (eds) *Measuring environment across the life span: Emerging methods and concepts*, Washington, DC: American Psychological Association, pp 357-92.

Wacquant, L. (2008) *Urban outcasts: A comparative sociology of advanced marginality*, Cambridge: Polity Press.

Wahl, H.W. (2001) 'Environmental influences on aging and behavior', in J.E. Birren and K.W. Schaie (eds) *Handbook of the psychology of aging*, New York: Academic Press, pp 215-37.

Wahl, H.-W. and Lang. F. (2006) 'Psychological aging: a contextual view', in P.M. Conn (ed), *Handbook of models for human aging*, Amsterdam, Elsevier, pp 881-95.

Wahl, H.W. and Weisman, G.D. (2003) 'Environmental gerontology at the beginning of the new millennium: reflections on its historical, empirical, and theoretical development', *The Gerontologist*, vol 43, no 5, pp 616-27.

Wainwright, M. (1999) 'The gritty city goes lookie-feely', *The Guardian*, 7 September.

Walker, A., Barnes, M., Cox, K., and Lessof, C. (2006) *Social exclusion of older people: Future trends and policies*, London: Department of Communities and Local Government.

Wang, C.C. (1999) 'Photovoice: a participatory action research strategy applied to women's health', *Journal of Women's Health*, vol 8, no 2, pp 185-92.

Wanless, D. (2006) *Securing good care for older people: Taking a long-term view*, London: King's Fund.

Warnes, A.M., Friedrich, K., Kellaher, L. and Torres, S. (2004) 'Diversity and welfare of older migrants on Europe', *Ageing and Society*, vol 24, no 3, pp 307-26.

West, R.A (2002) 'Place psychological experience: a Native American perspective', Dissertation, Antioch University/New England Graduate School.

Western, J. (1993) 'Ambivalent attachments to place in London: twelve Barbadian families', *Environment and Planning D: Society and Space*, vol 11, pp 147-70.

Wey, S. (2007) *The ethnical use of assistive technology: Dementia*, Leicester: at dementia (accessed at www.atdementia.org.uk/).

WHO (World Health Organization) (1989) *European Charter on environment and health*, Geneva: WHO.

WHO (2007) *Global age friendly cities: A guide*, Geneva: WHO.

Wiggins, R.D., Higgs, P.F.D., Hyde, M. and Blane, D.B. (2004) 'Quality of life in the Third Age: key predictors of the CASP-19 measure', *Ageing and Society*, vol 24, no 5, pp 693-79.

Wiles, J (2005) 'Home as a new site of care provision and consumption', in G.J. Andrews and D.R. Phillips (eds) *Ageing and place*, London: Routledge, pp 79-97.

Williams, G. (1996) 'City profile: Manchester', *Cities*, vol 13, no 3, pp 203-12.

World Bank (2001) Making Sustainable Commitments: An Environment Strategy for the World Bank.

Worpole, K, and Knox, K. (2007) *The social value of public spaces*, York: Joseph Rowntree Foundation.

Wright, S.D. (2000) 'Gray and green? Stewardship and sustainability in an aging society', *Journal of Aging Studies*, vol 14, no 3, pp 229-50.

Yeates, M. and Garner, B. (1976) *The North American city*, New York: Harper and Row.

Young, A.F., Russell, A. and Powers, J.R. (2004) 'The sense of belonging to a neighbourhood: can it be measured and is it related to health and well-being in older women?', *Social Science and Medicine*, vol 59, no 12, pp 2627-38.

Zwingle, E. (2002) 'Cities: challenges for humanity', *National Geographic*, 22 November (last accessed May 2009: http://ngm.nationalgeographic.com/ngm/0211/feature3/).

Index

D

E